Contents

Global Englishes and Transcultural Flows

'*Global Englishes and Transcultural Flows* is remarkable for the depth of its insight and the breadth of its scholarship. Drawing on theories of performativity and transculturation, Alastair Pennycook brings a fresh perspective to debates on the relationship between local and global cultural practices. His outstanding analysis of international hip-hop culture, in particular, offers a window on a wide range of contemporary topics, including globalization, world Englishes, identity, popular culture, and linguistic imperialism. Written with eloquence and style, the book is a "must read" for applied linguists, language educators, and cultural studies enthusiasts.'
Bonny Norton, *University of British Colombia, Canada*

'An exciting, thought-provoking and entertaining study of the transnational flows of Hip-Hop, and their implications for applied linguistics research and practices, combining up-to-date theoretical debates with a wealth of original data and detailed text analysis. Written with refreshing clarity and flair, the book makes an innovative contribution not only for scholars of transnationalism in the interface of linguistics and cultural studies, but provides an accessible textbook for students and interested readers.'
Ulrike Meinhof, *University of Southampton, UK*

The English language is spreading across the world, and so too is hip-hop culture: both are being altered, developed, reinterpreted, reclaimed.

This timely book breaks new ground in exploring the relations between global Englishes (the spread and use of diverse forms of English within processes of globalization), and transcultural flows (the movements, changes and reuses of cultural forms in disparate contexts). Drawing on transgressive and performative theory, Pennycook looks at how hip-hop, global Englishes, transcultural flows and pedagogy are interconnected in ways that oblige us to rethink language and culture within the contemporary world.

With the language of hip-hop and English woven together in new and creative ways, Alastair Pennycook argues that the use of English becomes not merely imitative, but part of a localized subculture in many parts of the world: hip-hop operates as a global code, while simultaneously demonstrating and creating a sense of locality.

This wide-ranging and informative discussion of English and hip-hop includes discussions from many contexts, from Australia to Japan and from Malaysia to Senegal, and focuses on the ways English is embedded in other linguistic contexts, including those of East Asia, Australia, West Africa and the Pacific Islands.

Global Englishes and Transcultural Flows will be a valuable resource to applied linguists, sociolinguists, and students on cultural studies, English language studies, TEFL and TESOL courses.

Alastair Pennycook is Professor of Language in Education at the University of Technology, Sydney. His previous publications include *The Cultural Politics of English as an International Language* (1994), *English and the Discourses of Colonialism* (Routledge, 1998) and *Critical Applied Linguistiscs: A critical introduction* (2001).

Global Englishes and Transcultural Flows

Alastair Pennycook

LONDON AND NEW YORK

First published 2007
by Routledge
2 Park Square, Milton Park, Abingdon, Oxon OX14 4RN

Simultaneously published in the USA and Canada
by Routledge
270 Madison Ave, New York, NY 10016

Reprinted 2008

*Routledge is an imprint of the Taylor & Francis Group, an informa
business*

Typeset in Sabon by Saxon Graphics Ltd
Printed and bound in Great Britain by Antony Rowe Ltd,
Chippenham, Wiltshire

British Library Cataloguing in Publication Data
A catalogue record for this book is available from the British Library

Library of Congress Cataloguing in Publication Data
Pennycook, Alastair, 1957–
   Global Englishes and transcultural flows / Alastair Pennycook.
      p. cm.
   Includes bibliographical references.
   1. English language – Slang. 2. Hip-hop – Influence. 3.
Communication, International. 4. Intercultural communication. I.
Title.
   PE3711.P46 2006
   427`.09–dc22
                                        2006018389

ISBN10: 0-415-37480-4 (hbk)
ISBN10: 0-415-37497-9 (pbk)
ISBN10: 0-203-08880-8 (ebk)

ISBN13: 978-0-415-37480-4 (hbk)
ISBN13: 978-0-415-37497-2 (pbk)
ISBN13: 978-0-203-08880-7 (ebk)

Preface and acknowledgements

A few years ago, a seminar on global hip-hop in the Faculty of Humanities and Social Sciences at the University of Technology Sydney caught my attention. I knew virtually nothing of hip-hop but the theme of globalization and localization intrigued me. As I listened to the talk by Tony Mitchell, I was struck by a range of issues. First, this topic in itself was fascinating: the ways in which hip-hop becomes a local cultural practice around the world opens up many questions of ownership, culture and change; second, the debate within cultural studies on these matters had, in a sense, already dealt with and moved on from many of the concerns we were still dealing with in language studies; and third, the connections between the global spread of language (particularly English) and the global spread of cultural forms was in desperate need of further investigation. And so this project was born. It has been a fascinating journey, taking me into a realm of music, graffiti, dance and sound that I had never paid much attention to, and giving me the great privilege of talking to hip-hop artists and researchers from many parts of the world. This has opened my eyes to many new ideas, people, sounds, movements and ways of being, and I am deeply grateful to all those who have helped with this.

First of all, then, my thanks to Tony Mitchell, author of *Global Noise* (Mitchell, 2001), for getting me into all this, for being such a generous and thoughtful colleague, and more recently an inspiring co-researcher on our joint project *Local Noise: Indigenising Hip-hop in Australasia*. The Australian Research Council (ARC) should also be duly thanked for funding both this project and my own *Postoccidental Englishes and Rap*, which forms the basis for much of this book. I owe a great deal of thanks to the many artists I have talked to, many of whom, such as Too Phat, Teh Tarik Crew, Daara J and K'Naan, found time backstage during a busy schedule to field my endless series of questions. And thanks to other artists and record labels, such as DJ Jun and Positive Tone, who gave me great access to materials and artists. Much of what I have come to understand in recent years has also been through working collaboratively with a number of research assistants (who have also, of course, been responsible for the hard background work: translations, transcriptions, interviews, readings and so on): Adam LeNevez, Jason Seeto, Celina McEwen, Astrid Lorange, Nick Keys, Emi Otsuji, Young Hee Park, Tomoko Takasaki and Go Eun Kim.

These projects have also introduced me to a new and exciting group of researchers following similar trajectories around language, culture, hip-hop and education, with whom more collaborations are planned. It has been an inspiration and a pleasure to talk, work, write and collaborate with: Samy Alim, Awad Ibrahim, Mela Sarkar, Michael Newman, Elaine Richardson, Tope Omoniyi, Rinaldo Walcott, Brownen Low, Jannis Androutsopoulos and others. The work being done by this group of scholars and some of their collaborators is some of the most exciting to emerge in applied linguistics for a long time. I am also grateful to all those who have taken an interest in my research and sent me a CD, a newspaper clip, a connection, an idea, and even on occasions, as happened to Lee Su Kim and Dominique Estival, found themselves unexpectedly backstage and helping out with an interview. It has also been my great fortune over the past few years to work with an exciting and intellectually stimulating group of doctoral students who have pushed my thinking in many different directions. In particular, I would like to thank Constance Ellwood, Adam LeNevez, Emi Otsuji, Ros Appleby, Anita Devos, Ross Forman, Sisamone Sithirajvongsa, Janis Brodie-Grant, Young Hee Park, Celia Thompson, Rana Chandrasoma, Maria Harissi and Marianne Grey for the intellectual struggles and pleasures we have had over the past few years.

I have had the chance to try out some of my ideas in print prior to the publication of this book, and I would like to thank Lawrence Erlbaum for permission to publish revised versions of: Pennycook, A. (2004b) Performativity and language studies. *Critical Inquiry in Language Studies: An International Journal*, 1(1), 1–19, and Pennycook, A. (in press) Language, localization and the real: hip-hop and the global spread of authenticity. *Journal of Language, Identity, and Education*, 6(2); to Blackwell for Pennycook, A. (2003a) Global Englishes, Rip Slyme and performativity. *Journal of Sociolinguistics*, 7(4), 513–533; and Taylor & Francis for Pennycook, A. (2005) Teaching with the flow: fixity and fluidity in education. *Asia Pacific Journal of Education*, 25(1), 29–43.

Meanwhile, I remain incredibly fortunate to be able to continue the long-term critical applied linguistic conversations (about language, life, death, politics, culture, change, identity, gender, sexuality, learning, teaching, words, landscapes and more) with my many friends and colleagues who constantly inspire, criticize and encourage my ideas. I am so grateful for all the wonderful conversations. Many thanks to Elana Shohamy, Tim McNamara, Bonny Norton, Brian Morgan, Vaidehi Ramanathan, Ryuko Kubota, Sinfree Makoni, Angel Lin, Claire Kramsch, Lee Su Kim, Suresh Canagarajah, Stephen May, Cynthia Nelson, Alison Lee, Allan Luke, Lynn Mario Menezes de Souza, Luiz Paulo Moita Lopes, and many others. Apologies to those I have left out. And finally my thanks, comme toujours, to Dominique Estival, who has listened to music she never expected to have to, heard arguments that made little sense, tolerated the moods, the work, the textual struggles, and always supported me in my new lunacies. Merci, encore.

1 Hip hop be connectin'

In the atmosphere: the wilder shores of English

December 2003. The Atmosphere nightclub in Kuala Lumpur, Malaysia. Joe Flizzow and Malique[1] – Too Phat – come on stage; their gait has a loose rhythm, a languid movement of the body, a hinging of the knees that feels like a walk from elsewhere. Their hands wave in the air, fingers pointing, gesticulating with the urgent rhythm of the music. Their matching clothes hang loosely from their bodies: white trainers, baggy jeans, shirts hanging out (one a black T-shirt, the other an orange basketball shirt). Both wear baseball caps set off at a slight angle to the side. Against the background beat from large speakers at the side of the stage they rap at speed, microphones held up in front of them. Behind them, a break-dancing crew, also in baggy jeans, caps and T-shirts, do back spins, windmills, head spins. Joe Flizzow at the mic:

> Hip hop be connectin' Kuala Lumpur with LB
> Hip hop be rockin' up towns laced wit' LV
> Ain't necessary to roll in ice rimmed M3's and be blingin'
> Hip hop be bringin' together emcees[2]

How do we understand this English rap in a Malaysian night-club, with its African American influences on pronunciation and syntax (Hip hop be connectin') its references to the world of hip-hop (blingin', bringin' together emcees) and current popular culture (Louis Vuitton clothes, BMW 3 series wheel rims)? Is this just a flow of culture from the centre to the periphery? Is the whole world becoming a stage for American culture? Does this suggest the gradual death of the rich heritage of Malaysian song and dance as American culture sweeps across the region, led by MTV, music channels, iPods, clothing fashions? Is this the ultimate triumph of global marketing, of the spread of American culture to take over the world, rendering traditional local cultural forms as nothing but a fetishist interest of cultural nationalists and anthropologists? And is the global spread of English the vanguard of the army of Western cultural imperialism, the Trojan Horse from which squadrons of cultural demons spread during the night? Or is it the other way round: is this fascination with copying Western cultural forms the precursor that opens the floodgates of English?

Or are there other ways of thinking about this? The language of hip-hop[3] forms something of a subcultural code itself. An allegation in the UK that the lyrics of a song by Andrew Alcee, a writer of garage music, had been used on Heartless Crew's album Crisp Biscuit, an album which, Alcee claimed, had references to drugs and violence, was dismissed in a decision by the British High Court in June 2003. Alongside the issue of rap's tendency to borrow lyrics and sounds from other sources – an issue to which I shall return – were the judge's comments on his inability in any case to make a judgement on the meaning of the rap lyrics: Mr Justice Lewison said the claim 'led to the faintly surreal experience of three gentlemen in horsehair wigs examining the meaning of such phrases as "mish mish man" and "shizzle my nizzle"'. In spite of searching the web to try to understand some of the lyrics, he concluded that although they were in a form of English, they were 'for practical purposes a foreign language' and he had no expert evidence as to what they meant (Judge fails to unravel rap lyrics, *Guardian Unlimited*, 9 June 2003). As another report of the case (Hamilton, 2003) described the problem, 'A High Court judge as good as admitted yesterday that the wilder shores of the English language were utterly beyond his comprehension'. The case had been unable to 'bridge the linguistic divide between Queen's Council English and the patois of young black England'.

Now if the 'wilder shores of the English language' are incomprehensible to speakers of mainstream varieties, and if it is these versions of English that are spreading as part of the global culture of hip-hop, we may well need a different way of looking at both English and English language pedagogy in the global context. Preisler (1999, p. 244), for example, argues that it 'is impossible to explain the status of English in, and impact on, Danish society ... without understanding the informal function of the English language, and indeed its sociolinguistic significance, in the Anglo-American-oriented subculture'. Using the example of the vocabulary of a group of Danish hip-hop 'street dancers', 'Out of Control', a vocabulary which includes break-dancing styles (boogie, windmills, back spin, head spin, turtle, cracking, waves, isolation, back spreads, locking, skeets), graffiti (tag, bomb, jams, cipher, burn-off, wild-style, straight-letters, piece, throw-up), MC-ing and DJ-ing (ragamuffin, scratch, mixer, cut-backs, cross-fader, break-beat) and the broader hip-hop culture (battle, biting, wanne-be, dope, pusher, graffiti-trip, hang-out, low-life, riot, stick-up), Preisler goes on to argue that there is far less variation in the forms of 'English from above' ('the promotion of English by the hegemonic culture for purposes of "international communication"') than in 'English from below' ('the informal – active or passive – use of English as an expression of subcultural identity and style') (p. 259). When we look at the global spread of English in relation to the global spread of subcultural style, then, this can also be seen in terms of an emergence of English from below, of the wilder shores of English bubbling up into everyday life.

The term *Blinglish* has been used either to refer to Black English or, more commonly, to disparage white kids' (or 'wiggers'') use of black hip-hop language (see *Urban Dictionary*, 2006). The term *Blinglish* combines not only Black English but also *bling bling*, a term that the *Hip Hoptionary* (Westbrook, 2002, p. 14) explains as '1) jewelry. 2) material showoff. 3) the glitter of diamonds.' Of course, the very existence of a *Hip Hoptionary* and of online rap dictionaries suggests the need for assistance with the wilder shores of the English language. While the notion of Blinglish points us back at one level to the idea of a homogenizing spread of language and culture, as kids around the world imitate African American speech forms, it is also worth considering that if it is indeed disenfranchised African Americans who are spearheading the global dominance of North American language and culture, if hip-hop is indeed 'a black cultural expression that prioritizes black voices from the margins of urban America' (Rose, 1994, p. 2), then we are looking at forms of expression of resistance to dominant white culture becoming a dominant global cultural form (Osumare, 2001). As we shall see in later chapters (5 and 7), the debates over the origins and spread of hip-hop complexify this picture further.

While these lyrics by Too Phat are clearly laced with African American derived forms, imported cultural references and borrowed terms from the subcultures of hip-hop, there are other things at work here too: there is a clear sense of both locality and a global hip-hop community. They are based in Kuala Lumpur (KL), yet hip-hop as a cultural form is connecting Kuala Lumpur with LB (Long Beach, California, where a collaborator on this track, Warren G, is located); and at the same time that they celebrate the way emcees (MCs – rappers) are connected across time and space, there is also a rejection of the bling world (blatant crass materialism) of some hip-hop culture. Worth noting too are the ways in which the global language and culture of hip-hop are both inclusive and exclusive. While on the one hand Too Phat claim membership of this global culture, they simultaneously use the in-house register of hip-hop that excludes many with its cultural references. Thus, while locating themselves within the linguistic and cultural world of hip-hop, which links across the globe yet operates as a cultural code, they are also locating themselves in Malaysia and positioning themselves in particular ways in relation to hip-hop culture.

Different Too Phat lyrics open up another perspective. Here is Joe Flizzow again:

> If I die tonight, what would I do on my last day
> I know I'd wake early in the morn' for crack of dawn's last pray
> Then probably go for breakfast like I used to do
> Fried kuey teow FAM and roti canai at Ruja's with my boo[4]

If we accept the world Englishes definition of Malaysia as a country located in the Outer Circle (for further discussion, see Chapter 2), a country in which

English has had a continuing role since the days of British colonialism, a country in which English has become localized, vernacularized to serve local purposes, a country where indeed we might say that English has become a local language, can we assume that Too Phat's English use is an external imposition rather than an internal choice? Clearly in the lyrics above, we have local references to food, one of the most common features of local Englishes, as well as a reference to Muslim prayers at dawn. Here, the inclusions and exclusions are operating on a different level. Rather than global hip-hop as the cultural context, we are now dealing with local Malaysian references, Muslim prayers, and Chinese and Indian food eaten at stalls for breakfast: fried kuey teow or *char kway teow* is a popular dish of fried flat noodles, while roti canai (or *roti prata* in Singapore) is Indian bread (roti) with canai or channa: boiled chickpeas in spicy sauce. With the even more specific reference to Ruja's, we are taken into the local world of Malaysia. And if English can thus become a local language, could not hip-hop also become a local cultural practice? When are the different elements of hip-hop – rapping (MC-ing), break-dancing, graffiti, DJ-ing, the clothes, the walk, the talk – reflexes of a global industry, and when can we see them as localized practices? Does Malaysian song and dance have to be traditional Malay *gamelan* or *rebana ubi* drums, or *silat* or *joget*,[5] or lion dances, dragon dances or Chinese opera, or Indian *Bharatnatyam* or *Kathakali* dances? Or could hip-hop also be Malaysian? If English can be used to express local cultural practices, can such practices include more recently localized forms such as hip-hop?

Indeed, more important than a notion of Blinglish (the inauthentic use of African American English) is the way in which rap and English are woven together in new and creative ways. The use of English becomes not merely imitative, but part of a localized subculture in many parts of the world. The forms of identification with African Americans are multiple and complex. And the flows of hip-hop are far more intricate than merely from North America to the rest of the world; there are elaborate circuits of influence in different languages across many parts of the world (see Chapter 7). The participation in this global form, and the use of a major language such as English (or French or Spanish), have particular implications for the ways in which a global community is imagined. My interest, then, is in how the global role of rap in relationship to English produces particular understandings of what it means to partake in multilayered modes of identity at global, regional, national and local levels: How can we understand this use of English, as it locates its users both as part of the global imagined community of English users and as participants in the global music industry, creating links through the 'international language' and yet relocating through its juxtaposition with local languages? How do these new global *raplishes*[6] work as tools for the performance of identities?

And when this moves one stage further, as in these 'rap Melayu' lyrics from Joe Flizzow in Ala Canggung (do you wanna have a party?), is the process of localization perhaps complete? Here, the inclusions and exclusions operate on another level, since most of what is said here is available only to speakers of Malay (or *Bahasa Indonesia*). Clearly, then, this is something different again. This is not recognizably part of African American culture, or global culture, yet nor is it easily located within Malaysian traditions. It is something else again:

> Ya!!! Kau tertarik dengan liriks, baut lu terbalik
> Mr Malique, Joe Flizzow dan T-Bone spit it menarik
> Kita hit terbaik bisa bikin goyang
> Tukang karut moden bercerita pasti girang
> Inilah kugiran yang kan menghilangkan rasa sayu
> Pertama kali gilang gemilang ku rap Melayu[7]

These are some of the questions that inform this book. On the one hand we have the many struggles and debates over English: How is English related to cultural forms and practices? Does its global spread now make it a culturally neutral language? Is the spread of English part of the gradual homogenization of the world? Is the world getting smaller? Or is English part of the greater diversification and heterogenization of the world? Is the world getting bigger? And how and why does a set of cultural practices such as hip-hop spread across the world? As the Japanese site 'Nip Hop' puts it, 'Hip-hop is a culture without a nation. Hip-hop culture is international. Each country has its own spin on hip-hop. Japan has one of the most intense hip-hop cultures in the world ... Japanese Hip-Hop has its own culture, but a culture that has many similar aspects of Hip-Hop around the world. These aspects include the DJ, MC, dancers and urban artists (taggers, spray paint art)' (Nip Hop, 2004). Such statements raise many questions. If Japanese hip-hop has its own culture, is this global hip-hop with a Japanese flavour, Japanese culture with a global orientation, or something new altogether?

Global Englishes and transcultural flows

I use the term *global Englishes* to locate the spread and use of English within critical theories of globalization. English is closely tied to processes of globalization: a language of threat, desire, destruction and opportunity. It cannot be usefully understood in modernist states-centric models of imperialism or world Englishes, or in terms of traditional, segregationist models of language. Thus, while drawing on the useful pluralization strategy of world Englishes, I prefer to locate these Englishes within a more complex vision of globalization. This view seeks to understand the role of English both critically – in terms of new forms of power, control and destruction – and in its complexity – in terms of new forms of resistance, change, appropriation and identity. It suggests that we need to move beyond arguments about homogeneity or heterogeneity, or imperialism and nation states, and instead focus on translocal and transcultural flows. English is a translocal language, a language of fluidity and fixity that moves across, while becoming embedded in, the materiality of localities and social relations. English is bound up with transcultural flows, a language of imagined communities and refashioning identities. I am interested, then, in locating English within a complex view of globalization here, not one that assumes that we are necessarily witnessing increasing levels of global similarity, but one that tries to understand the effects of cultural flows. I will discuss globalization and English in Chapter 2 in much greater depth.

The focus on the flows and appropriations of English and hip-hop, furthermore, will also mean that I will look at English in relationship with other languages. It has been observed at various times that the constant focus on English as a global language reinforces the position of English by incessantly reiterating its role. In this book, I will try to mitigate this focus on English through discussions of English use in relation to languages in East Asia, such as Japanese, Korean and Tagalog. I will also look at circuits of hip-hop that involve a range of other languages, from the French circuit that involves France, West African countries such as Mali, Senegal and Gabon, and Quebec, and which incorporates a wide variety of other languages, particularly from North Africa and the Caribbean (see Durand, 2002; Huq, 2001a, b), to the Pacific Island circuit with its use of Maori, Samoan, Tongan, Tok Pisin, and other languages. Indeed, one of the arguments that emerges in this book is that the use of languages in a domain such as hip-hop raises serious questions for our understanding of what languages are, particularly when considered as discrete entities. The focus on global Englishes, therefore, will also be aimed at rethinking many of the ways in which we view English and language more generally.

I use the term *transcultural flows* to address the ways in which cultural forms move, change and are reused to fashion new identities in diverse contexts. This is not, therefore, a question merely of cultural movement but of take-up, appropriation, change and refashioning. While not ignoring the many detrimental effects of globalization on economies and ecologies across the world – increased exploitation of workers, forced migration, global 'wars' to serve particular interests, destruction of the environment – I am interested centrally here in the cultural implications of globalization, the ways in which cultural forms spread and change. Following Appadurai (1996) and Clifford (1997), the focus is not so much on how music works culturally in a specific location but on the effects of the many encounters and hybrid co-productions of languages and cultures. From this point of view, locality, tradition and place are produced, not given, a result of particular ways of constructing identity (see Chapter 7). Transcultural flows therefore refer not merely to the spread of particular forms of culture across boundaries, or the existence of supercultural commonalities (cultural forms that transcend locality), but rather to the processes of borrowing, blending, remaking and returning, to processes of alternative cultural production.

Unlike Phillipson (1999), therefore, who views the global spread of English as indelibly linked to the Americanization and homogenization of world culture and to media imperialism, I am interested here in the ways in which the flows of cultural forms produce new forms of localization, and the use of global Englishes produces new forms of global identification. As Levy (2001, p. 134) suggests, hip-hop constitutes 'a global urban subculture that has entered people's lives and become a universal practice among youth the world over .... From a local fad among black youth in the Bronx, it has gone on to become a global, postindustrial signifying practice, giving new parameters of meaning to otherwise locally or nationally diverse identities.' While any such statements also need to be treated with a degree of caution – both in terms of the institutions that make it possible for hip-hop to achieve such spread and of the dangers of talking about a 'universal practice among youth the world over' as if global hip-hop affected everyone everywhere irrespective of classes, economies and localities – it is nevertheless useful to see this massive take-up in so many parts of the world as a *postindustrial signifying practice*, as new parameters of meaning that are neither simple adoptions of global practices nor local practices that have always been there.

As Appadurai (2001, p. 5) notes, 'we are functioning in a world fundamentally characterized by objects in motion. These objects include ideas and ideologies, people and goods, images and messages, technologies and techniques. This is a world of flows.' Central to Appadurai's vision of a world in motion is the argument that rather than globalization being 'the story of cultural homogenization' (1996, p. 11), it is better understood as a 'deeply historical, uneven and even *localizing* process. Globalization does not necessarily or even frequently imply homogenization or Americanization', since 'different societies appropriate the materials of modernity differently' (p. 17). Thus, while remaining attentive to the deeply historical and uneven aspects of globalization, I am interested here in cultural and linguistic flows not so much as processes of homogenization but as part of a reorganization of the local. In talking of transcultural flows, therefore, my focus is not merely on the movement of cultural forms across the globe but of the local take-up of such forms. Transculturation may be understood as a 'phenomenon of the contact zone' describing how 'subordinated or marginal groups select and invent from materials transmitted to them by a dominant or metropolitan culture' (Pratt, 1992, p. 6).

By taking up metaphors of movement and the spatial frames of 'trans' theories (see Chapter 3), I am trying here to escape from the debates over globalization versus localization, or neologisms such as glocalization that, be eliding the two polarities, flatten the dynamics of what is occurring here. I am interested instead in looking at language and culture in terms of 'fluidity', which refers to the movement and flows of music across time and space, and 'fixity', which refers to ways in which music is about location, tradition, cultural expression (Connell and Gibson, 2003). As Connell and

Gibson argue, a focus on fluidity and fixity takes us beyond the static dialectic of the global and the local, reflecting 'more dynamic ways of describing and understanding processes that move across, while becoming embedded in, the materiality of localities and social relations' (p. 17). Working with this contrast between the fluidity of cultural and linguistic scapes and the fixity of place, I am interested in how music and language – with a particular focus on hip-hop and English – are simultaneously fluid and fixed, move across space, borders, communities, nations but also become localized, indigenized, re-created in the local. Caught between fluidity and fixity, then, cultural and linguistic forms are always in a state of flux, always changing, always part of a process of the refashioning of identity.

The socioblinguistics of hip-hop

For those who do not know the wonderful world of hip-hop, this eclectic mixture of ugly vandalism (graffiti), angular athletics (break-dancing), grating noises (DJ-ing) and angry lyrics (MC-ing), not to mention the swagger, conspicuous consumption and antisocial attitudes of its well-known performers, might appear a very unlikely candidate for a serious study of language, culture and globalization. Such simplifications of a complex subculture, however, overlook the ways in which hip-hop has a diversity of ways of being, and has been taken up and localized in many diverse parts of the world. Responding to challenges that rap/hip-hop is on the one hand indelibly tied to African American culture and, on the other, nothing but a reflection of the imperialism of US media, Mitchell (2001, pp. 1–2) argues that 'Hip-hop and rap cannot be viewed simply as an expression of African-American culture; it has become a vehicle for global youth affiliations and a tool for reworking local identity all over the world.' As Krims points out, 'There is now scarcely a country in the world that does not feature some form of mutation or rap music, from the venerable and sophisticated hip-hop and rap scenes of France, to the "swa-rap" of Tanzania and Surinamese rap of Holland' (2000, p. 5). This, then, raises one of the central questions of globalization.

According to Condry (2001, p. 222), 'Japanese hip-hop and other versions around the world are interesting in part because they help us understand the significance of what seems to be an emerging global popular culture.' Is, then, the global spread of hip-hop an overarching cultural form that connects different practices around the world, or is it the sum-total of all its appropriations? The same question may be asked of the global spread of English: Is the global spread of English held together by some ontology of English or is it rather the product of all its different uses? The exploration in this book of relations between English and hip-hop will therefore draw not only on the uses of English within hip-hop but also on lessons to be learned by the comparison of two sets of cultural practices. While this focus on 'both the local and the global forces by which rap helps to form imagined identities in non-American contexts' (Krims, 2000, p. 5) is a central reason why hip-hop is possibly the best candidate for such an exploration, there are a number of other reasons why hip-hop should be taken seriously. According to Morgan, 'Hip-hop youth battle through the theoretical houses of Michel Foucault, Mikhail Bakhtin, Judith Butler, Antonio Gramsci, Jürgen Habermas, and more, "shouting out," testing, and challenging theories and philosophies, trying to bring it back to their young bodies in motion, trying to keep theory real. Instead of Descartes's split, they spit rhymes as they reason about their existence' (Morgan, 2005, p. 211). While we should perhaps never take such claims too seriously – we might, in a sense, undermine hip-hop by doing so – we should also be very wary of dismissing them. Hip-hop, as I shall argue in this book, has significant cultural, linguistic, philosophical and educational implications.

As a form of popular culture, hip-hop can tell us much more about how people engage with global culture than can the common focus on domains such as literature. While studies of the language of postcolonial literature (e.g. Talib, 2002) shed light on some domains of language use, the language of popular culture has been largely overlooked in applied linguistics and TESOL. For too long, discussions of language use and variation in global Englishes have focused on the writings of Roy, Rushdie and Rao, while popular culture has been largely ignored as not conforming to the norms of locally emergent standardized Englishes. As Connell and Gibson (2003) put it, popular music 'has the ability to mediate social knowledge, reinforce (or challenge) ideological constructions of contemporary (or past) life and be an agent of hegemony' (p. 270). Among the many lacunae of applied linguistics, the lack of attention to popular culture is one that needs rectifying. Rasolofondraosolo and Meinhof (2003) show the 'significance of the language of popular music in Madagascar for one of the central concerns of our times: the construction, performance and confirmation of cultural identities' (p. 145). In order to do this, they had to stretch the constraining frameworks of applied linguistics 'so as to capture the interplay between multi-modal textual forms, their performance and uptake by audiences, and ... processes of identification' (p. 145). Similarly, as Auzanneau (2002) comments, 'the study of rap is a means of examining the relationships between urban processes and sociolinguistic situations' (p. 120). It is this connection between sociolinguistics and hip-hop that has led me on occasions to use (tongue in cheek) the neologism *socioblinguistics*. While the attention this draws to the 'bling' of hip-hop makes it ultimately a distracting term for what I wish to get at here, it nevertheless can capture a central part of the focus on the interrelationship between the global spread of hip-hop and the study of languages in context. In this book, I shall be pushing the boundaries of applied linguistics by interlinking an understanding of global Englishes, the transmodal practices of hip-hop, and questions of performativity, identity and pedagogy.

As Rasolofondraosolo and Meinhof (2003) suggest, the study of popular music often requires attention to multimodal practices. A broad cultural formation such as hip-hop, which includes MC-ing (rapping), break-dancing, graffiti and DJ-ing, pushes us to open up more diverse and complex modes of analysis of which language is only one part. While there has been a great deal of interest in recent years in issues of multimodality (see e.g. Kress, 2003; Kress and van Leeuwen, 2001), the focus has often been on the (re)discovery of the integrated nature of visual and gestural modes of communication, or of writing and text. The upfront multimodality of hip-hop, however, presents a different challenge, since hip-hop overtly views its different genres as part of a broader set of cultural practices. Learning to read the multimodal tags and grafs (graffiti) of urban landscapes, for example, is one part of the broader multimodal engagement of the hip-hop world (Adams and Winter, 1997; Chalfant and Prigoff 1987; Macdonald, 2001). Within rap (MC-ing), furthermore, we also have to understand the relationship between musical rhythm and lyrics, or rather the *flow*. As Krims (2000) observes, the 'rhythmic styles of MCing, or "flows," are among the central aspects of rap production and reception, and any discussion of rap genres that takes musical poetics seriously demands a vocabulary of flow' (p. 48). And the notion of flow has implications for rapping in different languages (particularly in multilingual rap) as well as echoing the transcultural flows discussed above. Taken as a whole, hip-hop culture presents a challenge for an integrationist (see Harris, 1998) model of language, where language use is understood within a broad array of semiotic relations.

On the other hand, within this broad multimodal sphere, the highly skilled oral performance of MC-ing also makes rap of particular interest to those of us who place a strong emphasis on language. Rapping is a skill that requires immense verbal and mental dexterity, described by Rose (1994) in terms of *postliterate orality*: orally influenced traditions embedded in a postliterate technological context that breaks down the distinction between oral and literate modes of communication. The lyrics of rap are far more central than they are in many other forms of popular culture. Indeed, there is an indulgence in the uses, meanings, cadences and possibilities of language that Morgan (2001) captures when she claims that 'the *Word* is both the bible and the law; a source of worship and competition. Through both commercial and underground media, the music and words of Hip Hop transcend language, neighborhoods, cities, and national boundaries resulting in international varieties where marginalized groups and political parties appropriate Hip Hop as a symbol of resistance' (p. 204). One of the questions for this book, then, is: What happens to this *Word* when it is transposed to other contexts? What does it mean when the word of hip-hop transcends languages and boundaries? Ultimately, Morgan suggests, 'the *Word* in Hip Hop is at once the realization of Foucault's *The Discourse on Language* (1972), Bakhtin's *Dialogic Imagination* (1981), and Labov's *Language in the Inner City* (1972)' (p. 205). In the context of this book, the *word, la parole, el palabra na mi boca* (as GHOST 13 from the Philippines put it in Chavacano) is in many languages, and is a realization not only of

Foucault, Bakhtin and Labov but of Senegalese historian Cheikh Anta Diop, Martinican writer Édouard Glissant, Somalian poet Arays Isse Karshe, and many others (see Chapter 7). Taking up such bold challenges, I will also be arguing in this book that we need therefore not only to take the lyrics of rap very seriously, but also to take the language use of hip-hop seriously for the questions it presents to notions of language, literacy, authorship and text.

As Morgan suggests, hip-hop is often viewed as a form of resistance music. For Connell and Gibson (2003), 'it can and does enable resistance to globalising trends; rap and the ever-evolving hip hop scenes of particular inner-city areas are manifestations of this. Local musics remain vital' (p. 271). In his study of the ways in which African students in Canada 'become Black' as they redefine their identities in terms of the available social and cultural categories on the new continent and increasingly start to identify with forms of Black culture and Black language, particularly hip-hop and Black English, Ibrahim (1999) concludes by arguing that this was 'simultaneously an act of investment, an expression of desire, and a deliberate counterhegemonic undertaking'. Rap, he goes on to suggest, 'must be read as an act of resistance' (pp. 365–366). Similarly, Akindes' study of Hawaiian rappers Sudden Rush suggests that they use hip-hop as 'a liberatory discourse for Hawaiians seeking economic self-determination in the form of sovereignty. Sudden Rush ... have borrowed hip hop as a counter-hegemonic transcript that challenges tourism and Western imperialism' (Akindes, 2001, p. 95). Once again, of course, we need a note of caution here. There is nothing inherently oppositional and resistant about rap: it is equally capable of being as commercialized, conformist and conservative (as well as violent, misogynest and homophobic) as many other popular cultural forms (sometimes more so). But hip-hop nevertheless often carries with it a sense of opposition. As Potter (1995) argues, 'Given that hip-hop's problematics of race and class take place on the level of language', the issue of hip-hop as resistance vernacular 'is best addressed through an analysis of the possibility of resistance *via* language' (p. 17). As I shall argue below, it is in part through the very uses of language rappers engage in that we can see its potential for transformation.

Rap and hip-hop may be viewed as quintessential arts of postmodern times. As Krims (2000) suggests, 'rap music would have to have been invented by postmodern theory, had it not been there, poised to exact its tribute' (p. 8). Rap, suggests Shusterman (2000), is a 'postmodern popular art that challenges some of our most deeply entrenched aesthetic conventions, conventions which are common not only to modernism as an artistic style and ideology but to the philosophical doctrine of modernity and its differentiation of cultural spheres' (p. 61). Rap music's appropriation of sound and music bites and questioning of authorship and creation, its eclectic mixing of styles and use of new technology challenge 'modernist notions of aesthetic autonomy and artistic purity' and emphasize 'the localised and temporal rather than the putatively universal and eternal' (Shusterman,

2000, p. 61). Potter (1995) similarly views rap as a form of postmodernism, suggesting too that Black cultures conceived of postmodernism long before an intellectual avant-guarde in Europe started to question the intellectual inheritance of modernity, since they 'glimpsed the fundamental rottenness of European modernism from its very intestines long before Europe noticed any trace of indigestion' (p. 6). 'Hip-hop's triad of graffiti, dance, and rap', he suggests, 'are post-apocalyptic arts, scratches on the decaying surfaces of post-industrial urban America' (p. 8). And, as I argue here, not only on the decaying surfaces of postindustrial urban America, but also on the favoured favela walls of urban Brazil, the sanitized surfaces of Singapore, the multi-lingual matrices of Malaysia, the non-pacific spaces of the Pacific Islands.

A springboard to a wider world

This book, then, looks at the 'global, postindustrial signifying practice' of hip-hop, in order to shed light on globalization, global Englishes, flows of popular culture, and performance and performativity in relationship to identity and culture. Drawing on examples of hip-hop in Australia and East Asia (particularly Japan, Korea and Malaysia), I will argue that this tran-scultural use of English raises many new questions for how we understand language, identity, culture and locality. Chapter 2 – Other Englishes – looks at debates about the global spread of English, arguing that rather than the model of language implied by a globalization-as-imperialism thesis, a posi-tion which suggests that the world is being homogenized through English, or the view of language suggested by a world Englishes framework, which focuses on the heterogenization of varieties of English, we need an under-standing of global Englishes that focuses on both a critical understanding of globalization and a critical understanding of language. The dominant paradigms that have informed much of our discussion to date of the global spread of English – linguistic imperialism and world Englishes – are too tied to the linguistics and politics of the twentieth century and ill-equipped to deal with current modes of globalization. Instead, we need to start to look at all those other Englishes and new identities that these debates seem to over-look. Chapter 2 suggests the need to rethink what we mean by language in general and English in particular. The terms 'global Englishes' and 'other Englishes' in this chapter signal a move away from previous ways of con-ceptualizing the global position of English.

In order to pursue such a project further, I open up in chapters 3 and 4 some new theoretical spaces. Transgressive theory is discussed in Chapter 3 as a means to get beyond the 'critical' and the 'post' and as a way of think-ing that can deal with the transgressive acts of hip-hop. Like hip-hop at its transgressive best, transgressive theory needs both political and episte-mological tools to transgress the boundaries of mainstream thought and politics. A critical philosophy of transgression is not a set of anarchist incur-sions, tokenistic border-crossings or haphazard critiques of what is deemed to be wrong with the modern world, but rather a continuous questioning of how we come to be as we are, how our ways of understanding have been set, and how this could look different if we started to think otherwise. It is also thought for action and change, both Fanon and Foucault. On the one hand it demands that we confront relations of power – dominion, disparity, difference and desire – while on the other it maintains a constant scepticism, never allowing us to rest on the satisfaction of our own self-conception. Chapter 3 also develops the transgressive analytic framework of transculturation (the fluidity of cultural relations across global contexts), transmodality (language use in terms of mixed modes of semiotic diffusion), transtextualization (texts and signs within the historical, local, discursive and interpretive elements of context), and translation (translingual meaning as an act of interpretation across boundaries of understanding). The spatiality of the 'trans', it is suggested, may be more useful than the temporality of the 'post'.

Performativity and performance are the focus of Chapter 4. I suggest a need to focus on performance rather than competence (or better still, to do away with the distinction) since this focuses our attention on language use as a social and embodied act. This way of thinking makes the somatic turn towards the body and performance crucial to any understanding of language and being. In order to further the themes in this book of exploring different ways of thinking about language and identity within globalization, I take up Butler's development of the notion of performativity (and see Pennycook 2004b). The notion of performativity opens up a way of thinking about language use and identity that avoids foundationalist categories of language, identity, culture or gender. From this point of view, we are not as we are because of some inner being but because of what we do. This position not only opens up a non-essentialist view of identity, but also provides the ground for considering languages themselves from an anti-foundationalist perspective, part of the theme of Chapter 2. Languages are not so much entities that pre-exist our linguistic performances as the sedimented products of repeated acts of identity.

Chapters 5 to 8 look in greater depth at language, hip-hop and globalization. In Chapter 5 I develop the above discussion about hip-hop by making a case for taking popular culture seriously. This is an argument that would not be necessary for a cultural studies audience but remains a more contentious issue within applied linguistics. The tendency to dismiss 'pop culture' has a long history: from a culturally conservative point of view, popular music and entertainment are the shallow interests of a populace devoid of an interest in higher culture; from a more leftist point of view, popular culture is mass culture, soporific entertainment to passify the people. This view clearly underlies positions that equate the global spread of English with a 'dumbing down' of world culture. I argue by contrast that there are social, cultural, political, aesthetic, philosophical and educational grounds for seeing popular culture in more complex terms. Chapter 5 then goes on to look in greater depth at hip-hop, debates about its origins, and different ways of under-standing its global spread. A central issue here is whether the global take-up of hip-hop has to do with an engagement with African American cultural forms or whether it becomes something quite different again.

Looking not only at the parallel spread of English and hip-hop but also at the interconnectedness of this spread, Chapter 6 focuses on the hip-hop emphasis on authenticity, 'keepin' it real'. There is a constant tension here between the 'global spread of authenticity' – a culture of being true to the local, of telling it like it is – and the constant pull towards localization that this implies, a compulsion not only to make hip-hop locally rele-vant but also to define locally what authenticity means. This focus on the relationship between a call for authenticity, its relocalization in other con-texts, and the use of English raises questions about how we think about local and global language use, and what it means to represent local expe-rience. Authenticity for some insists that African American hip-hop is the only real thing and that all other forms are inauthentic deviations; others insist that hip-hop must be a culture of the streets, and to become pop-ular, to become a commercial success, is to sell out, to lose authenticity; some insist that to be authentic one needs to stick to one's 'own' cultural and linguistic domain, to draw on one's own traditions, to be overtly local; others argue that to be authentically local is a question of using a true local variety of a language, be that a local English, a creole, or any lan-guage of the streets; for others, being authentic is a matter of just speaking from the heart: the expression of one's feelings is an inherently authen-tic activity; yet another position suggests that authenticity is a question of style and genre, of finding ways to tell a story that resonates with an audi-ence, of achieving agreement about what matters; and some suggest that any recontextualization of language and culture renders it authentic anew. Sorting out these competing discourses takes us far beyond simple dichot-omies which suggest that English is for global use and local languages for local identity. Rather, as this chapter suggests, the authenticity that hip-hop insists on is not a question of staying true to a prior set of embedded languages and practices but rather an issue of performing multiple forms of realism within the fields of change and flow made possible by multiple language use.

Chapter 7 looks at the use of mixed codes, creoles and local cultural traditions to explore the ways in which the global flows of hip-hop and English intersect. Rather than viewing the direction of hip-hop as always from the centre to the periphery, it is more useful to look at the multiple and interlocking circuits of flow that operate across the globe. From the French circuit with its multiple languages and mixes, to the Pacific circuit linking island populations through appeals to Pacific identity, from collab-orative CDs in South East Asia to Islamic hip-hop, there is a vibrant world of circuits of flow. Within these circles, the mixed codes of the street and the hypermixes of hip-hop pose a threat to the linguistic, cultural and political stability urged by national language policies and wished into place by frameworks of linguistic analysis that posit separate and enumerable languages. The world of global hip-hop is one of language mixing, transidiomatic practices and refashioned identities: The flow is always remixed. As hip-hop engages with diverse local practices in different contexts, it draws on multiple local influences, raising questions about its origins. If Italian hip-hop draws on traditions of operatic recitative, if Somali-Canadian hip-hop finds inspiration in the tradition of Somalian oral poetry, if Fijian-Australian hip-hop may be seen in terms of island traditions of dance, song, story-telling and carving, if Turkish hip-hop can draw on seventeenth-century minstrels, Malaysian on traditional Malay song, and Senegalese on the *griots* of West Africa, it becomes less clear whether this is the localization of hip-hop, the delocalization of local traditions, or something else again.

Education is the central focus of the final chapter. Hip-hop pedagogies may involve anything from using popular culture as a motivational factor in the curriculum, the inclusion of student culture in the classroom, or opening up education to the challenge of student voice, to awareness raising through rap lyrics, helping students to understand the connections between the languages of the street and the codes of education, or hip-hop workshops to engage disadvantaged youths in community centres and correctional facilities. The broader cultural challenge posed by the transgressive art of hip-hop, however, also opens up new ways of thinking about education that are not merely to do with experiential or lifelong learning, about informal education in the streets, but rather offer a new and transgressive set of opportunities for connecting education, the streets, disadvantage, language and culture, redrawing the lines of language, learning and engagement. If we believe that education needs to proceed by taking student knowledge, identity and desire into account, we need to engage with multiple ways of speaking, being and learning, with multilayered modes of identity at global, regional, national and local levels. Unless we get in touch with this as educators, the flow will pass us by.

Congolese-Belgian hip-hop artist Pitcho describes his engagement with hip-hop culture not as an end-point but as a starting point, a springboard for exploring a much wider world:

> Il ne faut pas considérer le hip-hop comme une finalité, mais bien comme un tremplin. C'est un domaine artistique où les gens évoluent dans les directions les plus diverses. La culture hip-hop est, à mon avis, l'une des cultures les plus ouvertes. C'est en écoutant du rap que j'en suis venu à écouter du jazz, du funk, de la musique traditionnelle .... C'est en lisant du rap que je me suis intéressé aux livres de Martin Luther King, de Malcom X .... Même dans le breakdance on repère des influences venues des arts martiaux, des danses africaines .... C'est cela la culture hip-hop, l'ouverture d'esprit.
>
> (Africultures, 2004)

Hip-hop should not be seen as a finality, but rather as a springboard. It is an artistic field where people evolve in the most diverse directions. Hip-hop culture, in my opinion, is one of the most open cultures. It was by listening to rap that I came to listen to jazz, funk, traditional music .... It was by reading rap that I was interested in books by Martin Luther King, Malcom X .... Even in break-dance you can find influences from the martial arts, African dances .... That's what hip-hop is all about, open-mindedness. (my translation)

I also hope to be able to use hip-hop as a springboard to open up a range of contemporary concerns. It is, I hope, with such 'ouverture d'esprit', such open-mindedness, that those interested like myself in broad questions to do with language, culture and education can start to consider how hip-hop, global Englishes, transcultural flows and pedagogy are interconnected in ways that we need to understand in order to engage with the current world.

2 Other Englishes

September 2005, late afternoon, *La Place des Cocotiers* in central Noumea, New Caledonia. A performance of *capoeira*, the Brazilian martial art/ dance form: a chanting circle surrounding the spinning, weaving, circling motions of pairs of players. The islands of New Caledonia have been crossed by many different flows of people: Austronesians, Melanesians, Polynesians, Indonesians; European explorers, whalers and sandalwood traders; Protestant missionaries from Tonga and Samoa, newly converted and ready to spread the word to their Pacific cousins; Catholic missionaries, traders and colonial officers from France; political prisoners shipped out after the Paris Commune in 1871, alongside Arab and Berber anti-colonial fighters from the Maghreb; Chinese, Vietnamese and other Pacific islanders looking for work in the sprawling nickel mines; American military troops stationed noisily by the harbour during the Second World War; Japanese, French, Australian and other tourists, sitting on beaches, taking a trip out to Le Phare Amédée, browsing through the Centre Culturel Tjibaou. While divided on one level between the *Kanaks* (indigenous population) and the *Caldoches* (settlers of French background), such islands have always had shifting populations, people moving back and forth, colonizations; cultures have mixed, changed, rejected, appropriated, adapted.

And today, passing through, a *capoeira* group, singing, beating drums, as two contestants weave and shadow fight around each other in graceful movements. In many ways this is just a continuation of the same – a stopping-off point in the Pacific for a Sydney-based *capoeira* group, bringing their version of this art – developed in Brazil by African slaves in the sixteenth century – to work with New Caledonian practitioners. *Capoeira* was a form of resistance, a way of passing on cultural traditions, an underground and for a time illegal activity that later developed into a widely practised art, with two players surrounded by a circle (*rodo*) and rhythmic music and singing. *Capoeira* is also seen as having had a strong influence on break-dancing, that cornerstone of the hip-hop world, whether through more direct links from Brazilians in New York in the 1970s or through more general borrowings and cross-overs from these related art forms that emphasize competition and athleticism, linking the traditions of the African diaspora through physical movement against a musical background as a means to transgress circumstances of oppression.

It is this world of cross-overs, mixes, borrowings and appropriations that is central to many of the concerns of this book. The appearance of this Sydney-based *capoeira* group in the *Place des Cocotiers* raises questions about the circles of cultural flow that make such connections possible; questions about authenticity when a Brazilian slave-based cultural practice travels in other bodies across the globe; questions of desire and identification as different members of the Noumea community relate to the African diaspora, physical movement, or the English used by the *mestre*; questions of origins and interconnectedness in the mixing of cultural pathways and histories. While many of the current conditions of the global world – the movement of people and money, the new forms of exploitation and environmental damage, the technologically driven availability of sounds and images from across the globe – could only happen at this juncture of the twenty-first century, forms of globalization have also been with us for a long time. It may only be at this historical juncture that cultural forms of African origin can drift casually through a Pacific island, but these forms were developed in Brazil under colonial rule several hundred years ago. This tension between the historical origins of globalization and the particularity of the present will be discussed below.

This chapter seeks to connect globalization and English. The use of the term 'global Englishes' might suggest a blend on the one hand of critical theories of globalization, where globalization is seen as an inherently destructive force homogenizing the world, and world Englishes on the other, where English is seen as a pluralized entity. While in some ways this term is intended to capture these two polarities – a critical theory of globalization and a pluralist vision of Englishes – I will also be distancing myself from these two ways of viewing English in the world (imperial or pluralist) since both have considerable shortcomings. As the discussion of *capoeira* in Noumea suggests, my interest in globalization is not merely with the ugliness of a world dominated by a rampant superpower, by a war on terror, by the rise of fundamentalist ideologies, by the imposition of crippling social and economic policies on those who can least afford it, but also by the possibilities that the global flows of languages and cultures open up. My interest in English concerns not only the detrimental effects of its spread on education systems, other languages and cultures, nor only its development into new, world Englishes, but also the ways in which it can be used outside these strictures, and the ways we can start to think about English in other ways.

Beyond homogeny and heterogeny

This chapter will therefore focus on both globalization and English. Reviewing David Crystal's (1997) book on the global spread of English, Sir John Hanson, the former Director-General of the British Council, proclaims: 'On it still strides: we can argue about what globalisation is till the cows come – but that globalisation exists is beyond question, with English its accompanist. The accompanist is indispensable to the performance' (Hanson, 1997, p. 22). Phillipson (1999, p. 274), by contrast, in his review of the same book, takes a more critical line, suggesting 'Crystal's celebration of the growth of English' is tied to 'an uncritical endorsement of capitalism, its science and technology, a modernisation ideology, monolingualism as a norm, ideological globalisation and internationalisation, transnationalisation, the Americanisation and homogenisation of world culture, linguistic, culture and media imperialism'. If Hanson's and Crystal's position simply fails to engage with questions of globalization and English, Phillipson's position rather problematically presents us only with an image of homogenization within a neocolonial global polity (which I have elsewhere categorized as the 'homogeny' position on global English; see Pennycook, 2003b).[1]

Given that there is now a vast range of work looking at the complexities of globalization (e.g. Appadurai, 1996; Castells, 2000; Giddens, 1999; Hardt and Negri, 2000; Mignolo, 2000), studies of global English deserve better than this. At the very least, we need to understand how English is involved in global flows of culture and knowledge, how English is used and appropriated by users of English around the world, how English colludes with multiple domains of globalization, from popular culture to unpopular politics, from international capital to local transaction, from ostensible diplomacy to purported peace-keeping, from religious proselytizing to secular resistance. The incessant invocation of 'English as an international language' avoids the obligation to deal with the complexity of English in relation to globalization while simultaneously reiterating the existence of English as if this were an issue not in doubt. As Kramsch (1999) observes, 'If there is one thing that globalization has brought us, and that the teaching of English makes possible, it is travel, migration, multiple allegiances, and a different relationship to time and place' (p. 138). The global spread of English inevitably raises questions not only of homogenization but also of difference. While Phillipson (1992, 1999, 2003) has usefully taken us beyond views of global English that fail to engage critically with the current world, continually striking a note of caution where English is concerned, a version of global English as only a force in the direction of greater similarity closes down an exploration of the complexity of current global conditions.

'Phillipson's account of linguistic imperialism', as Holborow (1999) notes, also 'leads in nationalist directions' (p. 79), since it fails to take class sufficiently into account in its centre–periphery model, and focuses predominantly on support for minority languages. This framework (imperialism versus local rights) frequently inspires nationalist responses, such as the recent *Combat pour le Français* by Claude Hagège (2006) in which the author argues for greater support for French in opposition to the global spread of English. Drawing on Phillipson's (2003, 2005) critique of the role of English in Europe, Hagège, as the subtitle of the book suggests (*Au nom de la diversité des langues et des cultures*: In the name of the diversity of languages and cultures), argues that support for French is support for cultural and linguistic diversity more broadly. Yet this *diversité* is not the global vision of *diversalité* (see Chapter 7) of the creolists Confiant, Chamoiseau and Glissant, or the translingual musicality of francophone hip-hop in Marseille, Dakar, Libreville or Montreal, but rather a nationally oriented vision of French as the guarantor of diversity in the face of imperial English. A similar case can be made for some Japanese responses to the threat of English imperialism (Tsuda, 1995), which switch from useful critiques of inequitable interactions between Japanese and non-Japanese in English, to strong nationalist defences of Japanese language and culture.

In a number of ways, therefore, the idea of world Englishes may be a better candidate for an understanding of globalization and English, since it seeks to challenge the notion of a monolithic English emanating from the central Anglo-institutions of global hegemony. While the homogeny position suggests that English is playing a role in world homogenization, here we get the other side of the coin, the *heterogeny position,* focusing on the 'implications of pluricentricity ... the new and emerging norms of performance, and the bilingual's creativity as a manifestation of the contextual and formal hybridity of Englishes' (Kachru, 1997, p. 66). The world Englishes paradigm has focused on the ways in which English has become locally adapted and institutionalized to create different varieties of English (different Englishes) around the world (Kachru, 1985, 1986, 1992; Kachru and Nelson, 1996). This work has been very significant in a number of ways. It has opened up a large field of study of difference in terms of new Englishes and has made it possible to argue that different forms of English are local varieties rather than misformed central English calumnies. On the other hand, this framework has also held back a more dynamic exploration of global Englishes. While the homogeny position operates with an over-determined political framework, the World Englishes framework has consistently avoided the broader political implications of the global spread of English: The 'pleas for the neutrality of English in the post-colonial contexts are as ubiquitous and as insistent as they are unsubstantiated and unexplained', suggests Parakrama (1995, p. 22). As Canagarajah (1999b) laments, 'We are urged to bury our eyes ostrich-like to the political evils and ideological temptations outside' (p. 210).

Alongside its political quietism, the world Englishes (WE) framework also presents a number of other limitations to a broader exploration of global Englishes. If the imperialism framework tends towards nationalist responses, the world Englishes framework places nationalism at its core. As Krishnaswamy and Burde (1998, p. 30) observe, if Randolph Quirk represented 'the imperialistic attitude' to English, the world Englishes approach represents a 'a nationalistic point of view', whereby nations and their varieties of English are conjured into existence: 'Like Indian nationalism,

"Indian English" is "fundamentally insecure" since the notion "nation-India" is insecure' (p. 63). As Dasgupta (1993, p. 137) laments, 'seldom have so many talented men and women worked so long and so hard and achieved so little', since the linguistics on which it relies cannot capture the complexity of language use it claims to investigate, a point emphasized by Krishnaswamy and Burde's (1998, p. 64) call for 'a reinvestigation of several concepts currently used by scholars'. By focusing centrally on the development of new national Englishes, the world Englishes approach reproduces the very linguistics it needs to escape.

Probably the best-known and most often cited dimension of the WE paradigm is the model of concentric circles: the 'norm-providing' inner circle, where English is spoken as a native language (ENL), the 'norm-developing' outer circle, where it is a second language (ESL), and the 'norm-dependent' expanding circle, where it is a foreign language (EFL). Although only 'tentatively labelled' (Kachru, 1985, p. 12) in earlier versions, it has been claimed more recently that 'the circles model is valid in the senses of earlier historical and political contexts, the dynamic diachronic advance of English around the world, and the functions and standards to which its users relate English in its many current global incarnations' (Kachru and Nelson, 1996, p. 78). Yano (2001, p. 121) refers to this model as the 'standard framework of world Englishes studies', and of all current discussions around global Englishes it is probably this model that is most widely referred to. While it has clearly therefore served some purposes in providing labels for different contexts of language use, it also suffers from several flaws: the location of nationally defined identities within the circles, the inability to deal with numerous contexts, and the privileging of ENL over ESL over EFL.

As Bruthiaux (2003, p. 161) points out, the descriptive and analytic inconsistency of the concentric circle model gives it little explanatory power. This 'superficially appealing and convenient model conceals more than it reveals', since it attempts to compare varieties of English, different speaker types and geographical locations all at once. Its use of inconsistent criteria to categorize so-called varieties of English is confounded by a 'primarily nation-based model'. According to Holborow (1999), the concentric circle model fails 'to take adequate account of social factors and social differences *within* the circles' (pp. 59–60). It thus overlooks difference within regions and ascribes variety based on postcolonial political history: where a nation state was created, so a variety emerged. By positing these new Englishes, it perpetuates the myth of national languages that the global spread of English allows us to start to rethink, and does so by focusing on a narrow selection of standardized forms in particular communities. As Parakrama (1995) argues, 'The smoothing out of struggle within and without language is replicated in the homogenizing of the varieties of English on the basis of "upper-class" forms. Kachru is thus able to theorize on the nature of a monolithic Indian English' (pp. 25–26). While appearing, therefore, to work from an inclusionary political agenda in its attempt to have the new Englishes acknowledged as varieties of English, this approach to language is remorselessly exclusionary. Ultimately, concludes Bruthiaux, 'the Three Circles model is a 20th century construct that has outlived its usefulness' (2003, p. 161).

The process of constructing these new national varieties of English involves a host of exclusions. Mufwene (1994, 1998) laments that the distinction between native and indigenized varieties of English 'excludes English creoles, most of which are spoken as native languages and vernaculars' (1994, p. 24). This exclusion, he suggests, ultimately concerns the identity of creole speakers: 'the naming practices of new Englishes has to do more with the racial identity of those who speak them than with how these varieties developed and the extent of their structural deviations' (2001, p. 107). The inclusion of creoles, furthermore, would profoundly challenge the notion of world Englishes: not only would it challenge the racial exclusion of the wrong sorts of speakers, but it would also challenge what is understood by language in general and English in particular. As Sebba (1997, p. 289) notes, following Mühlhäusler (1992), 'the study of pidgins and creoles forces us to stop conceptualising language as a *thing*, an *object* which can be captured and put under a microscope and dissected using a set of tools developed by linguists'. The dynamism of creoles, therefore, throws out a challenge to all study of languages as objects, an issue to which I return in Chapter 7.

The inclusion of creoles within an understanding of English, furthermore, questions not only the reification of English and world Englishes as objects on which linguists can do their work, but also how we think about languages more broadly. The inclusion of creole languages, with their hybrid lexicons and grammars, immediately destabilizes the concept of world Englishes, which by and large relies on a belief in a core, central grammar and lexicon of English (which is what makes new Englishes still English), with new Englishes characterized by various grammatical shifts, new lexical items and different pragmatic and phonological features. In this view, divergences from the core are viewed as 'localizations' so long as the overarching system remains intact. English from a creole-inclusive point of view, however, not only embraces a wide variety of mutually incomprehensible uses of language but also potentially a wide variety of grammars. Creole languages have to be excluded from *world* Englishes therefore, since they perforce destabilize the very definitions of language and grammar that underlie this version of a global language. Creole languages are therefore very much part of the notion of *global* Englishes, since they aim precisely at such destabilization.

Pluralization of English, therefore, does not take us far enough and remains an exclusionary paradigm. Just as Makoni (1998a, b) has argued that the concept of multilingualism may do little more than pluralize monolingualism, so I am suggesting that the concept of world Englishes does little more than pluralize monolithic English. The notion of world Englishes leaves out all those other Englishes which do not fit the paradigm of an emergent national standard, and in doing so, falls into the trap of mapping centre linguists' images of language and the world on to the periphery. As Parakrama (1995) argues, the world Englishes approach to diversity of English 'cannot do justice to those Other Englishes as long as they remain within the over-arching structures that these Englishes bring to crisis. To take these new/other Englishes seriously would require a fundamental revaluation of linguistic paradigms, and not merely a slight accommodation or adjustment' (p. 17). Or, as Canagarajah (1999a, p. 180) puts it, in Kachru's 'attempt to systematize the periphery variants, he has to standardize the language himself, leaving out many eccentric, hybrid forms of local Englishes as too unsystematic. In this, the Kachruvian paradigm follows the logic of the prescriptive and elitist tendencies of the center linguists.' The irony here is that while resembling a pluralist, localised version of English, this paradigm reinforces both centrist views on language and dangerous myths about English.

If we take a step back from this myth, it is indeed puzzling to observe the extraordinary continuation of the idea that something called English exists, a myth perpetuated by strategies of exclusion and circularity. It is assumed a priori that there is such a thing as English, a view reinforced by excluding those types of English, and, as Mufwene notes, those types of speakers, that don't fit what is deemed to be English, and by then employing the circular argument that if it doesn't fit, then it isn't English. A core system of English is assumed, with deviations from this core that destabilize the notion of system discounted. The world Englishes paradigm, while attempting to achieve sociolinguistic equality for its varieties, is not epistemologically different from this model of core, variation and exclusion: for a world English to be such, it must adhere to the underlying grammar of central English, demonstrate enough variety to make it interestingly different, but not diverge to the extent that it undermines the myth of English. If we acknowledge creole languages, however, if we refuse to draw a line down the middle of a creole continuum (exclaiming that one end is English while the other is not), if we decide that those 'other Englishes' may be part of English, then we are not dealing with a language held in place by a core structure but rather a notion of language status that is not definable by interior criteria.

Rather than the model of language implied by a globalization-as-imperialism thesis, a position which suggests that the world is being homogenized through English, or the view of language suggested by a world Englishes framework which focuses on the heterogenization of varieties of English, I am arguing for an understanding of global Englishes that focuses on both a critical understanding of globalization and a critical understanding of language. The dominant paradigms that have informed much of our discussion to date of the global spread of English – linguistic imperialism and world Englishes – are both mired in a linguistics and a politics of the last century, focusing inexorably on languages and nations as given entities, and ill-equipped to deal with current modes of globalization. It is common to view globalization in terms of two axes, the global and the local: on the one hand the dominance of particular cultural and linguistic practices, on the other the maintenance or development of local practices. The argument of this chapter and this book, however, is that we need more complex and flexible ways of thinking about this. The multidimensional nature of both dominating modes of globalization – corporatization, capitalization, conceptualization – and of resistant and localizing modes – transculturation, translocalization, transformation – lead to very different linguistic and cultural practices than international domination or national localization. It is a far more dynamic space of flows. As Sonntag (2003) suggests, 'global integration may be a better indicator of similarities in the local politics of global English than the usage-of-English categories' (p. 114).

Globalization, worldliness and transgression

We therefore need ways of mapping Englishes against a reasonably complex understanding of globalization. It is important first of all to separate different versions of globalization. One version sees it as more or less akin to Americanization. From this perspective, drawing on the tradition of economically focused world-systems models, globalization refers to the increasing domination of predominantly US-based economic and political power. Yet this version is already limited by its attempts to turn globalization into a state-based phenomenon. While it would be equally foolish to ignore the global role of the US and its reversal of the common adage to 'think globally, act locally' by acting globally and thinking locally, as Slavoj Žižek (2004) has remarked, it is of greater concern to understand the role of both transnational corporations and bodies such as the International Monetary Fund (IMF) in the constant creation rather than alleviation of poverty. As Joseph Stiglitz (2002), Nobel Prize-winning economist and former chief economist of the World Bank between 1997 and 2001, argues in his book *Globalization and its Discontents*, the IMF is peopled by economic fundamentalists who insist, without regard for local conditions and constraints, on a monetarist creed that prescribes cuts in government spending, privatization of public institutions, removal of subsidies and the opening up of the economy to transnational corporatizations. It is this process that I shall call 'corporatization' (see below), since it follows a model both of turning publicly owned sectors into privately run corporations and emphasizes a free market to which large corporations should have access.

But corporatization and economics are not the only factors worth considering here. While corporatization usefully describes one dominant aspect of the current state of affairs, as both a cultural design on and for the world, as well as an economic model for the world, several other factors need to be understood. As Giddens (1999), Castells (2000) and others have shown, globalization is not only about economic processes, but political, technological and cultural processes as well. Globalization may be better understood as a compression of time and space, an intensification of social, economic, cultural and political relations, a series of global linkages that render events in one location of potential and immediate importance in other, quite distant locations. To suggest that globalization is only a US or Western domination of the world is to take a narrow and ultimately unproductive view of global relations. The very point about globalization is that it is global, and thus is inevitably caught up in multiple influences. Indian call centres, indigenous education conferences, Japanese animated cartoons, anti-globalization networks, fast-moving fashions, gay and lesbian travel organizations, the ubiquity and similarity of urban graffiti are all part of globalization. To view culture and language in terms only of reflections of the economic is to miss the point that new technologies and communications are enabling immense and complex flows of people, signs, sounds, images across multiple borders in multiple directions. Education is a good example of this, with students moving in increasing numbers to take up educational possibilities elsewhere (Singh and Doherty, 2004), resulting in changing practices in the new 'educational contact zones', and new, appropriated knowledges travelling across borders.

According to Mignolo (2000), 'The current process of globalization is not a new phenomenon, although the way in which it is taking place is without precedent. On a larger scale, globalization at the end of the twentieth century (mainly occurring through transnational corporations, the media, and technology) is the most recent configuration of a process that can be traced back to the 1500s, with the beginning of transatlantic exploration and the consolidation of Western hegemony' (p. 236). Mignolo traces three principal phases. The first, the *Orbis Universalis Christianus*, was consolidated by the defeat of the Moors, the expulsion of the Jews from the Iberian peninsula and the 'discovery' of America. The second phase 'replaced the hegemony of the Christian mission with the civilizing mission' with a new basis of mercantile expansion and trading based around Amsterdam, and the emergence of France and England as the new imperial powers. The civilizing mission took over from the Christian mission but also co-existed with it. This mission went through various configurations in the twentieth century, particularly the development and modernization paradigms following the Second World War. Finally, the third phase has gradually taken precedent with the emphasis on efficiency and expanding markets. But, as Mignolo emphasizes, we need to understand 'the coexistence of successive global designs that are part of the imaginary of the modern/colonial world system' (p. 280).

This conception of the historical continuity of globalization is widely contested on the basis that what we are now experiencing is fundamentally new. On the one hand, efforts to construct a more benign view of globalization have been keen to distance the current age from previous eras of imperial expansion. On the other hand, analyses that place the expansion of capital at their core, and argue that globalization is nothing more than the logical next step of imperialism, have been critiqued for their failure to grasp that there is something fundamentally different going on. Hardt and Negri's (2000) Empire is significant here since they argue that most analyses fail to account for 'the novelty of the structures and logics of power that order the contemporary world. Empire is not a weak echo of modern imperialisms but a fundamentally new form of rule' (p. 146). Unlike the old imperialism(s), which were centred around the economic and political structures and exchanges of the nation state (indeed, the two were in many ways mutually constitutive), and which may be best portrayed in terms of world maps with different colours for different empires, the new Empire is a system of national and supranational regulations that control and produce new economies, cultures, politics and ways of living.

It is possible, I want to suggest, to reconcile these apparently divergent views on globalization, the one arguing for historical continuity, the other for a radical break with the past. On the one hand, if we lose sight of the historical precedents of the current state of globalization, we lose a crucial understanding of how current global conditions have come into being; on the other, if we focus too much on continuity, we fail to see that the forces of globalization demand new ways of thinking, new solutions to new problems. Drawing on Mignolo's (2000) and Hardt and Negri's (2000) views of globalization, therefore, I suggest we can expand on Mignolo's threefold model of European designs by considering five overlapping processes: the first is the age of Christianizing and discovering, where Europeans set out on voyages of discovery, driven both by mercantile interests and a fundamental belief in their own religious rectitude; second is the civilizing and enlightening design for the world, where European beliefs in their cultural and philosophical superiority formed the basis for an era of civilizing the world; third came conceptualizing and developing, a period when the goal became to conceptualize other countries and to help them develop in the European image (a period when Western academic knowledge and the disciplines of anthropology, linguistics and economics came to the fore) (Cohn, 1996); this merged into the capitalizing/universalizing design, when international capital and a concept of human universality governed human relations in the latter part of the twentieth century; and finally corporatizing/ globalizing, when globalization takes over from universal and international concepts of the world, and it is the corporatization of many levels of society – from business to institutions that had formally been seen as part of the state (education, health, transport) – that predominates within a new neo-liberal politics for the world. Unless we incorporate this historical vision into an understanding of globalization, we will lose sight of the many current overlapping designs of the world. As will be discussed in Chapter 7, for example, while Senegalese hip-hoppers Daara J may be part of current global circuits of the music industry, when they invoke the history of slavery to explain that hip-hop started in Africa and is returning to Africa (and calling their track that refers to this 'Boomerang' for good measure), they locate themselves firmly within an historical understanding of globalization.

In addition to the basic argument that globalization has a long history, there are a number of significant considerations here. Most important are the observations that this is not a purely economic model, and that the designs overlap each other. Thus we are not looking only at a history of capital expansion but also at a model of cultural expansion, which is not necessarily driven by prior capitalist goals. While trade and capitalism played significant roles within imperial expansion, so too did beliefs in the imperatives to spread Christianity and Western knowledge. English was also bound up with many elements of these global designs, as Read attested over 150 years ago:

> Ours is the language of the arts and sciences, of trade and commerce, of civilization and religious liberty .... It is a store-house of the varied knowledge which brings a nation within the pale of civilization and Christianity .... Already it is the language of the Bible .... So prevalent is this language already become, as to betoken that it may soon become the language of international communication for the world.
>
> (Read, 1849, p. 48, cited in Bailey, 1991, p. 116)

These designs have not replaced each other; rather, they co-exist. The Christian design on the world does not appear to be any weaker in the twenty-first century than it was in the sixteenth century (see Pennycook and Coutand-Marin, 2003; Pennycook and Makoni, 2005), but now it co-exists with civilizing, conceptualizing, capitalizing and corporatizing designs.

A new era of Empire, as Hardt and Negri (2000) argue, requires new ways of thinking: 'We should be done once and for all with the search for an outside, a standpoint that imagines a purity for our politics. It is better both theoretically and practically to enter the terrain of Empire and confront its homogenizing and heterogenizing flows in all their complexity, grounding our analysis in the power of the global multitude' (p. 46). While imperialism was a territorial expansion of the nation state, Empire is decentred and deterritorialized. The modern nation state 'was structured in part by new capitalist productive processes on the one hand and old networks of absolutist administration on the other. This uneasy structural relationship was stabilized by the national identity: a cultural, integrating identity, founded on a biological continuity of blood relations, a spatial continuity of territory, and linguistic commonality' (p. 95). Just as we need to think outside the notion of the nation state, so too we need to rethink language. Modernist theories of power, they argue, considered language to be external, transcendent, superstructural, above productive and social relations. Hardt and Negri suggest, by contrast, that it is 'immanent' to such relations (p. 33). 'Power, as it produces, organizes; as it organizes, it speaks and expresses itself as authority. Language, as it communicates, produces commodities but moreover creates subjectivities, puts them in relation, and orders them' (p. 33).

Such views have serious implications for any understanding of global Englishes, since they relocate language and power outside the nation but immanent to global relations. This helps to clarify the problems with viewing current global relations in terms either of imperialism versus national opposition or spread versus national standardization, both of which are strategies of the old regime. Although Empire wields enormous powers of oppression and destruction, we should neither become nostalgic for earlier forms of oppression, nor overlook the new possibilities for change it offers. Just as Marx argued that capital was a necessary stage to pass through – and preferable to earlier formations of power, particularly feudalism – Hardt and Negri argue persuasively that there is no going back: trying to use the nation state or localization as strategies of resistance is largely reactionary nostalgia. While I shall focus in some detail in Chapters 6 and 7 on forms of localization – seen not so much as nostalgic returns to earlier forms but as reinventions of the local – this view of Empire has great significance for how we understand issues such as linguistic imperialism, language rights or world Englishes, since it suggests that all such concepts fail to grasp current modes of power. And so, finally, we come to the last crucial point that the new conditions of Empire require and produce new strategies of resistance.

To see the development of globalization as only a set of European (and latterly American) designs on the world overlooks two important considerations: first, the role of other significant empires over the past 500 years, such as the Russian, Chinese and Japanese. If we are to talk about globalization, we surely need to see more interlocking relationships here, both in terms of historical empires and contemporary circles of influence. Thus, even though these imperial designs may well have coalesced in the current form of globalization – indeed, it is this coalescence that may make this new era different from the past stages – there are nevertheless more complex interwoven histories than only that of European colonialism. And second, there have always been strategies of opposition: the new conditions of Empire require and produce new strategies of resistance. Resistance and change, argue Mignolo (2000) and Hardt and Negri (2000), are possible, but they will not be achieved through a wistful longing for old forms of identification. While processes of resistance, appropriation and hybridization also have a long history (indeed, they may be mapped alongside global designs), they become something new under new conditions of power. For Hardt and Negri (2000, p. 393), new conditions of opposition are produced due to the direct confrontation between Empire and people: 'Empire creates a greater potential for revolution than did the modern regimes of power because it presents us, alongside the machine of command, with an alternative: the set of all the exploited and the subjugated, a multitude that is directly opposed to Empire, with no mediation between them.'

Here, however, by dismissing the local and being seduced by a form of romantic, global neo-Marxism,[2] Hardt and Negri miss the point that resistance is more a question of Mignolo's 'local histories', 'subaltern knowledges' and 'border thinking' than of global revolution or democracy.

As Mignolo suggests, there has always been opposition and resistance to global designs: they have been changed, appropriated and remade. Drawing on the distinction used by Renato Ortiz and Edouard Glissant between globalización/globalization and mundialización/mondialization, Mignolo suggests that the first may be used to refer to these global designs, while the second term, which I am here translating as worldliness,[3] may be seen in terms of 'local histories *in* which global histories are enacted or where they have to be adapted, adopted, transformed, and rearticulated' (Mignolo, 2000, p. 278). This, then, is the site of resistance, change, adaptation and reformulation. It is akin to what Canagarajah (1999a) in his discussion of resistance to the global spread of English describes as a 'resistance perspective', highlighting the ways in which postcolonial subjects 'may find ways to negotiate, alter and oppose political structures, and reconstruct their languages, cultures and identities to their advantage. The intention is not to reject English, but to *reconstitute* it in more inclusive, ethical, and democratic terms' (p. 2). From this point of view, then, there is always a response to the designs of Empire, processes of resistance, rearticulation, reconstitution.

Thus I want to suggest that in response to the Christianizing and discovering, civilizing and enlightening, conceptualizing and developing, capitalizing and universalizing, and corporatizing and globalizing designs there have always been reactions. Responses to such designs may take many forms, as Kubota (2002) notes in her discussion of the cultural, linguistic and educational responses to globalization in Japan. Globalization, she suggests, implies not only 'cultural homogenization influenced by global standardization of economic activities and a flow of cultural goods from the centre to the periphery' but also 'increased local diversity influenced by human contact across cultural boundaries as well as speedy exchange of commodities and information' (p. 13). This has been met by three responses: increased local community diversity, increased emphasis on English, and increased linguistic and cultural nationalism. As Kubota's comments suggest, there is not only resistance and reaction to globalization, but these are also of many kinds, from the defensive and reactionary to the activist and transformative. Likewise, drawing on his extensive research on the processes of opposition and resistance, Willis (2003) describes 'three waves' of youth response to imposed structures of modernity: the response to universal schooling, the response to the decline of manual labour in (post)industrial societies, and the creative response 'to a plethora of electronic signals and cultural commodities in ways that surprise their makers, finding meanings and identities never meant to be there and defying simple nostrums that bewail the manipulation of passivity of "consumers"' (p. 392). There will, then, always be reactions, interpretations, rearticulations of whatever is spread by globalization.

For the purposes of this book, I shall focus on a set of interrelated processes that have transgressive or transformational orientations: transgression and resistance, translation and rearticulation, transformation and reconstitution, translocalization and appropriation, transculturation and hybridization. These will be discussed in greater depth in Chapter 3 on transgressive theories. Overall, the point here is to understand globalization not only in terms of economic relations, but also in terms of social, cultural and political relations. Such processes, I have argued, need to be understood both in terms of historical continuity and in terms of historical disjuncture: while we are being presented with radically new conditions and theories, we also need to understand their historical precedents. Globalization brings new forms of power, control and destruction; but it also always becomes relocated in new forms of worldliness, engendering processes of resistance, change and appropriation. If we want to deal with global Englishes, I suggest, we need to do so against such a background, viewing English as a crucial part of globalization and worldliness, though not a mere reflection of economic relations. We need to challenge the many myths of English (see Pennycook, in press) that give it a priori ontological status and instead ask what kinds of desires and mobilizations are at stake when English is invoked.

Postoccidentalism and kaleidoscopic, ludic Englishes

I argued above that the frameworks for dealing with global English with which we have been operating are limited in various ways. Phillipson (1992) gives us an impossible view of imperialistic English which Bhatt (2005) describes as a 'new form of linguistic colonialism, expressed in terms of expert discourse' that overlooks 'the role various Englishes play in different social, economic, and political market-places in India' (p. 33). While linguistic imperialism has perhaps inadvertently reinforced states-centric visions of language and politics, a world Englishes focus has made this central to its understanding of variety. As Bruthiaux (2003) describes it, 'while the Three Circles model has provided us with a convenient shorthand for labeling contexts of English worldwide, the categories that the model created have also had the unfortunate side-effect of reifying the content of these categories and of encouraging the notion that Englishes are Englishes, regardless of circle' (p.174). By focusing all too often on national varieties of English as represented through the 'high culture' activities of English-language writers (for more discussion, see Chapter 5), World Englishes operate in a way similar to what Hutnyk (2000) calls the 'liberal exoticist enthusiasm' (p. 12) for hybridity in world music, the 'global sampling' (p. 22) of WOMAD (World of Music and Dance) festivals. My point here, of course, is not to discount postcolonial writing in English, but to seek a more complex, contemporary understanding of cultural production in relationship to English, nations, culture, representation and the world.

In order to get beyond these frameworks, I have been trying to stake out a view of global Englishes which suggests that various linguistic uses that used to be more localized are now occurring on a global scale; these global language uses are not determined by economic relations alone, but rather are part of complex networks of communication and cultural flows. In order to grasp such language use, we need to understand that we are dealing here with radically new conditions and theories. Such use of other Englishes needs to be understood both in terms of their historical continuity and in terms of historical disjuncture; they also need to be understood critically in terms of new forms of power, control and destruction, as well as new forms of resistance, change and appropriation. We need to ask here how it is that 'English' became 'English', not in terms of a standard history of the English language but rather in terms of how this and other languages were constructed in particular ways. As I argue at greater length in Chapter 3, we need theoretical tools that address not only relations of power – dominion, disparity, difference and desire – but that also maintain a constant scepticism towards the categories we take for granted. One way forward here is to think in terms of postoccidentalism.

Occidentalism may be understood in several different ways,[4] though perhaps most important is Mignolo's (2000) assertion that 'without Occidentalism there is no Orientalism' (p. 58). From this perspective, as Europe orientalized other parts of the world, it was always constructing itself as the counterpart. Singh (1996) points to the 'characteristic Orientalizing tropes of difference producing an ontological distinction between West and East, defining the Orient in terms of everything the Occident is not: decadent, weak, barbaric, feminine' (p. 59). The British view of India, for example, 'as a land of dirt, disease, and sudden death' (Metcalf, 1995, p. 171) only became possible in relationship to a construction of Britain as a land of health, cleanliness and longevity: 'Calcutta, one might say, became filthy only as London became clean' (Metcalf, 1995, p. 173). Occidentalism, then, may be understood as 'the Western version of Western civilization (its own self-description) ingrained in the imaginary of the modern/colonial world' (Mignolo, 2000, p. 328). As Venn (2000, p. 19) argues, the notion of occidentalism

> directs attention to the becoming-modern of the world and the becoming-West of Europe such that Western modernity gradually became established as the privileged, if not hegemonic, form of sociality, tied to a universalizing and totalizing ambition. Occidentalism indicates a genealogy of the present which reconstructs a particular trajectory of modernity, inflected by the fact of colonialism and of capitalism.

A post-Occidentalist position, according to Mignolo (2000), takes us beyond postmodern and postcolonial critiques since 'they fail to recognize adequately the contemporary object of critique' (p. 137). While they critique the binaries of modernism and colonialism, they do not focus enough on the contemporary world. It is for related reasons that I take up the notion of transgressive theory in Chapter 3. Here, I want to use the insights of a post-Occidentalist position to ask how it is that particular versions of language gained ascendancy and to open up alternative ways of thinking about global Englishes. Sinfree Makoni and I (Makoni and Pennycook, 2005, in press) have approached this issue through the lenses of disinventing and reconstituting language, similarly asking how it is that languages became languages, English became English. Our argument here is that the ways in which language and languages are understood has been constructed through particular metadiscursive regimes (Bauman and Briggs, 2003) and is dependent on the analysts' cultural and historical 'locus of enunciation' (Mignolo, 2000, p. 116).

Taking up the post-Occidentalist question of how it was that certain formations were able to describe themselves as 'modern', Bauman and Briggs (2003) suggest that Latour (1993) and Foucault (1970), both of whom have done much to help us understand the construction of modernity, offer inadequate accounts of the role of language. Latour, they suggest, 'misses language, that is, the role of its construction as autonomous and the work of purification and hybridization this entails in making modernity' (p. 8). By viewing language as only a mode of mediation between the primary domains of science and society, Latour remains 'simply modern here, having succumbed to the definition of language as real and its relegation to the role of carrying out particular modernist functions, such as conveying information' (p. 8). This is akin to the problems with Anderson's (1983) well-known account of imagined communities. As Joseph (2004) points out, 'Anderson's constructionist approach to nationalism is purchased at the price of an essentialist outlook on languages. It seems a bargain to the sociologist or political scientist, to whom it brings explanatory simplicity not to mention ease. But ... it is a false simplicity. National languages and identities arise in tandem, "dialectically" if you like, in a complex process that ought to be our focus of interest and study' (Joseph, 2004, p. 124). Similarly, while Foucault's (1970) account of language 'provides an excellent starting point for discerning how reimagining language was crucial for imagining modernity', Bauman and Briggs (2003) argue that 'the story needs to be retold if its broader significance – particularly for understanding how modernity produces and structures inequality – is to become more intellectually and politically accessible' (p. 10).

For Bauman and Briggs, the key question is how modernism (through the work of philosophers such as Locke) created language as a separate domain, how language 'came into being' (p. 7) and the 'process involved in creating language and rendering it a powerful means of creating social inequality' (p. 9). As Mühlhäusler (2000) points out, the notion of 'a language' 'is a recent culture-specific notion associated with the rise of European nation states and the Enlightenment. The notion of "a language" makes little sense in most traditional societies' (p. 358). Crucial to this construction of language, according to Bauman and Briggs (2003), was Locke's 'positioning of language as one of the three "great provinces of the intellectual world" that are "wholly separate and distinct"' (p. 299). As they go on to explain, 'separating language from both nature/science and society/politics, Locke could place practices for purifying language of any explicit connections with either society or nature at the center of his vision of modern linguistic and textual practices' (pp. 299–300).

My argument here is that current ways of looking at global Englishes have inherited this view of languages as isolated, autonomous and enumerable entities. They are thus seeking to operate with the very epistemological tools that were developed under the conditions they seek to critique (imperialism and Anglo-centrism). Rajagopalan (1999) raises this issue when he suggests that 'the very charges being pressed against the hegemony of the English language and its putative imperialist pretensions themselves bear the imprint of a way of thinking about language moulded in an intellectual climate of excessive nationalist fervour and organized marauding of the wealth of alien nations, an intellectual climate where identities were invariably thought of in all-or-nothing terms' (p. 201). Looking at the discourses of language rights in relation to the global spread of English, Sonntag (2003) makes a similar point, suggesting that 'the willingness to use the language of human rights on the global level to frame local linguistic demands vis-à-vis global English may merely be affirming the global vision projected by American liberal democracy' (p. 25). Unless we can escape these frameworks for thinking about English, therefore, we run the danger of constantly remaking precisely those conditions we aim to critique.

An integrationist redefinition of linguistics (Harris, 1990, 1998) provides one possible way forward here. As both Mühlhäusler (2000) and Toolan (2003) argue, an integrationist view of language suggests not merely that language is integrated with its environment, but rather that languages themselves cannot be viewed as discrete items, rejecting as a 'powerful and misleading myth,' any assumption that a language is essentially an autonomous system which humans can harness to meet their communicational needs' (Toolan, 2003, p. 123). This, then, takes seriously Harris's claim that 'linguistics does not need to postulate the existence of languages as part of its theoretical apparatus' (1990, p. 45). As Harris goes on to argue, the question here is whether 'the concept of a language, as defined by orthodox modern linguistics, corresponds to any determinate or determinable object of analysis at all, whether social or individual, whether institutional or psychological. If there is no such object, it would be difficult to evade the conclusion that modern linguistics has been based upon a myth' (p. 45). And as I would suggest for global Englishes, paraphrasing Harris, the question is whether the concept of English or Englishes, as defined by linguistic imperialism or world Englishes or any other current attempt to deal with global English, corresponds to any object of analysis at all, whether social or individual, whether institutional or

psychological. If there is no such object, it would be difficult to evade the conclusion that current views of global English have been based upon a myth.

A focus on the notion of language ideologies or regimes of language
(Kroskrity, 2000) within linguistic anthropology raises the question of how
it is that languages are understood locally. As Woolard (2004) notes, such
work has shown that 'linguistic ideologies are never just about language, but
rather also concern such fundamental social notions as community, nation,
and humanity itself' (p. 58). For linguistic anthropologists, the problem was
that the 'surgical removal of language from context produced an amputated
"language" that was the preferred object of the language sciences for most
of the twentieth century' (Kroskrity, 2000, p. 5). By studying language ideologies as contextual sets of belief about languages, or as Irvine (1989, p.
255) puts it, 'the cultural system of ideas about social and linguistic relationships, together with their loading of moral and political interests', this
line of work has shown the significance of local knowledge about language.
As Branson and Miller (2000) argue, we 'must not only revel in linguistic
difference but cope with that difference analytically. Let us recognize the
culturally specific nature of our own schemes and search for new modes of
analysis that do not fit other languages into a mould but celebrate and build
on their epistemological differences' (p. 32).

To this picture of culturally specific understandings of language we may
also add sociolinguistic investigations of what Rampton (1995) has called
'crossing' – ways in which members of certain groups use forms of speech
from other groups – or 'styling the Other' – 'ways in which people use language and dialect in discursive practice to appropriate, explore, reproduce
or challenge influential images and stereotypes of groups that they *don't*
themselves (straightforwardly) belong to' (Rampton, 1999, p. 421). Instead
of focusing on a 'linguistics of community' (which is often based on a circularity of argument which suggests that a speaker of a particular community
speaks a certain language because he or she belongs to the community which
speaks that language, while the fact that they speak this language in turn
proves they are a member of this community), this work focuses more on a
'linguistics of contact' (Pratt, 1987), 'looking instead at the intricate ways
in which people use language to index social group affiliations in situations
where the acceptability and legitimacy of their doing so is open to question,
incontrovertibly guaranteed neither by ties of inheritance, ingroup social-
isation, nor by any other language ideology' (Rampton, 1999, p. 422).
Significant too in this work has been the focus on popular culture, word
play and contextual interaction. As Hill suggests, the 'kaleidoscopic, ludic,
open flavor' of much of the language use described profoundly challenges
the methods of mainstream sociolinguistics 'by transgressing fundamental
ideas of "speakerhood"' (1999, pp. 550–511). Cutler's (1999) study of a
white American teenager's identification with hip-hop culture shows how
this can be a contested space that 'may not match the standards of authenticity laid out in traditional sociolinguistics' (p. 439). This work raises key

questions about communication, community, contact, identity and play. And as I shall be arguing in this book, it is precisely the 'kaleidoscopic, ludic, open flavor' of language use in hip-hop that needs to be taken seriously as performance and transgression.

As Cameron (1990, 1995, 1997) has observed, while the sociolinguistics that lies at the core of most studies of global Englishes has operated all too often with fixed and static categories of class, gender and identity membership as if these were transparent givens on to which language may be mapped, a more critical account suggests that 'language is one of the things that constitutes my identity as a particular kind of subject' (1995, p. 16). This opens up the possibility of thinking in terms of semiotic reconstruction and performativity. As Kandiah (1998, p. 100) argues, most approaches to the new Englishes miss the crucial point that these Englishes 'fundamentally involve a radical act of semiotic reconstruction and reconstitution which of itself confers native userhood on the subjects involved in the act'. The crucial point here, then, is that it is not so much whether or not one is born in a particular type of community but rather what one does with the language. It is in the performance that the identity is created. I shall discuss performativity in much greater depth in Chapter 4. In the next chapter, I will look more closely at what I call transgressive theory.

3   Transgressive theories

Graffiti have been described as a form of 'transgressive semiotics' (Scollon and Scollon, 2003, p. 147): while they are often conspicuously authored, they are also crucially not authorized, transgressing public space. Hip-hop more broadly may be seen as a set of transgressive semiotic practices, *breaking* the rules of dancing, *scratching* against the groove, *rapping* against the status quo, *tagging* the public space. Indeed, Riley (2005) argues for an interpretation of gangsta rap in terms of the 'transgressive sacred' (p. 303), which links such forms of popular culture to traditional sites of festivity and ritual that may be seen as either reverential or transgressive (Caillois, 1988; Durkheim, 1961). From its destabilization of notions of authorship and originality to its often aggressive challenges to aesthetics, politics and social norms, hip-hop transgresses a sense of what is possible and permissible, a set of 'post-apocalyptic' cultural forms set against decaying, postindustrial urban spaces around the world (Potter, 1995, p. 8). As we saw in Chapter 2, the 'kaleidoscopic, ludic, open flavor' of language in hip-hop can profoundly challenge many assumptions about ownership, community and language use 'by transgressing fundamental ideas of "speakerhood"' (Hill, 1999, pp. 550–551).

Like the *trans* of transgender, transvestite and transsexual, to think and be trans is not only to cross over, to transcend the bounded norms of social and cultural dictates, but also to question the ontologies on which definitions of sex, gender and sexuality rest (Butler, 2004). As Jervis (1999) points out, 'transgressive sexuality is an offence against the "real", the modern structure of reality and illusion; it is an ontological "crime", before it is a moral one' (p. 177). In this chapter I propose a form of transgressive theory that seeks both to account for the transgressions of hip-hop and to disrupt some standard ontologies. In the previous chapter I raised a number of questions about the ontology of language in general and English in particular (and see Pennycook, 2006b). I also suggested the need to move beyond some of the 'post' frameworks because of the inevitable ways in which they are always looking over their shoulders at the past. Obsessed with structuralism, modernism and colonialism, poststructuralism, postmodernism and postcolonialism have too often been concerned with critique and with looking for solutions in the wrong place. In order to avoid the pitfalls of the realist/non-realist debate, I shall suggest, following David Scott (1999), that we can only move forward if we accept the reality of struggle and the particularity of knowledge, Fanon and Foucault. I am therefore arguing for the idea of transgressive theory, as a necessary way of dealing with a transgressive form such as hip-hop, as an approach that takes us beyond the 'posts' and the 'critical', and as an overarching framework that pulls together numerous 'trans' concepts (transculturation, translation, transtextuality, transmodality).

From critical to transgressive applied linguistics

I have discussed at length elsewhere (Pennycook, 2001, 2003c, 2004a, 2006c) the tensions and difficulties in the development of a critical applied linguistics. Rather than a method, a set of techniques or a fixed body of knowledge, I see critical applied linguistics as a *movable praxis*, a constantly shifting and dynamic approach to questions of language in multiple contexts. Rather than viewing critical applied linguistics as a new form of interdisciplinary knowledge, I prefer to view it as a form of *anti*-disciplinary or transgressive knowledge, as a way of thinking and doing that is always problematizing. This means not only that critical applied linguistics implies a hybrid model of research and praxis, but also that it generates something which is far more dynamic. Critical applied linguistics from this perspective is not about the mapping of a fixed politics on to a static body of knowledge, but rather is about creating something new. As Foucault (1980) put it, 'the problem is not so much one of defining a political "position" (which is to choose from a pre-existing set of possibilities) but to imagine and to bring into being new schemas of politicisation' (p. 190).

One of the limitations of common understandings of interdisciplinarity is that while work across disciplines is encouraged, the notion of disciplinary knowledge itself remains relatively fixed. From this point of view applied linguistics as a discipline (or an interdiscipline) can draw on other disciplines such as linguistics, psychology and education to inform its work. Such a view, however, overlooks the ways in which both applied linguistics and the other disciplines on which it draws are shifting spaces of intellectual inquiry, especially in the wake of the linguistic and cultural turns in the social sciences. Discussing the signs of maturity in applied linguistics (AL) suggested by its moving away from a reliance on linguistics to become a theory-generating discipline in its own right, Rajagopalan (2004) talks of the 'growing need to conceive of AL as a *trans*disciplinary field of inquiry', which means 'traversing (and, if it comes to the push, *trans*gressing) conventional disciplinary boundaries in order to develop a brand new research agenda which, while freely drawing on a wide variety of disciplines, would obstinately seek to remain subaltern to none' (p. 410, emphasis in original). This, then, is one sense of the notion of transgressing: in the domain of disciplinary knowledge, it suggests not merely inter- or transdisciplinary pluralism, but also a more illicit sense of traversing forbidden boundaries, and perhaps, in the process, starting to trample down some of these disciplinary fences.

According to Elder (2004), 'the very existence of a transgressive critical applied linguistics which attacks the foundations and goals of applied linguistics is perhaps a sign that applied linguistics is a discipline which has come of age' (p. 430). Thus, while Davies (1999) may lament the critique of applied linguistics and the moves towards a broader interdisciplinary conception of the area as 'dismissive totally of the attempt since the 1950s to develop a coherent applied linguistics' (p. 141), it is also possible to see in these developments a greater maturity, a breaking away from the shackles of disciplinarity that an older generation of applied linguists has sought to impose. By drawing on a far broader range of 'external' domains than is often the case with applied linguistics, transgressive applied linguistics not only opens up the intellectual framework to many diverse influences, but also makes debates over 'linguistics applied' versus 'applied linguistics' at best of peripheral interest (linguistics in most of its current manifestations is of limited use) and at worst a major distraction from the concerns we need to deal with. By taking not only a broad but also a political view of knowledge, transgressive applied linguistics takes us beyond a conception of applied linguistics as a fixed discipline, beyond even a view of applied linguistics as a domain of interdisciplinary work.

The opening up of applied linguistics to this diversity of concerns and perspectives has caused some concern, bringing warnings that critical applied linguistics must not be 'allowed to take over, cuckoo-like' (Davies, 1999, p. 142), or admonitions that 'by making a virtue of the necessity of partiality we in effect deny plurality and impose our own version of reality, thereby exercising the power of authority which we claim to deplore' (Widdowson, 2001, p. 15). While such warnings need to be heeded – the impetus of a critical or transgressive approach to applied linguistics can never be to 'take over' the discipline, and the emphasis on the partial should never lead to the denial of difference – it is time to move forward from these debates over the nature of applied linguistics. Following David Scott (1999), I would like to be able to take various long-fought-over political and epistemological stances more or less for granted: 'positions are to be read as contingent, histories as local, subjects as constructed, and knowledge as enmeshed in power' (p. 4). Let us take these as givens, as positions made evident through poststructuralist, postmodern and postcolonial critiques of knowledge, and move on. In order to ground a new approach to *transgressive applied linguistics*, we need to find ways of maintaining both a relentless focus on the workings of power and a restless questioning of the terms we use, or, as Scott suggests, we need to work both with the postcolonial politics of Frantz Fanon – 'the revolutionary architect par excellence of anticolonial liberation' (p. 200) – and also with the epistemological scepticism of Michel Foucault – to warn us that 'politics must never be allowed to rest on the satisfaction of its own self-conception, on the identities it affirms as the constituents of its community' (p. 207). On the one hand, the urgency and realities of political struggle, on the other hand, the need to always question our own and others' assumptions.

Fanon requires us to focus on complex relations of power, resistance and struggle; on race, postcolonial politics and inequalities constructed through forms of difference (gender, sexual orientation, language use). Adapting Janks's (2000) discussion of power and critical literacy, any critical project needs to focus on the constant interplay among *dominion* (the contingent and contextual effects of power), *disparity* (inequality and the demand for access), *difference* (engaging with diversity) and *desire* (understanding how identity and agency are related). If we take any domain of applied linguistics (e.g. workplace communication, literacy, translation), we can start to see the conflictual interplay of these concerns. Dominion: In what multiple ways does power operate in workplace communication? What texts have power in what contexts? What is the power behind different versions of translation? Disparity: How can the silenced in the workplace start to speak? How can people gain access to powerful texts? Can others gain access to the processes of translation? Difference: What other kinds of communication are possible? How do people read texts differently? What forms of difference emerge in alternative translations? Desire: Why do people take up particular modes of communication? What subject positions are available to different readers? Why still are certain interpretations preferred?

At the same time, Foucault brings a constant scepticism towards cherished concepts and modes of thought. Taken-for-granted categories such as man, woman, class, race, ethnicity, nation, identity, awareness, emancipation, language or power must be understood as contingent, shifting and produced in the particular, rather than having some prior ontological status. As we analyse and promote critical/transgressive approaches to applied linguistics, we must always be wary lest the very terms and concepts we use are at the same time doing damage to the communities we are working with. Thus while remaining responsive to and engaged with the interplay among difference, dominion, disparity and desire, we need simultaneously to be responsive to the contingent nature of our terminologies. Just as Chakrabarty (2000) seeks to bring the Marxian project of the demystification of ideology into conversation with the Heideggerian project of hermeneutic understanding, so this use of Fanon and Foucault seeks to bring into conversation postcolonial critique and transgressive philosophy.

In his discussion of Fanon and Foucault, Said (2001) suggests a discomfort with the latter's all-embracing view of power, and what he sees as 'a kind of quietism that emerges at various points in Foucault's career: the sense that everything is historically determined, that ideas of justice, of good and evil, and so forth, have no significance, because they are constituted by whoever is using them'. Fanon's work, by contrast, is 'based upon the notion of genuine historical change by which oppressed classes are capable of liberating themselves from their oppressors' (pp. 53–54). But in combination rather than opposition, in spite of the apparent incommensurabilities here, Fanon and Foucault, as Aravamudan (1999) suggests, come together in their attempt to free us, politically and theoretically, from the chains of history. Once they are used together, suggests Aravamudan (1999), 'global theorists give way to local intellectuals, metropolitan readers are trumped by their colonial cousins, and cosmopolitans give way to tropicopolitans' (p. 331). As David Scott (1999) puts it, 'we need *both* Fanon and Foucault' for a project of refashioning futures. They can work together 'not in a relationship of harmonious settlement, nor in a relation of dialectical displacement, but in a relation of strategic supplement' (p. 219). Fanon becomes the Rastafarian *ruud bwai*[1] of Bob Marley's politics of refusal (the connection to hip-hop politics is evident here). Foucault constantly reminds us of the exclusions inherent in all roads to liberation, of the need never to allow politics to rest on the satisfaction of its own self-conception.

Transgressive theories

In her argument for transgressive pedagogies, bell hooks (1994) talks of being 'most inspired by those teachers who have had the courage to transgress those boundaries that would confine each pupil to a rote, assembly line approach to learning' (p. 13). To transgress, hooks suggests, is to oppose, to push against and to traverse the oppressive boundaries of race, gender and class domination. Here we have an image of teachers who both transgress the normal boundaries of pedagogy and teach their own students to transgress: pedagogy both as and for transgression. As Namulundah Florence (1998) explains, while transgression is often viewed in negative terms, hooks' concept of transgression suggests 'moving past boundaries, the right to choice, to truth telling and critical consciousness, the right to recognize limitations, the shift of paradigms, and the desire to "know" beyond what is readily perceptible' (p. xvii). Here, then, is both the Fanonian obligation to struggle against oppression and the Foucauldian imperative to think differently. Transgressive applied linguistics likewise pushes beyond normative boundaries; it seeks to imagine otherwise, maintaining both the political action of hooks's teaching to transgress as well as the questions embedded in teaching as transgression.

Hence I take transgressive to refer to the need to have both political and epistemological tools to transgress the boundaries of conventional thought and politics. Any critical project needs both a political agenda and a preparedness to question the concepts with which it deals, both Fanon and Foucault. Transgressive theories not only trespass on forbidden territory but also attempt to think what should not be thought, to do what should not be done. Transgression 'is that conduct which breaks rules or exceeds boundaries' (Jenks, 2003, p. 3). As Jenks goes on to argue, transgression must be carefully distinguished from disorder or chaos, since it always implies an order that is being transgressed. Modernity, he goes on, following Nietzsche, has been 'a process of the oppression and compartmentalization of the will' which has 'generated an ungoverned desire to extend, exceed, or go beyond the margins of acceptability or normal performance. Transgression therefore becomes a primary postmodern topic and a responsible one' (p. 8). Thus transgression may be seen as the desire to go beyond, to think otherwise, to transcend the boundaries of the modern.

Jervis (1999) maintains that transgression is more than mere reversal, inversion, subversion or opposition; it involves instead 'hybridization, the mixing of categories and the questioning of the boundaries that separate categories' (p. 4). Thus the transgressive is a reflexive questioning of 'the culture that has defined it in its otherness'. Rather than overtly challenging the status quo, it investigates the ways in which common sense, the normal, the law, the taken-for-granted, the given are often arbitrarily fixed around relations of power yet also complicit with what they exclude. Transgressive theory thus not only challenges the boundaries and mechanisms that sustain categories and ways of thinking but also produces other ways of thinking. In the same way that Foucault presents us with the need to seek new schemas of politicization, transgressive theory is not so much about establishing a fixed and normative epistemology as it is about seeking new frames of thought and conduct, or, as Kearney (1988) puts it, 'the ethical demand to imagine *otherwise*' (p. 364).

Transgression is not only an epistemological question but it is also central to desire. For Lacan, 'without a transgression there is no access to *jouissance*,[2] and that is precisely the function of the Law. Transgression in the direction of *jouissance* only takes place if it is supported by the oppositional principle, by the forms of Law' (Lacan, 1992, p. 177). There is no *jouissance,* no pleasure/desire, without the cultural and legal proscriptions that regulate our desires. Our desires are constantly produced within the confines of social and cultural regulation, and *jouissance* thus becomes dependent on the transgression of these boundaries. To transgress, therefore, is always connected with forms of pleasure and desire, and forms of pleasure and desire are dependent on transgression. What it is possible to think is always formulated within highly regulated contexts of thought and action; and thought and desire are intertwined in ways that rationalist philosophies of mind cannot account for: without transgression of boundaries there is neither thought nor pleasure, and transgressive theorizing is also about desire. 'At the root of sexuality, of the movement that nothing can ever limit', argues Foucault (1977), 'a singular experience is shaped: that of transgression' (p. 33). Limit and transgression depend on each other, for 'a limit could not exist if it were absolutely uncrossable and, reciprocally, transgression would be pointless if it merely crossed a limit composed of illusions and shadows' (p. 34). Transgression, therefore, 'is not related to the limit as black to white, the prohibited to the unlawful, the outside to the inside, or as the open area of a building to its enclosed spaces. Rather, their relationship takes the form of a spiral which no simple infraction can exhaust' (p. 35).

The notion of transgression, then, escapes the limits of dialectical thinking and instead, as David Scott (1999) suggests, develops a relation of strategic supplement, pushing us to think of that which has not been thought. The notion of transgression refutes the modernist hope of ideology critique and demystification and moves towards alterity. This is what makes a notion of transgression so important for thinking about domains such as popular culture, hip-hop and, I would like to argue, language. We need ways of thinking about the pleasure of doing things differently. We do not live in a world where people conform mindlessly to the putative rules of language; we live in a world of language transgressions, impossible without some presumed order worth transgressing, and made possible by the desire for difference. Transgression is not merely, therefore, an act of going against what is accepted, of testing the possibilities of difference, but is also an exploration of boundaries of thought. In his discussion of Kant's answer to the question 'What is Enlightenment?' (*Was ist Aufklärung?*), Foucault (1984) argues that if Kant's position was one of 'knowing what limits knowledge has to renounce transgressing', we need now to turn this into a more positive orientation, 'to transform the critique conducted in the form of necessary limitation into a practical critique that takes the form of a possible transgression' (p. 45). The obvious consequence of this, suggests Foucault, is that 'criticism is no longer going to be practiced in the search for formal structures with universal value, but rather as a historical investigation into the events that have led us to constitute ourselves and to recognize ourselves as subjects of what we are doing, thinking, saying' (pp. 45–46).

The point, therefore, is that transgressive work cannot operate from our current knowledge of ourselves in an attempt to delimit what we can know, but rather works in a more positive and practical sense to undertake those moves that were deemed impossible. Rather than Kant's version of an Enlightenment that establishes the limits of possibility, this vision is one that seeks transgressively to understand how it is we come to think, speak and act as we do. Foucault (1984) characterizes this critical philosophy as a 'historico-practical test of the limits that we may go beyond' (p. 47). What Foucault is proposing here is 'an attitude, an ethos, a philosophical life in which the critique of what we are is at one and the same time the historical analysis of the limits that are imposed on us and an experiment with the possibility of going beyond them' (p. 50). Here, then, is a critical philosophy of transgression. It is not a project of random, pointless transgressive interruptions but rather a profound and methodical investigation of how to understand ourselves, our histories and how the boundaries of thought may be traversed. Such a transgressive stance seeks to 'give new impetus, as far and wide as possible, to the undefined work of freedom' (p. 46).

For some, the notion of transgression might appear too ungrounded, a series of token border raids that achieve little. The notion of transgressive theory I am developing here is far more than this, however: while it does attempt to avoid the limiting position of those critical stances for which all analysis is already pre-decided (globalization is per se to be critiqued, English is a pernicious evil, pop culture is the consumerist fast food of the eyes and ears), it also demands a reflexive stance about what and why it crosses; it is thought in movement rather than thought looking over its shoulder at what it is 'post'; it is about desire, alterity and freedom. A critical philosophy of transgression is therefore anything but a series of random incursions into other territory or border-crossings for their own sake since it demands a continuous and simultaneous questioning of how we come to be as we are, how such limits have been imposed historically, and how we can start to think and act beyond them. It is therefore thought for action and change, it is Foucault and Fanon, problematizing practice and political practice. Transgressive applied linguistics is applied linguistics both as and for transgressive thought and action.

I am also using the notion of transgressive as linked to a larger set of 'trans' rather than 'post' theories. A problem with the position of the 'posts' is that although they have taken our thinking usefully forward in many domains, they remain tied to the domains beyond which they claim to go: poststructuralism struggles to escape the bondage of structuralist linguistics; postmodernism has always been tied to its definitions of modernism; and postcolonialism, although often tied to both historical reappraisal and oppositional politics (Young, 2001), nevertheless carries with it overtones of an 'afterwards', which, if nothing else, runs the danger of obscuring the ongoing nature of colonial relations. It is as if these theoretical stances move forward while always looking backward, marching into the future with their eyes firmly on the past. Like Walter Benjamin's (1969) image of the 'angel of history', his face turned towards the rubble of the past, 'post' theory always seems to tie the postcolonial irredeemably to the colonial, the poststructural irrevocably to the structural, and the postmodern incessantly to the modern, thereby also rendering the problems we need to address to be those of modernism, structuralism and colonialism.

This attempt to get beyond the 'post' by a move towards the transgressive by no means indicates a rejection of the many theoretical gains made by the combination of post theories. We ought now to be able to take for granted an understanding of how the binaries and essentialisms of modernism, structuralism and colonialism produced modes of analysis that narrowly constrained the possibilities of thought while simultaneously constructing pernicious otherings; we ought to be able to assume the particularity and locality of thought and knowledge and its relation to power; we should now no longer have to argue that subjects are discursively constructed, that interpretations are contingent, that there is no position outside discourse. A move to look at 'trans' rather than 'post' theories, however, shifts the relationship from a temporal to a more spatial domain, from time to movement, shifting dependency away from a former set of theoretical paradigms (modernism, structuralism, colonialism) to a more contemporary array of contexts. This shift from the temporal to the spatial is important for a move towards understanding globalization, movement, flows and linkages. More specifically, by emphasizing the spatiality of the *trans* within the domain of transgressive theories, it is possible to integrate concepts of transculturation and translocalization, opening up the processes of cultural interaction in terms of a fluidity of relations across global contexts; to develop the notion of transmodality as a way of thinking about language use as located within multiple modes of semiotic diffusion; to think of semiotics in terms of transtextualization, as a way of looking at texts and signs within the historical, local, discursive and interpretive elements of context; and translation as a way of thinking about translingual meaning as an act of interpretation across boundaries of understanding. These interrelated theories are discussed below, while further connections to linguistic, somatic and performative turns are developed in Chapter 4.

Transculturation and transidiomatic practices

As Connell and Gibson (2003) suggest, 'transnational cultural products, in whatever direction they appear to be travelling, do not simply replace local ones, but are refashioned and given new meaning' (p. 191). Notions of the transcultural, transnational and translocal present a way of thinking about flow, flux and fixity in relation to location that move beyond both dichotomies of the global and local, and dialectics between global homogenization and local heterogenization. Critiquing static definitions of cultural identity in ethnography, Clifford (1997) argues that rather than using localizing strategies by which people are considered to exist culturally in a specific location, a more useful image is one of *travel*, with its emphasis on movement, encounter and change, for 'once the representational challenge is seen to be the portrayal and understanding of local/global historical encounters, co-productions, dominations, and resistances, then one needs to focus on hybrid, cosmopolitan experiences as much as on rooted, native ones' (p. 24). From this point of view, locality is produced, not given, a result of particular ways of constructing identity, 'a phenomenological property of social life, a structure of feeling that is produced by particular forms of intentional activity and that yields particular sorts of material effects' (Appadurai, 1996, p. 182). Thus, 'when borders gain a paradoxical centrality, margins, edges, and lines of communication emerge as complex maps and histories. To account for these formations, I draw on emerging conceptions of translocal (not global or universal) culture' (Clifford, 1997, p. 7). The notion of the translocal, then, gives us a way of thinking about the wider occurrence of local relations and the mobile space of cultural relations.

Many have questioned the use of the category *culture* in popular, political and academic writing over the past 150 years. From Said's (1978) classic study of the construction of the Orient in the Western imaginary to all the subsequent studies of postcolonial discourse and the complicity of culture and colonialism (Thomas, 1994; Young, 1995, 2001), from Bhabha's (1994) ponderings on the 'location of culture' to McConaghy's (2000) critique of 'culturalism' in the context of indigenous Australia, which incorporates 'particular anthropological notions of "culture"' and 'the ideologies of and discursive regimes of universalism, cultural racism, and cultural incompatibility in order to construct and perpetuate a "two race" binary' (p. xi), the notion of fixed cultures attached to ethnic or national identities has come under massive critical scrutiny. So much so that Clifford questioned whether the concept of culture had perhaps 'served its time' (1988, p. 274). Notwithstanding all the problems with the way the notion of culture has been mobilized to orientalize, reify, categorize and divide, however, some notion of culture may still be useful as a way of describing human difference. Thus, after asking if the culture concept had perhaps served its time, Clifford (1988) attempts to employ the term differently, to imply movement and contingent difference.

In order to get beyond the fixed categories of deterministic behaviour all too often implied by the notion of culture, various propositions for new terminology and conceptualizations have been proposed: Bhabha (1994) in particular has developed the notions of 'third space' and 'hybridity', 'where difference is neither One nor the Other but *something else besides, in-between*' (p. 219). Kramsch has taken up this notion in the context of language education, suggesting that the 'third place' opened up by cultural exchange is a 'third culture in its own right' (1993, p. 9). For McConaghy, it is useful to think in terms of 'postculturalism', which 'seeks to problematise issues of culture and identity and to position cultural considerations within a wider framework' (p. 9). Following her extended critique of orientalism in TESOL literature (with a particular emphasis on the constructions of Japanese culture), Ryuko Kubota (2004) has taken up the notion of *critical multiculturalism*, which 'critically examines how inequality and injustice are produced and perpetuated in relation to power and privilege' (p. 37) by focusing directly on issues of racism – on 'collective, rather than individual, oppression' (p. 37) – and by problematizing, rather than presupposing difference, exploring 'a critical understanding of culture' (p. 38).

While much of this work and terminology has helped us to move forward in ways of thinking about cultural difference, I want to explore in greater depth here the notion of *transculturation* (or transculturality). Critiquing traditional notions of culture for their 'unificatory' principles of social homogenization (it is presumed that all people within a given culture always act out instances of that culture), 'ethnic consolidation' (whereby cultures are the properties of independent and autonomous ethnic groups) and 'intercultural delimitation' (which limits the possibilities of movement, understanding and communication between these supposed cultures) (pp. 194–195), Welsch (1999) proposes the notion of *transculturality* (*Transkulturalität* in German). He suggests that transculturality is preferable to both interculturality and multiculturality since both keep the concept of culture whole while suggesting plurality or communication across or between cultures (and compare the discussion of transmodality and multimodality below). Transculturality, Welsch suggests, is a consequence of the internal complexity of societies (with their many differential social divisions), the external relations through which cultures interact, and the processes of hybridization (cultures are always mixing with each other).

The most widely cited use of the term is in Mary Louise Pratt's (1992) key book *Imperial Eyes: Travel Writing and Transculturation*, where she explains transculturation as a 'phenomenon of the contact zone' (the space of colonial encounters, in which people from different historical and geographical spaces encounter each other), hence Kramsch's (1999) 'critical pedagogy of the contact zone' (p. 138). Pratt notes the first use of the term in Cuban sociologist Fernando Ortiz's (1940) book *Contrapunto Cubano*, in which Ortiz argued that Malinowski's notions of acculturation and deculturation were inadequate to describe 'the extremely complex transmutation of culture that has taken place' in Cuba (1940/1995, p. 98; cited in Mignolo, 2000, p. 14). Mignolo, however, while noting the significance of this term, prefers to avoid it in order to escape the sense of a 'biological /cultural mixture of people' (p. 14). For Mignolo, the notion of *cultural semiosis* is preferable because it emphasizes the centrality of 'social–semiotic interactions' and attempts to 'dispel the notion of "culture"' because it is 'precisely a key word of colonial discourses classifying the planet' (pp. 14–15). Like the notion of hybridity, which also derives from a colonial construction of biological mixing (see Young, 1995), transculturation runs the risk, like all cultural terminology, of reproducing the bonds of difference that were central to the colonial enterprise.

Mignolo's cautionary note notwithstanding, the term 'transculturation' may still be able to do more useful work than the concept of cultural semiosis. For Pratt, the term describes how 'subordinated or marginal groups select and invent from materials transmitted to them by a dominant or metropolitan culture' (p. 6). As she explains, while it is difficult for such people to control or regulate the flows of materials, there are possibilities for determining how much will be taken up and what it will be used for. And as well as asking how 'metropolitan modes of representation' are taken up in the periphery, it is also possible, she suggests, to look at transculturation from the colonies to the metropolis. It is this understanding of transculturation that is of central significance for the themes of this book, since it is precisely such processes of selection and invention in the dynamic appropriations of hip-hop that are of interest here. And, as I will argue, the complex circles of flow (see Chapter 7) across the globe not only make the centre's take-up of peripheral cultural forms a real possibility, but also raise many questions about the centre–periphery framing of this relation.

Transculturation may also be seen in relation to what Jacquemet (2005) calls *transidiomatic practices*: 'the communicative practices of transnational groups that interact using different languages and communicative codes simultaneously present in a range of communicative channels, both local and distant.' Transidiomatic practices, Jacquemet explains, 'are the results of the co-presence of multilingual talk (exercised by de/reterritorialized speakers) and electronic media, in contexts heavily structured by social indexicalities and semiotic codes'. For Jacquemet, such practices are dependent on 'transnational environments', the mediation of 'deterritorialized technologies', and interaction 'with both present and distant people' (p. 265). As we shall see in Chapters 6 and 7, such transidiomatic practices are an integral part of global hip-hop. I want to suggest, however, that such transidiomatic practices, such uses of different modes, codes and channels, are not necessarily so dependent on technologies and current modes of global integration as Jacquemet suggests. Although there are very particular forces at work in the globe today that make it very different from earlier eras, and although the global spread of hip-hop is very dependent on the mediation of deterritorialized technologies, the assumption that it is only now that we have transculturation or transidiomatic practices, that this is a phenomenon produced by the postmodern world, a product of increased global flows and movements, may miss the historical understanding of globalization discussed in Chapter 2. Rather, I would argue that there has always been transculturation, and that it is the massive weight of the fixed concept of culture that has made it invisible.

Taken in conjunction, the notions of transidiomatic and transcultural practices refer not merely to the spread of particular forms of culture across boundaries, nor only to the existence of supercultural commonalities (cultural forms that transcend locality). They draw our attention instead to the constant processes of borrowing, bending and blending of cultures, to the communicative practices of people interacting across different linguistic and communicative codes, borrowing, bending and blending languages into new modes of expression. Transcultural and transidiomatic practices point to the ways in which those apparently on the receiving end of cultural and linguistic domination select, appropriate, refashion and return new cultural and linguistic forms through complex interactive cultural groups (defined not in ethnic terms but along subcultural affiliations of gender, class, sexual orientation, profession, interest, desires and so on). Transcultural and transidiomatic practices therefore refer not to homogenization or heterogenization but to alternative spaces of cultural production. This allows us to get beyond the question of uniformization or particularization, and opens up an understanding of cultural movement while never losing sight of the uneven terrain (global economies, the music industry) over which such movements occur.

Transmodality

As Auzanneau (2002) points out, too much work around hip-hop has tended to remain as juxtaposed interdisciplinarity, overlooking the ways in which 'the social, musical, and linguistic dimensions – among others – of the songs are interrelated and call for a "pluridisciplinary approach of collaboration"' (p. 109). Hip-hop presents several layers of modality. As a broad cultural sphere, it encompasses DJ-ing, MC-ing, break-dancing and graffiti. Within these different domains, furthermore, there are also levels of multimodality, so that MC-ing as performance includes dress, posture and voice. Rap lyrics, meanwhile, also need to be understood within the context of the flow of rap, the musical context in which they are embedded (Krims, 2000). Such integrated, multimodal, cultural production challenges us to rethink in several ways our understanding of language, culture and modality. As van Leeuwen (1999) shows, speech, music and sound are semiotically interrelated. Much of the meaning of speech is carried in its rhythm, intonation and cadence; music brings interpretive frameworks of mood to the sounds it may accompany. In the context of hip-hop, and in particular rap, it would be a mistake to try to read the lyrics without an appreciation of the music. As we shall see in Chapters 6 and 7, an interpretation of language without an understanding of the musical accompaniment misses an important aspect of localization. And, as I suggested at the beginning of Chapter 1, it is not only the lyrics and music but also the dress, the body, the attitude and the b-boys in the back, that give meaning to a hip-hop event. Rap, suggests Shusterman (2000), challenges the separation of cultural spheres and disembodied voices. As will be discussed further in Chapter 4, Shusterman's interest is particularly in the philosophical rejection of what is deemed to be below the level of the word, and the need to engage with what he calls the 'somatic turn', the turn towards the body.

Kress and van Leeuwen (2001) argue that the dominance of 'monomodality' in Western cultural production – novels, reports, academic writing without pictures; paintings in the same oil-and-canvas medium; identically dressed classical musicians – has been changing and requires new tools for analysis. Instead, they propose 'a theory of multimodal communication' which attempts to deal with the 'use of several semiotic modes in the design of a semiotic product or event, together with the particular way in which these modes are combined' (p. 20). Kress and van Leeuwen (2001) move beyond the more minimalist step elsewhere in literacy studies (Kress, 2003; Kress and van Leeuwen, 1996) that focuses predominantly on relations between texts and images or on text-based analyses of visual representation, to look at film, physical space, body movement in relation to classroom discourse, voice quality in speaking and singing, and so forth. In a similar vein, Norris (2004) presents a framework for analysing multimodal interaction based on the premise that language 'is only one mode among many, which may or may not take a central role at any given moment in an interaction'

(p. 2). While there will not be space in this book to engage in the close multimodal analysis advocated by Norris, the view that language can only be understood in relation to other forms of semiosis is significant for the understanding of hip-hop as a popular transcultural form.

In the same way that Makoni (1998a, b; and see Makoni and Pennycook (2005, 2006)), however, has suggested that multilingualism all too often becomes little more than a pluralization of monolingualism (multilingualism champions the use of separate codes rather than challenging their existence; see Chapters 2 and 7 for further discussion), so I would suggest that multimodality tends to celebrate the use of a plurality of modes rather than pursue the more transgressive enquiry into their initial construction as separate entities to start with. In the same way that it can be useful to draw a distinction between postmodernity and postmodernism (see Pennycook, 2006), the first focusing on real changes to language and culture in a new era of global communication, the second on the ways in which language and culture have been constructed through the discourses of modernity, so it may be useful to distinguish between multilingualism and multimodality on the one hand, which focus on languages and modes as pluralized entities within a new era of globalized communication, and translingualism and transmodality on the other hand, which question the very separability of languages and modes in the first place.

The point here, then, is that not only are languages not discrete entities in relation to each other but the separation of language from the complexity of signs with which its use is associated has limited our understanding of a broader semiotics. Segregrationalist linguistics (as Harris (1990, 1998) calls this) has constructed language as a separate entity. An integrational view of language, by contrast, suggests not merely that language is integrated with its environment but rather that languages themselves cannot be viewed as discrete items, cannot be treated as autonomous systems outside the other meaning-making practices of the bodies, texts, contexts and histories in which they are embedded. For these reasons I prefer the term *transmodality* to multimodality, since it implies not so much that meaning occurs within different related channels, but rather that it occurs across modes of meaning-making in ways that transgress established beliefs in discrete channels. Kress (2003) uses the term *transduction* to refer to the 'process in which something which has been configured or shaped in one or more modes is *re*configured, *re*shaped according to the affordances of a quite different mode' (p. 47). The term 'transduction' is also used by Massumi to refer to 'the transmission of an impulse of virtuality from one actualization to another and across them all (what Guattari calls transversality)' (Massumi, 2002, p. 42). I prefer the term 'transmodality', implying both that such reconfiguring occurs across modes and that these modes are also integrated.

The notion of transmodality I am proposing here, then, draws on the notion of multimodality as put forward by Kress and van Leeuwen (2001), challenging the notion that 'meaning resides in language alone' or that 'language is the central means of representing and communicating even though there are "extra-linguistic", "para-linguistic" things going on as well' (p. 111). Transmodality also draws on Scollon and Scollon's (2003) *geosemiotics*, 'the ways in which language or discourse is part of this perennial weave of individuals, objects, time and space'. Geosemiotics emphasizes that 'indexicality, action, and identity are all anchored in the physical spaces and real times of our material world' (p. 14). Transmodality implies not only that meaning occurs in multiple modes, or that language cannot be understood in isolation, but also that there is no such thing as language in isolation. The notion of transmodality I am developing here draws not only on semiotic theory – the multimodality of signs – but also on somatic, musical and spatial theories, so that the embodiment, flow and location of meaning may be understood in the complexity of their relations (Connell and Gibson, 2003; Krims, 2000; Shusterman, 2000). By taking further the notion of transmodality, and relating it to notions of performativity (see Chapter 4), I am seeking to explore ways by which transgressive meaning-making (writing on the walls of the city, mixing languages, sampling sound texts, walking the walk, wearing the clothes) may be seen not so much as adding meaning-making practices to a pre-existing language but rather as a performative making of meaning across many sites.

Transtextuality and transsignification

At the heart of some of these moves to develop a multimodal form of analysis is a call for a rethinking of the cornerstone of semiotic theory, the sign. In contention is the central linguistic notion of the arbitrariness of the sign. It is crucial, however, in order to understand what is at stake here, to appreciate what is and what is not meant by this concept. For Saussure (1915/1983), to whom we owe this notion of arbitrariness, all signs consist of two elements: the signifier (the form of the word) and the signified (what is meant). The relationship between the two, he argued, is in most cases arbitrary; that is to say there is no inherent relationship between a meaning (say, tree) and a word form ('tree'), a position obviously supported by the use of different words in different languages to refer, more or less, to the same concept (arbre, Baum, ki). It is important to note here, first, that this view of signs, which has become a bedrock of mainstream linguistic thought, has nothing to do with the social use of signs. This notion of arbitrariness does not suggest that, say, a choice to call an event a 'riot' or a 'demonstration' is arbitrary; rather, it suggests only that the word forms 'riot' or 'demonstration' are arbitrarily linked to their meanings. Second, the notion of the signified refers not to an object in the world (a referent) but to a concept. Structuralism is interested in the relationships between signs themselves, not in a relationship between signs and objects in the world. Unfortunately, a lot of discussion of the sign has conflated these issues, suggesting that to refer to a certain object or person with a certain sign (to label a particular person a terrorist or guerrilla, for example) is not an arbitrary act (Fairclough, 1992). The problem is that the arbitrariness referred to in structuralist linguistics (the relationship between sound/writing (signifier) and meaning (signified)) is not the arbitrariness that others are rejecting: the Saussurean notion of the sign is only talking about the relation between abstract form and meaning, not use. Therein, of course, lies one of its great weaknesses.

What I want to suggest in this section is that we need to move beyond both this structuralist conception of the sign and its poststructuralist reinterpretation. As I suggested above, a problem with the 'post' theories has been their constant reference to that which they supposedly succeed. Poststructuralism has therefore been ineluctably tied to a rethinking of Saussurean structuralism, keeping parts of the semiotic theory of signs in place while opening up others. Thus, while poststructuralism has maintained an interest in signs abstracted from any notion of the 'real world', the stability of the sign – the assumption that signs have a socially agreed-upon meaning – has been replaced by a view of meaning that is always in flux or discursively mediated. This has been of immense importance for escaping both a structuralist supposition of commonality and a functionalist supposition of materiality, allowing for a much more flexible understanding of meaning as discursively mediated (Pennycook, 2002b). And yet, as Harland (1987) notes, this 'superstructuralist' position has more in common across structuralism and poststructuralism than debates would like to admit. The logocentrism of poststructuralism – all is discourse – has always made it hard to deal with either context or a notion of 'the real'. While retaining many of the crucial insights of poststructuralism – its anti-essentialist position, its understanding of discourse, its view of subjectivity – I want to move on here to a notion of transsignification.

A weakness of the Saussurean sign has been its abstraction from contexts of use, as if signs have meaning without reference to people, places, contexts and history. As Harris (1990) explains, from an integrationalist point of view the orthodox principle of arbitrariness is 'simply an irrelevance'. Whether the relation between signifier and signified is arbitrary or not makes no difference, since the significance of a sign 'is always a function of its integration into a particular communication situation'. From this point of view, the constant reiteration of the arbitrariness of the sign is part of the attempt to isolate language from its surrounds, 'the result of treating the linguistic sign as a decontextualized unit, having a form and a meaning whose relationship can be considered in isolation from the actual employment of the sign in any given situation' (p. 48). From Harris's integrational view of linguistics, then, just as I argued above that language needs to be integrated into a transmodal conception of meaning-making, so the sign itself cannot be understood as having meaning outside of its contexts of use. Rather than a version of linguistics that assigns a priori meaning to signs within a system, we need an approach to language that 'makes the sign itself subject to the exigencies of communication and assigns ontological priority to the fact of communication itself' (Hopper, 1998, p. 157). Thus a sign is 'provisional, and is dependent, not as an essential inner core of constant meaning, but on previous uses and contexts in which the current speaker has used or heard it' (p. 157).

From a slightly different point of view, Kress (2003) argues that the notion of the arbitrariness of the sign 'embodies a fundamental error, a confusion which has gone unrecognized by and large, and endlessly repeated' (p. 41). Kress suggests this is a problem of level, since 'the level of the signified tree – the meaning – is matched by the level at which the signifier is lexical form – the word: not phonetic or phonological form' (p. 41). Thus the 'signifier/form for the signified/meaning *tree* is the lexical form/signifier "tree"'. Kress goes on to 'reject the idea of arbitrariness', assuming that 'the relation between signifier and signified is always motivated, that is, that the shape of the signifier, its "form", materially or abstractly considered, is chosen because of its *aptness* for expressing that which is to be signified' (p. 42). While the example Kress often uses to make this point – a child drawing a car using a series of circles – may not be sufficiently generalizable to broader contexts of language (a child's manipulation of drawn signs – circles, as wheels, to represent a car – is very different from other forms of social semiosis such as writing), and while the question of aptness begs the question of how a sign becomes apt, this view that signs are socially motivated allows us to see meaning-making in more dynamic terms than using pregiven and agreed-upon signs.

Drawing, as does Kress, on the work of the semiotician C.S. Peirce (1992, 1998), Scollon and Scollon (2003) argue that the 'meaning of a sign is anchored in the material world whether the linguistic utterance is spoken by one person to another or posted as a stop sign on a street corner' (p. 3). This notion of *indexicality* 'is the property of the context-dependency of signs, especially language' (p. 3). Scollon and Scollon also question the notion of arbitrariness, suggesting that 'it has been emphasized by semioticians that the relationship between signs and the objects they represent is entirely arbitrary' (p. 27). As with Kress's example of the child drawing, however, the examples Scollon and Scollon use – predominantly street signs – show the context-dependency and indexicality of signs well but raise questions as to whether such signs are so easily generalizable to all semiotic relations (Scollon and Scollon also appear to conflate the relation between signs and objects with the relation between signifiers and signifieds). This view of the indexicality and the materiality of the sign nevertheless points in some useful directions. Using Peirce's distinction between *iconic* (where the form of the sign parallels the signified/referent: a running figure to show an emergency exit, for example), *indexical* (where the sign points to something in the world, such as a directional arrow suggesting which way to run) and *symbolic* (where the relation is more abstract) signs, Kress takes 'Peirce's iconic sign as the model of all relations of signs to their referents' (p. 42) while Scollon and Scollon take the concept of indexicality as central. Van Lier (2004) likewise argues that while indexicality may be 'the most important key to becoming a member of a community', it is also the 'workbench or desktop on which the learner may negotiate the free flow among signs and the construction of options for life' (p. 68).

Thus while Peirce's semiotic theory usefully gets us out of the decontextualized binarisms of Saussurean theory (particularly since it incorporates the *interpretant* in the model), Scollon and Scollon overemphasize the contextuality (indexicality) of the sign while Kress overemphasizes the choice of apt signs (iconicity). A problem here has been the tendency to try to understand semiotics by looking at simple signs or early stages of sign acquisition. Neither position provides us with a rich enough theory for considering how it is that signs *symbolically* come to have meaning in complex textual contexts. What Kress and Scollon and Scollon show here is that we need a different version of the sign that locates the sign in physical space and human interaction, making language use central to a concept of meaning. As van Lier (2004) and Kramsch (2000) show, by combining C.S. Peirce's semiotics with Vygotskyan (1986) and Bakhtinian (1986) understandings of language and thought, we can move towards a more useful view of semiotics as carrying traces of meaning over time, located in particular contexts, open to interpretation and dialogical. What I want to argue for is a version of the contextual use of signs that is neither iconically nor indexically determining, a view of a signs in terms of *transtextuality* that does not suggest that it mirrors its referent or points to the world as transparently as do drawings and street signs.

I shall use a notion of textuality to refer to signs or signs in combination, or, to put it another way, I am using the notion of transtextuality here to refer to a form of social semiotics that may deal with anything from a single sign to an extended text. Drawing on the insights above and on an earlier formulation of textual relations (Pennycook, 2001), I therefore want to suggest that signs/texts have meaning not in themselves but only when used; they need to be understood productively, contextually and discursively; i.e. they have histories, they are contextually influenced, and they occur within larger frameworks of meaning. From this point of view, then, the context of a sign includes the *pretextual history* of the sign (which gives a context for its iconic status); the *contextual relations* in which its use occurs (the physical location, the participants, the indexical pointing to the world); the *subtextual meanings* according to the discourses within which it operates (the discourses and ideologies that mobilize and are mobilized by the sign); the *intertextual echoes* by which signs and texts refer to each other (meaning occurs not only in contextual relation but also across texts), and the *posttextual interpretations* of the actors (the meanings participants read into the sign). None of these exists in isolation from the others. The meaning of any sign (tree, riot, aptness, a stop sign), therefore, points back to its prior posttextual uses (both individually and socially), is embedded contextually (Where is it? Who utters it? Referring to what?), is bound up with larger frames of subtextual meaning (In what wider patterns of meaning is it used?), connects intertextually to other uses (What are its other textual contexts?), and is always open to posttextual interpretation. This is the social semiotics of transsignification.

Translation and translingualism

Finally, I want to make a case for the centrality of translation, which for too long has been marginalized as a secondary process within cultural and linguistic exchange. Translation, argues Cronin (2003), plays a crucial role within globalization, since one of its primary functions is 'to replenish the intertextual resources of a culture' (p. 133). While the responsibility of the translator is conventionally thought of in terms of giving a fair and accurate representation of a source text, such 'textual scrupulousness' addresses only part of the contemporary responsibility of the translator, since there must also be 'an activist dimension to translation which involves an engagement with the cultural politics of society at national and international levels' (p. 134). Such responsibility, he goes on, needs to be 'firmly situated in *transnational* translation history so that any politics of translation is explicitly situated in identifiable historical contexts' (p. 135). This notion of activist translation links to Venuti's (1998) *translingualism,* which aims to disrupt the assimilationary and domesticating tendencies that eradicate difference through translation. For Venuti, translingual differences need to be present in the translated text: 'Because the translingualism of colonial and postcolonial writing redefines authorship to embrace translation, it issues an implicit challenge to the concept of authorial originality, a hallowed tenet of European romanticism that continues to prevail regardless of where a culture is positioned in the global economy' (p. 175). Once again, the connections to hip-hop and its challenges to identity and authorship are apparent.

As Spivak (1993) remarks, drawing on a discussion with Michele Barrett, 'the politics of translation takes on a massive life of its own if you see language as the process of meaning-construction' (p. 179). From this perspective it is possible to view all language use as a process of translation, thus questioning the assumption that translation is a mapping of items from one code to another. According to Steiner (1975), 'inside or between languages, human communication equals translation. A study of translation is a study of language' (p. 47). That is to say that communication between languages presents not so much the central process of translation but rather a special case: all communication involves translation. This renders translation not the peripheral area it has been to much of applied linguistics, but rather the key to understanding communication. It also suggests that this boundary we set up between languages, making translation an issue when we speak 'different languages' but not when we speak the 'same language', is yet again a distinction that is hard to maintain. The notion of translation I am developing here is one that transgresses rather than maintains distinctions between languages (see Makoni and Pennycook, in press); in the transcultural field of hip-hop flows and appropriations, translation is not so much a process of encoding and decoding across languages but of making meaning across and against codifications.

For Chakrabarty (2000), the 'problem of capitalist modernity cannot any longer be seen simply as a sociological problem of historical transition ... but as a problem of translation, as well' (p. 17). What Chakrabarty is pointing to here is that we need to consider very seriously that translation produces 'neither an absence of relationship between dominant and dominating forms of knowledge nor equivalents that successfully mediate between differences, but precisely the partly opaque relationship we call "difference"' (p. 17). Mignolo (2000) describes Chakrabarty's position as signalling 'the death of history and the beginning of translation as a new form of knowledge that displaces the hegemonic and subaltern locations of disciplinary knowledge' (p. 205). Thus '*knowledge works as translation and translation works as knowledge,* that is *trans-* rather than *inter*disciplinary, undermining disciplinary foundations of knowledge' (p. 208; emphasis in original). As the fourth element of transgressive theory, therefore, translation, like transculturation (rather than the intercultural), makes difference and the need for boundary transgression central.

Similarly, Clifford (1997, p. 39) draws attention to the role of what he calls 'translation terms' in opening up questions of difference:

> By 'translation term' I mean a word of apparently general application used for comparison in a strategic and contingent way. 'Travel' has an inextinguishable taint of location by class, gender, race, and a certain literariness. It offers a good reminder that all translation terms used in global comparisons – terms like culture, art, society, peasant, mode of production, man, woman, modernity, ethnography – get us some distance *and* fall apart.

At the very least, such observations make salient the point that in talking, say, of rap, hip-hop, graffiti, globalization, music or language we need always to be aware that these are 'translation terms', concepts whose meaning cannot be assumed to hold across and within languages, terms which get us some distance and fall apart, concepts which in their supposed commonality and globality may conceal levels of difference that need to be opened up. More generally, however, they suggest the need to see translation as signalling both the constant opacity of language as well as the opportunity to open up questions of difference.

Semiotics, somatics and Dionysian excess

Transgressive theory, as I am trying to develop it here, is a way of thinking that can deal with the transgressive acts of hip-hop, both through its related analytic framework of translation, transmodality, transculturation and transtextuality, and through its openness to think differently. Like hip-hop at its transgressive best, transgressive theory needs both political and epistemological tools to transgress the boundaries of mainstream thought and politics. A critical philosophy of transgression is not a set of anarchist incursions, tokenistic border-crossings or haphazard critiques of what is deemed to be wrong with the modern world, but rather a continuous questioning of how we come to be as we are, how our ways of understanding have been set, and how this could look different if we started to think otherwise. It is also, as I have been insisting, thought for action and change, both Fanon and Foucault. On the one hand, it demands that we confront relations of power – dominion, disparity, difference and desire – while on the other it maintains a constant scepticism, never allowing us to rest on the satisfaction of our own self-conception.

For Shusterman, rap should be appreciated for its philosophical and transgressive stances on the world: 'What could be further from modernity's project of rationalization and secularization, what more inimical to modernism's rationalized, disembodied, and formalized aesthetic?' Shusterman (2000, p. 75) asks.

> No wonder the established modernist aesthetic is so hostile to rap. If there is a viable space between the modern rationalized aesthetic and an altogether irrational one whose rabid Dionysian excess must vitiate its cognitive, didactic, and political claims, this is the space for a postmodern aesthetic. I think the fine art of rap inhabits that space, and I hope it will continue to thrive there.

Hip-hop as transgressive cultural form opens the space to think differently, opens the space for a different, transgressive applied linguistics that is then able to reflect on the relations between popular culture, pleasure, difference and language in ways that its rationalized aesthetic has not been able to do. And in his invocation of the Dionysian, Shusterman raises the question of the pleasure and the body, issues that I shall pursue in Chapter 4.

In the next chapter on performance and performativity, I shall take some of these insights further by exploring implications of the linguistic, somatic and performative turns. As I suggested above, the transgressive theory I am proposing takes for granted various concerns of 'post' theory – that realist representation has been cast into radical doubt, that we need to understand the role of discourse in constituting the subject, that the subject is multiple and conflictual, that knowledge production needs reflexivity – yet at the same time it acknowledges that the logocentric idealism implied by too great an emphasis on discourse overlooks the ways in which the social order is not only about language, textuality and semiosis but is also about space, the body, time, social and institutional contexts, and differences constructed along the lines of sex, gender, race, ethnicity and much more. The somatic turn allows us to readdress the embodiment of difference, while the performative turn, on which the following chapter focuses, suggests that identities are formed in the linguistic and embodied performance rather than pregiven. As we shall see, this further provides the ground for considering languages themselves from an anti-foundationalist perspective, whereby language use is an act of identity which calls that language into being.

4 Performance and performativity

'Central to hip hop culture', argues Walcott (1999, p. 102), 'is the idea of performance or rather acts of performativity.' In this chapter I shall explore in some depth the concepts of performance and performativity. While the two notions share a number of allied meanings, it is important to distinguish between them. According to Cameron and Kulick (2003), performativity refers to 'the underlying conditions that make performance possible, or by virtue of which a given performance does or does not succeed' (p. 150). Thus to say that gender, sexuality or desire are performative is not to say merely that they are performed but rather that they are produced in the performance. Performativity therefore 'focuses attention on the codes of signification that underlie particular performances, and so challenges the common-sense perception that our verbal and other behaviour is merely a "natural" expression of our essential selves' (p. 150). It is this sense of the performative that is crucial to this chapter and to this book as a whole: understanding hip-hop performance is not only a question of appreciating the implications of 'performing live' but also of appreciating the ways in which both language and identity are produced in the performance.

From competence to embodied performance

The notion of performance has been played down in language studies in several ways: from the inception of modern linguistics via Saussure's *langue* (system)/ *parole* (use) dichotomy, and more particularly in Chomsky's competence /performance division, a distinction has been maintained between system and realization, with the focus of linguistics on the former term, the abstract, underlying abilities of language users rather than on the actual realization or use of language in daily life. Indeed, Chomsky (1965) was to dismiss data based on actual language use as 'fairly degenerate in quality', as full of 'false starts, deviations from rules, changes of plan in mid-course, and so on' (p. 31). From this point of view, not only was the focus of linguistic enquiry on the abstract competence to produce grammatical utterances, but the means to arrive at such an analysis was not through everyday use of language (an empirical mess) so much as through rationalist introspection: the performance of language in a social and cultural domain was simply not of interest. Hymes (1972, p. 272) described the ideological implications of this

> linking of performance to imperfection ... as ... rather a Garden of Eden view. Human life seems divided between grammatical competence, an ideal innately-derived sort of power, and performance, an exigency rather like the eating of the apple, thrusting the perfect speaker-hearer out into a fallen world .... The controlling image is of an abstract, isolated individual, almost an unmotivated cognitive mechanism, not except incidentally, a person in a social world.

There are a number of possible responses to the competence/performance problem. As Halliday (1978) suggests, you can on the one hand accept the distinction and try to 'formulate some concept (which is Hymes's communicative competence) to take account of the speaker's ability to use language in ways that are appropriate to the situation' (1978, p. 38). Thus for Hymes, 'a broad theory of competence' aims to show how 'the systemically possible, the feasible, and the appropriate are linked to produce and interpret actually occurring cultural behavior' (1972, p. 286). This move to include sociolinguistic rules for appropriate use has had a massive influence on language pedagogy, the argument being that in order for students to learn how to communicate they need to develop a broad communicative competence, defined in terms of 'the underlying systems of knowledge and skill required for communication' (Canale, 1983, p. 5). Numerous attempts have been made to expand an understanding of these underlying competencies beyond the grammatical, including sociolinguistic, discursive, strategic, paralinguistic, organizational and pragmatic competencies (Bachman, 1990; Canale, 1983; Canale and Swain, 1980; Pennycook, 1985).

Such an argument, however, still maintains competence as the underlying capacity and performance as its realization. While language pedagogy and assessment have moved to some extent towards performance-based models, few have grasped the implications of opening up the 'pandora's box' of performance (McNamara, 1995), operating instead with modified versions of the competence/performance division that still posits an underlying set of communicative capacities. We therefore need to distinguish between those areas of language studies that focus on everyday language use, but are nevertheless interested centrally in understanding underlying competencies, and work that is interested not only in the performance itself, but views the performance as primary. The effects of Hymes's strategic move to work with the competence/performance distinction and to devote his attention to broadening the former term has had significant and, it could be argued, detrimental effects on language education since it has focused attention on underlying competence as the driver of production, rather than seeing competence as the product of performance, or indeed doing away with the distinction completely.

As Halliday (1978) suggests, one can on the other hand 'reject the distinction altogether on the grounds that we cannot operate with this degree and this *kind* of idealization' (p. 38). From Halliday's point of view, 'Hymes is taking the intra-organism ticket to what is actually an inter-organism destination' (p. 38). Just as Bourdieu (see below) criticizes linguistics for looking for power within language when power in fact operates outside, so Halliday is here suggesting that Hymes makes the mistake of constructing a competence within the individual when he might more productively be looking at social relations. For Halliday the distinction is simply not useful, since social semiotics takes language use (function) to be primary, the language system being a product of its use. From this point of view, performance in language is not the end-point of competence, but rather language is the by-product of performance. For Hopper (1998), grammar is a consequence not a precondition of communication: grammar is *emergent*, since 'structure, or regularity, comes out of discourse and is shaped by discourse in an ongoing process. Grammar is, in this view, simply the name for certain categories of observed repetitions in discourse' (Hopper, 1998, p. 156). To learn a language therefore is

> not a question of acquiring grammatical structure but of *expanding a repertoire of communicative contexts*. Consequently, there is no date or age at which the learning of a language can be said to be complete. New contexts, and new occasions of negotiation of meaning, occur constantly. A language is not a circumscribed object but a confederation of available and overlapping social experiences.
>
> (Hopper, 1998, p. 171)

I shall expand below on the implications of this view of emergent grammar in relation to performativity. At this juncture it is worth noting how a view of language as performance at the very least inverts the relationship between competence and performance (the former is a product of the latter), or, more importantly, does away with it altogether: what ties performances together is not a competence that lies within each individual but a wide array of social, cultural and discursive forces. As Bauman (2004) puts it, 'a focus on the calibration of the intertextual gaps between successive reiterations of a text in the dialogic history of performance illuminates the discursive foundations of sociohistorical continuity' (pp. 10–11). This, then, ties in with the transtextual framework discussed in Chapter 3, where the meaning of a text is viewed in terms of its pretextual dialogic history of performance, intertextual relations between texts, contextual embeddedness in use, and sub- and posttextual frames of meaning and interpretation. A focus on performance undermines a belief in creativity as always having to have new form emerging from underlying competence; instead, it places a focus on texts in context. By making textual performance salient, furthermore, it highlights the bodily performance of texts in their transmodal recital.

In the sense of acting out for an audience, the notion of performance raises further questions for language studies, since it does not conform to the decree that real language use must be 'natural', unrehearsed, unscripted. From this point of view, to perform is to adhere to someone else's script, to engage in language behaviour that is 'only a performance', that is unnatural. For linguistic anthropologists such as Bauman (1992, 2004), however, the notion of language performance may take on a particular significance. Rather than viewing performance as 'any doing of an act of communication', it is viewed as 'a specially marked mode of action, one that sets up or represents a special interpretative frame within which the act of communication is to be understood' (1992, p. 44). In this sense of performance – dismissed by Austin (see below) as *etiolations*, but taken up by Derrida as part of general *iterability* – 'the act of communication is put on display, objectified, lifted out to a degree from its contextual surroundings, and opened up to scrutiny by an audience. Performance thus calls forth special attention to and heightened awareness of the act of communication' (Bauman, 1992, p. 44). From this perspective, then, language performances are social acts of a particular kind that make language use available for inspection. The performance of a text, as Bauman (2004) argues, may be seen in terms of 'the dynamics of recontextualization': 'A performed text may be subsequently – or, to be sure, antecedently – reported, rehearsed, translated, relayed, quoted, summarised, or parodied, to suggest but a few of the intertextual possibilities' (p. 10).

Performance also shifts the focus from internal, abstracted competencies to public, bodily enactments. The emergence of the body through the somatic turn (Shusterman, 2000) in the social sciences places language use in a different context. Much has been written about the linguistic turn based on the poststructuralist insight that 'the common factor in the analysis of social organization, social meanings, power and individual consciousness is *language*' (Weedon, 1987, p. 21). As Weedon went on to explain, language 'is the place where actual and possible forms of social organization and their likely social and political consequences are defined and contested. Yet it is also the place where our sense of ourselves, our subjectivity, is *constructed*' (1987, p. 21). An irony here, as Poynton (1993) points out, is that linguistics failed to register that this linguistic turn 'was not only asking different kinds of questions about language as a social phenomenon but was calling into question the premises of established ways of "knowing about language" within disciplinary linguistics itself' (Poynton, 1993, pp. 3–4; see also Pennycook, 2002b). The effects of this linguistic turn in language studies has been slow, and it is only recently, as Canagarajah (2004) explains, that we have started to 'understand identities as multiple, conflictual, negotiated and evolving. We have traveled far from the traditional assumption in language studies that identities are static, unitary, discrete, and given' (p. 117). While the linguistic turn has thus challenged and inverted assumptions about the processes of language production from interiority (competence) to exteriority (per-formance) by arguing that we are constructed *by* language rather than being the constructors *of* language, it is the *somatic turn* that takes us fully back towards a notion of embodiment.

The origins of this move towards the body, Shusterman (2000) suggests, may be multiple – from a 'need to find and cultivate a stable point of ref-erence in a rapidly changing and increasingly baffling world' (p. 162) to 'the weakening cultural hold of religious views that for many centuries demonized the body as the enemy of the divine immortal soul and hence a threat to true happiness' (p. 163) – but its significance lies in at least three crucial dimensions: a reaction against the logocentric idealism of poststruc-turalism, the attempt to reclaim domains of being that have been excised by rationalist philosophy, and the political, and particularly feminist, demand to account for our physical presence. The feminist critique of such disem-bodied approaches to research and knowledge has arguably been the most powerful, with writers such as Dorothy Smith (1999, p. 4) defining the notion of 'writing the social' in terms of taking

> one step back before the Cartesian shift that forgets the body. The body isn't forgotten; hence, the actual local site of the body isn't forgotten. Inquiry starts with the knower who is actually located; she is active; she is at work; she is connected up with other people in various ways; she thinks, eats, sleeps, laughs, desires, sorrows, sings, curses, loves, just here; she reads here; she watches television.

Philosophy, Shusterman (2000, p. 156) suggests, 'can engage somatics as a new domain for reconstructive critical theory'. As he continues, 'any robustly somatic philosophy may seem scandalous, because it bucks the idealism that still haunts philosophy and is manifest, for example, in the linguistic turn's resolution to exclude from philosophical inquiry anything below the level of language or *logos*' (p. 157).

From Foucault's (1986) increased interest in the 'care of the self' to fem-inist critiques of disembodied male knowledge, the body has returned as a significant site of engagement. As Threadgold (1997) suggests, we need to understand how the social order is '*both* imbricated in language, textuality and semiosis *and* is corporeal, spatial, temporal, institutional, conflictual, and marked by sexual, racial and other differences' (p. 101). For Bourdieu, we need to understand how dispositions are written on to our bodies, how cultural capital is not something we pull on and take off but is deeply bound up with how we act:

> The sense of acceptability which orients linguistic practices is inscribed in the most deep-rooted of bodily dispositions; it is the whole body which responds by its posture, but also by its inner reactions or, more specifically, the articulatory ones, to the tension of the market. Language is a body

technique, and specifically linguistic, especially phonetic, competence is a dimension of bodily hexis in which one's whole relation to the social world, and one's whole socially informed relation to the world, are expressed.

(Bourdieu, 1991, p. 86)

James Clifford draws on Bourdieu's work to suggest that in anthropology 'we may find it useful to think of the "field" as a habitus rather than as a place, a cluster of *embodied* dispositions and practices' (Clifford, 1997, p. 69). As he explains, 'a disciplinary habitus has been sustained around the embodied activity of fieldwork: an ungendered, unraced, sexually inactive subject interacts intensively (on hermeneutic/scientific levels, at the very least) with its interlocutors' (p. 72).

We observe here, then, a range of ways of thinking about language performance, not as the unregulated by-product of competence, but rather as the socially embedded and culturally embodied use of language. Notions of competence, system, core identity, origins or grammar are considered either as misplaced attempts to imagine essential essences or as by-products of performance. The perspective I am trying to open up here, then, suggests that 'history, tradition and identity are all performances, all the result of invested actors who position themselves vis-a-vis others in a complex and unfolding reality not of their own making' (Dimitriadis, 2001, p. 11). And in order to understand how it is that we are the products of our performances, we need to turn to the notion of performativity. Thus, rather than an underlying competence driving our performance, it is the repeated performances of language and identity that produce the semblance of being. In order to pursue this view further, I will turn in the next section to a discussion of the fascinating history of the performative, from Austin to Butler, via Derrida and Bourdieu.

Performativity: from speech act to sedimented performance

At first glance, performativity, as developed by the philosopher J.L. Austin and subsequently incorporated into speech act theory, may seem a rather lacklustre concept to invoke for rethinking language and identity within the global context of hip-hop, since it is generally relegated to a small category of verbs or acts that do what they say ('I sentence you to five years in prison' and so forth). Yet while, on the one hand, remaining a rather obscure corner of language philosophy and pragmatics, the notion of the performative has at the same time generated huge interest from a very wide range of thinkers, including Derrida, Bourdieu, Butler, Habermas, Deleuze and Guattari, and Laclau. It has become a key term in anti-foundationalist notions of gender, sexuality and identity. In this section I shall make a case for the importance of the notion of performativity as a term in applied linguistics, since it opens up several significant ways of thinking about language and identity, languages as entities, and language as part of transmodal performance. It also provides a useful means to bring back performance into the competence-heavy domain of mainstream applied and unapplied linguistics.

The term *performative* was coined by J.L. Austin (1962) in his book *How to Do Things With Words* to describe a particular type of speech act that does what it says, or performs an act in the doing. Typical examples of performatives include 'I pronounce you man and wife'; 'I sentence you to ten years in prison'; 'I name this ship' and so on. Austin distinguished between 'constatives' and 'performatives': the first describe a state of affairs (which can be true or false), while the latter accomplish something in their enunciation. The significance of this distinction needs to be understood in the context of a particular strand of twentieth century British language philosophy, with its concern for formal logic (and logical positivism) and truth conditions. For Austin, the significance of performatives was that they were not bound by truth conditions but rather could succeed or not succeed (felicitous or infelicitous rather than true or false), their success depending on contextual factors such as following the conventional procedure, the right words being uttered by the right people in the right circumstances, and the whole having the right effect.

Austin went on to divide his performatives into several subsets of verbs, including verdictives (for example, convict, diagnose), exercitives (appoint, excommunicate, recommend), commissives (promise, bet), behavitives (apologize, thank, welcome) and expositives (affirm, deny, inform). He also argued that it was possible for these verbs to be absent ('I'll do it' has the same performative force as 'I promise I'll do it'), thus opening the way for a distinction between explicit and implicit performatives (the first includes a verb that describes the action; the latter does not). There are a number of difficulties here, however. Once the concept of a performative is opened up to include all these possible items, and once a distinction is made to allow implicit performatives, it is hard to maintain any clear category of the performative. As Austin himself acknowledged, once you went down this route, it was not in fact so clear that his basic constative/performative distinction could be maintained: 'Now we must ask ourselves whether issuing a constative utterance is not, after all, the performance of an act, the act, namely, of stating. Is stating an act in the same sense as marrying, apologizing, betting, etc.?' (Austin, 1971, p. 20).

Austin attempted, and then abandoned, the idea that performatives could be linguistically defined. For a while, linguists attempted to define the syntactic structure of performatives, suggesting that performative utterances had the following characteristics: (1) first person subject (I/we); (2) simple present tense verb (state, ask); (3) indirect object *you*; (4) possibility of inserting *hereby*; and (5) not negative (see Leech, 1974). Such attempts immediately ran into problems, however, since they did not allow for the implicit performatives ('I bet you five dollars' versus 'Five bucks says you'll never make it'), left out those explicit performatives that did not adhere to this formula ('You are hereby warned that ...'), and did not allow for the possibility that even some of the 'pure performatives' like 'I name this ship' might not actually depend as much as it was claimed on the actual words being spoken (might not a judge just say 'Five years!' or a ship launcher proclaim 'Titanic!'?). Other attempts were made to construct categorizations over several levels; for example, (1) performatives where the 'I' and verb and ritual behaviour are central to the performance (I name this ship); (2) those that are not ritualized and where the verb may be omitted ([I promise] I'll do it); and (3) those which may or may not be performative depending on the context: 'There's a bull in the field' may be an implicit performative if it is intended as a warning.

For a short while, 'performative analysis' became a key theme in generative semantics, the argument being that the deep semantic structure of all utterances is a performative: 'It'll rain tomorrow', for example, having a deep structure: I state that [it'll rain tomorrow], or I predict that [it'll rain tomorrow]. Ultimately, however, the possibility of defining performative acts or of describing all language use in these terms was largely abandoned. The coverage of the notion of the performative was gradually reduced until it was back where it had started: that small, quirky and slightly undefinable category of language acts that perform the act in the saying as part of a ritual activity. By and large, the performative, from a linguistic point of view, has been relegated to a fairly insignificant corner of language theory. Austin himself had started afresh by exploring the notion of locutionary (the act of saying something), illocutionary (what we do in saying something – apologizing, describing) and perlocutionary (the purpose or effect of the utterance) acts. While a sense of performativity was still attached to Austin's use of illocutionary speech acts, this was largely lost as his ideas were appropriated by the language philosopher John Searle (1969), who sought a closer *rapprochement* between his view of speech acts and a Chomskyan version of competence (Rajagopalan, 2000). Performativity was back in the box.

The social magic of performatives

It is worth recalling, however, that while this is the history of the performative from the point of view of linguistics, which is primarily concerned with trying to define language use from the inside, as it were, Austin was a philosopher concerned with the question of how we do things with words (as part of a larger philosophy of action): how is it that language can function as a form of social activity, achieving different effects, causing people to act, bringing multiple reactions? If the take-up of such questions within the domain of linguistics was always hobbled by the linguistic obsession with the interiority of language, for many others, the question of how we do things with words (and how words do things to us) remained a key pursuit. Given the broader interest in the idea of how we do things with words – the role ascribed to discourse in poststructuralism, for example, as the site where our subjectivities are formed and reality is produced – the can of worms opened up by Austin has been regularly reopened. The question became not a linguistic one about how we can define a performative speech act, but rather how it is that words have effects. As Butler (1997) begins her book *Excitable Speech: A Politics of the Performative,* 'When we claim to have been injured by language, what kind of claim do we make? We ascribe an agency to language, a power to injure, and position ourselves as the objects of its injurious trajectory' (p. 1). From such questions a much wider series of issues open up, leading us to ask if it might not in fact be the case that all language is indeed performative, not in the sense that it depends on an underlying performative speech act (I believe that, I state that) but rather that it produces the conditions it describes.

Two major theorists who have engaged with Austin's work are Lyotard and Habermas, though I shall mention them only briefly here, since neither takes us in useful directions in terms of the agenda of this book. Lyotard (1984) defines performativity as 'the optimization of the global relationship between input and output' (p. 11). He links this to Austin's work, suggesting that this use of performativity 'in the new current sense of efficiency measured according to an input/output ratio' is not so far from Austin's performativity, since 'Austin's performative realizes the optimal performance' (p. 88, n. 30). This is a rather odd reading of Austin, it seems to me, though this sense of performativity – as efficiency measured according to an input/output ratio – is now widely used in many institutions (from education to business), and is akin to notions such as 'performance indicators' (a set of criteria to evaluate performance). This sense of performativity – which is very distinct from the way I am using it in this chapter – may be seen as part of the corporatization of the world (see Chapter 2), leading to increased use of such performance measures in many domains of both public and private life. It is worth reiterating, however, that although Lyotard develops this notion of performativity based on his reading of Austin, and although this is probably the most common use of the term currently, it is not the sense of performativity I am interested in here.

In Habermas's (1984) attempt to use the philosophy of language to justify the project of modernity, he also turned to Austin. In order to get beyond what he saw as critical theory's overreliance on instrumental reason – presupposed by a subject isolated from other subjects and a material world – Habermas set out to understand how a relationship to the world was intersubjectively established and how the communicative function of language was central to this process. In order to make this argument, he needed to demonstrate that the original and primary mode of language use was communication aimed at reaching understanding. As Rasmussen (1990) suggests, this 'thesis regarding the primacy of the communicative mode constitutes the major theoretical insight sustaining the entire edifice Habermas has built' (p. 28). Yet, although Habermas interestingly stresses performative aspects of language in the achievement of intersubjectivity (emphasizing the need to understand 'the meaning of the performative – and not the referential – use of the expression "I" within the system of personal pronouns' (1984, p. 397)), his attempt to show how both ideology and rational-purposive thought were perversions of the essential communicative function of language produces a highly normative account of language and intention that does not sit well with the arguments of this book.

A more useful engagement with Austin may be found in Derrida's debate with the language philosopher John Searle. Derrida (1982) challenged the type of speech acts that were excluded from Austin's model. In determining the conditions under which performatives were felicitous, such as being said sincerely by the right person in the right circumstances, Austin made a number of exclusions of what he termed *etiolations* – language uses that were not serious or real, such as jokes, plays and so on. For Derrida, however, such exclusions raised an important point about language use: 'Is not what Austin excludes as anomalous, exceptional, "non-serious," that is, citation, (on the stage, in a poem, or in a soliloquy), the determined modification of a general citationality – or rather, a general iterability – without which there could not even be a "successful" performative?' (1982, p. 325). For Derrida, then, the crucial issue was not so much one of trying to establish what made a performative felicitous – the right person saying it at the right time under the right conditions – but rather the way in which language use was made effective by repetition, by citation. 'Could a performative statement succeed', Derrida asked, 'if its formulation did not repeat a "coded" or iterable statement, in other words if the expressions I use to open a meeting, launch a ship, or a marriage were not identifiable as conforming to an iterable model, and therefore if they were not identifiable in a way as "citation"?' (p. 326). Derrida's insight here is significant since it not only questions the divisions between the serious and non-serious (with implications for how we understand performance), but it also raises questions about originality. For Austin, a signature was a performative – by signing one's name, one does the act of signing – but Derrida asks whether such acts as signing do not gain their power from the general citationality and iterability of language.

Bourdieu's (1982, 1991) argument is a different one, focusing centrally on how it is that words come to have power. The error that Austin makes (and Habermas after him, in his reliance on the notion of the ideal speech situation, devoid of relations of power), he suggests, is to believe that 'he has discovered the principal of the efficacy of language in discourse itself, in the truly linguistic substance of spoken language' (1982, p. 105).[1] Once we treat language as an autonomous object, Bourdieu argues, an error made possible by Saussure's radical separation of internal from external linguistics, of the science of language from the science of the use of language,

> we are condemned to look for the power of words within words, which is not where it is to be found .... By trying to understand linguistically

the power of linguistic manifestations, by looking for the principle of logic and efficacy of institutional language within language, we forget that authority is invested in language from outside .... Such authority is at best represented, manifested, symbolized by language.

(Bourdieu, 1982, pp. 103–105)

For Bourdieu, then, power is external to language. And thus performatives are dependent not so much on Austin's felicity conditions but rather on institutional authorization.

To understand Austin's performative utterances we 'cannot restrict ourselves to the limits of linguistics. The magical efficacy of these *institutional acts* is inseparable from the existence of an institution that defines the requisite conditions (agent, time, place) for the magic of words to operate' (1982, p. 69). To understand the illocutionary power of discourse, therefore, linguistic research has to give way to 'proper sociological research into the conditions under which people can find themselves and their speech invested with such power. The real source of the magic of performative utterances lies ... in the social conditions of the *institution* which invests legitimacy in its representative as an agent capable of acting on the social world through words' (p. 73). For Bourdieu, performative utterances must always fail if the speaker does not have the institutional power to speak. Austin identified a particular set of expressions which appear to 'hold *within themselves* the principle of power which in reality rests in the institutional conditions of their production and reception' (p. 111). The power of words, therefore, the possibility that language can have social effects, according to Bourdieu, is always dependent on prior social conditions of power.

Butler (1997) suggests, however, that Bourdieu's 'conservative account of the speech act presumes that the conventions that will authorize the performative are already in place' (p. 142), a view which fails to account for Derrida's discussion of context or the power of words in themselves. She argues that language should not be seen as 'a static and closed system whose utterances are functionally secured in advance by the "social positions" to which they are mimetically related' (p. 145). Thus, by 'making social institutions static, Bourdieu fails to grasp the logic of iterability that governs the possibility of social transformation' (p. 147); and 'by claiming that performative utterances are only effective when they are spoken by those who are (already) in a position of social power to exercise words as deeds, Bourdieu inadvertently forecloses the possibility of an agency that emerges from the margins of power' (p. 156). This is a crucial insight. While Bourdieu usefully shows that both the linguistic and the Critical Theory (Habermas) approaches to performativity fail to conceptualize the local contingencies of power that enable a performative to work, Butler shows that this implies a static vision of the relationship between language and the social, by which power in language is determined only by prior power in the social domain. As she explains (1999), the problem with Bourdieu's account of performative speech acts is the assumption that 'the subject who utters the performative is positioned on a map of social power in a fairly fixed way' and this position will determine the efficacy of the performative (p. 123). He thus confuses 'being authorized to speak' and 'speaking with authority'.

Butler, by contrast, wants to ask what forms of performative can be enacted by those who are not socially sanctioned to do so:

> I would argue that it is precisely the *expropriability* of the dominant, 'authorized' discourse that constitutes one potential site of its subversive resignification. What happens, for instance, when those who have been denied the social power to claim 'freedom' or 'democracy' appropriate those terms from the dominant discourse and rework or resignify those highly cathected terms to rally a political movement?
>
> (Butler, 1997, pp. 157–158)

And what, she asks, 'is the performative power of appropriating the very terms by which one has been abused in order to deplete the term of its degradation or to derive an affirmation from that degradation, rallying under the sign of "queer" or revaluing affirmatively the category of "black" or of "woman"?' (p. 158). We need, therefore, to have a theory of how social transformation operates through linguistic use rather than seeing all language use as mirroring the social. The performative is 'not merely an act used by a pregiven subject, but is one of the powerful and insidious ways in which subjects are called into social being, inaugurated into sociality by a variety of diffuse and powerful interpellations' (1999, p. 125). This tension between the interpellation of subjects into particular ways of being and the expropriability of dominant discourses for other ends is significant for the focus in this book on the relation between dominant discourses and performances of global hip-hop and their local appropriation.

Butler's understanding of performativity provides us with key ways of opening up an understanding of language, identity and performance. Focusing centrally on gender, she (1990a) argues that 'gender proves to be performative – that is, constituting the identity it is purported to be. In this sense, gender is always a doing, though not a doing by a subject who might be said to preexist the deed' (p. 25). Performativity, then, following Butler, may be understood as the way in which we perform acts of identity as an ongoing series of social and cultural performances rather than as the expression of a prior identity. As she goes on to argue: 'Gender is the repeated stylization of the body, a set of repeated acts within a highly rigid regulatory frame that congeal over time to produce the appearance of substance, of a natural sort of being' (p. 33). Butler's concern is that the foundational belief in gendered or sexed identities is paradoxical, since it predetermines and fixes the subjects it aims to liberate. These arguments have been most influential in queer studies, where the questioning of categories of sexual and gender identity have allowed a framing of sexuality that goes beyond lesbian and gay identification and instead embraces the broader categories of queer or trans (Butler, 2004; Nelson, 1999). As Jagose (1996) puts it, 'Debates around performativity put a denaturalising pressure on sex, gender, sexuality, bodies and identities' (p. 90).

Taking up Austin's concept of performativity as language that performs in the act of speaking, Butler insists that 'identity is performatively constituted by the very "expressions" that are said to be its results' (1990a, p. 25). Not only does the performative therefore constitute identity as a productive act, but what it constitutes is what it is purported to be. This process of self-production is by no means a question of free-willed choice to take up some form of identity or another but rather occurs within a 'highly rigid regulatory frame' (p. 33). Identities are a product of our ongoing performances of acts that are largely pre-scribed. Butler's conception has been taken up and challenged in a number of ways, some of which overemphasized the relationship to performance as theatrical and optional, suggesting that gender could be performed as an actor takes on a role. Butler carefully refutes this position in her 1993 book *Bodies that Matter*, arguing that 'performativity is neither free play nor theatrical self-presentation; nor can it simply be equated with performance' (1993, p. 95). As Butler conceives the term, it gives us important ways of understanding the local contingencies of identity formation.

In terms of my interest in this book of exploring different ways of thinking about language and identity within globalization, Butler's development of the notion of performativity has several significant implications: it opens up a way of thinking about language use and identity that avoids foundationalist categories. We are not as we are because of some inner being but because of what we do. Hence, rather than being a rejection of the materiality of the body – as some critiques of Butler have suggested – this way of thinking makes the somatic turn and performance crucial to any understanding of being. At the same time, however, it does not give to the body a prior ontological status outside its inscription into discourse, and it insists that the performance of identity is highly regulated. We do not write our own scripts, although we do have some space for change. This position not only opens up a non-essentialist view of identity, but it also provides the ground for considering languages themselves from an ant-foundationalist perspective. I explore these issues further below.

How to do identity and language with words

This discussion of performativity, then, has opened up several significant ways for rethinking language and identity. It provides a way of thinking about relationships between language and identity that emphasize the productive force of language in constituting identity rather than identity being a pregiven construct that is reflected in language use. As noted in Chapter 2, critics of traditional sociolinguistics, such as Cameron (1995, 1997), have pointed out that rather than assuming we speak in particular ways because of who we are, it might be more useful to consider the possibility that we are as we are because of how we speak. The question for language and gender studies, then, is not how men and women talk differently, as if males and females pre-existed their language use as given categories of identity, but rather – recalling Austin once again – how we do gender with words. This does not mean that we do not constantly perform gendered identities through language but rather that we constitute through language the identity it is purported to be. It is in the performance that we make the difference. As Butler (1999) suggests, 'Being called a "girl" from the inception of existence is a way in which the girl becomes transitively "girled" over time' (p. 120). Appropriating Althusser's notion of interpellation to the question of performativity, Butler argues that such processes of 'hailing' subjects into being are 'social performatives, ritualized and sedimented through time'. Thus 'the interpellation as performative establishes the discursive constitution of the subject as inextricable from the social constitution of the subject' (p. 120). Here, then, we are able to go beyond the language/society divide that Bourdieu perpetuates, and we are able to see how social subjects are constituted, and how the sedimented interpellation of the subject produces performative effects.

The notion of performativity helps fill that gap in poststructuralist theory to do with the making of the subject: from a poststructuralist point of view, the subject is produced in discourse. As Price (1996) points out, however, the ways in which this has been taken up in applied linguistic work (see, e.g., (Norton-) Peirce, 1995; Norton, 2000), leave the relationship between subject and discourse as largely static: a subject chooses to take up a subject position in a pregiven discourse. The problem here is that, like objects waiting to be named, these subject positions pre-exist the discursive engagement of the subject. Price (1999), by contrast, argues for a view in which 'discourse is seen as a practice in which both discourse and subject are performatively realized' (p. 582). An understanding of performativity, therefore, allows us to view the production of identity in the doing. As Laclau (1989) argues in his introduction to Žižek's (1989) *The Sublime Object of Ideology*, 'if the unity of the object is the retroactive effect of naming itself, then naming is not just the pure nominalistic game of attributing an empty name to a preconstituted subject'. Thus, if the process of naming objects amounts to the very act of their constitution, then the 'essentially performative character of naming is the precondition for all hegemony and politics' (p. xiv).

Questioning the ways in which sociolinguistic studies of variety assume the prior existence of languages within which variation occurs, Le Page and Tabouret-Keller (1985) argue that we need instead to understand how we constitute linguistic and cultural identities through the performance of *acts of identity*. If gendered and other identities are seen in a non-foundational light, so may language itself be seen as a product of performative acts. It is instructive in this context to compare Butler's comments on gender with Hopper's view of *emergent grammar*: 'The subject is not *determined* by the rules through which it is generated because signification is *not a founding act, but rather a regulated process of repetition*' (Butler, 1990a, p. 145; emphasis in original). For Hopper, the apparent structure or regularity of grammar is an emergent property that 'is shaped by discourse in an ongoing process. Grammar is, in this view, simply the name for certain categories of observed repetitions in discourse' (Hopper, 1998, p. 156). Thus, just as Butler (1999) argues that identities are a product of ritualized social performatives calling the subject into being and 'sedimented through time' (p. 120), so for Hopper:

> there is no natural fixed structure to language. Rather, speakers borrow heavily from their previous experiences of communication in similar circumstances, on similar topics, and with similar interlocutors. Systematicity, in this view, is an illusion produced by the partial settling or *sedimentation* of frequently used forms into temporary subsystems.
>
> (Hopper, 1998, pp. 157–158)

The concept of sedimentation links to Derrida's (1982) contention that a performative only works with the force of iterability: the performative achieves an accumulated force by dint of its 'citationality', which also simultaneously positions the speaker as the supposedly original and intentional utterer of the speech act. From this perspective, gender, like grammar, like many other forms of identity or apparently structured properties, is a sedimentation of acts repeated over time within regulated contexts (and see the discussion of transtextuality in Chapter 3). And while giving the appearance of substance, of representing an underlying reality, it is actually a result of the repeated layering of acts that purport to correspond to an identity but actually produce it in the doing. Such a position also ties in to Bakhtin's view of the dialogic nature of language, suggesting that all language use carries histories of its former uses with it. 'Our speech, that is, all our utterances' are therefore 'filled with others' words, varying degrees of otherness and varying degrees of "our-own-ness", varying degrees of awareness and detachment. These words of others carry with them their own expression, their own evaluation tone, which we assimilate, rework and reaccentuate' (Bakhtin, 1986, p. 89).

   The word, according to Bakhtin (1981, p. 293), 'is half someone else's, [and] becomes "one's own" only when the speaker populates it with his[/her] own intention, his[/her] own accent, when [s/]he appropriates the word, adapting to his[/her] own semantic and expressive intention'. Commenting on the importance of this idea of 'appropriating others' words' for language learning, Lensmire and Beals (1994) suggest that 'We are born and develop, learn to speak, read and write, awash in the words of others....Our words are always someone else's words first; and these words sound with the intonations and evaluations of others who have used them before, and from whom we have learned them' (p. 411). Hopper's view of sedimentation ties in interestingly here; indeed, in the very echoes of others' words, his argument appears to perform what it argues:

> We say things that have been said before. Our speech is a vast collection of hand-me-downs that reaches back in time to the beginnings of language. The aggregation of changes and adjustments that are made to this inheritance on each individual occasion of use results in a constant erosion and replacement of the sediment of usage that is called grammar.
>
> (Hopper, 1998, p. 159)

What this does, crucially, is challenge the centrality of competence (underlying system) over performance. Thus, by looking at the performativity of language – the ways in which in the doing it does that which it purports to be – we can start to question the foundation of linguistic belief in system, and go beyond mere reporting of performance. Instead, this opens up the space to explore how sedimentation occurs (and can be opposed). More generally, we can start to raise broader questions about the whole ontological status of the notion of language and languages (Makoni and Pennycook, 2005, 2006). Languages are no more pregiven entities that pre-exist our linguistic performances than are gendered or ethnic identities. Rather they are the sedimented products of repeated acts of identity.

Returning for a moment to the discussion of English begun in Chapter 2, we can now start to consider the language not so much in terms of an underlying set of structures but rather as a social, ideological, historical and discursive construction, the product of ritualized social performatives that become sedimented into temporary subsystems. These social performatives are acts of identity, investment and semiotic (re)construction (Kandiah, 1998). That is to say, the temporary sedimentation of English subsystems is a result of agentive acts, particular moves to identify, to use and adapt available semiotic resources for a variety of goals. English, like any other language, does not exist as a prior system but is produced and sedimented through acts of identity. Similar to the way that we perform identity with words (rather than reflect identities in language), we also perform languages with words. What we therefore have to understand is not this 'thing' 'English' that does or does not do things to and for people, but rather the multiple investments that people bring to their acts, desires and performances in 'English'.

Just as Butler describes her project as 'a poststructuralist rewriting of discursive performativity as it operates in the materialization of sex' (1993. p. 12), so my interest here is in a transgressive rewriting of discursive performativity as it operates in the materialization of language. If Foucault (1980) was concerned with the 'truth effects' of discourse, and Butler (1993) with the 'body effects' of discourse, I am here concerned with the 'language effects' of discourse, the ways in which languages are materialized through discourse. By analogy, then, with Foucault's (1980) argument that we need to give up asking if something is true or false and instead focus on the truth effects of making different epistemological claims, or the transgressive philosophy discussed in the previous chapter whereby the question becomes one of thinking outside the limits, so we would do better to go beyond asking whether English exists or not, and rather focus on the 'language effects' produced by the language industry. This points to the need for a much more contextualized understanding of language as locally derived. Something called English is mobilized by English-language industries with particular language effects. But something called English is also part of complex language chains, mobilized as part of multiple acts of identity; it is caught in a constant process of semiotic reconstruction.

Refashioning ourselves with words

Having pointed earlier to the need both to move beyond the competence/performance divide of linguistics and to distinguish carefully between performance and performativity, it is now useful to revisit the power of performance. As Derrida suggested in his critique of the etiolations rejected by Austin, there is good reason to take language performances more seriously. According to Bauman and Briggs (1996), 'performances are not simply artful uses of language that stand apart both from day-to-day life and from larger questions of meaning, as Kantian aesthetics would suggest. Performance rather provides a frame that invites critical reflection on communicative processes' (p. 60). Thus, while Austin claimed that performance weakens the performative force of utterances, the work of linguistic anthropologists interested in performance 'suggests that poetic patterning, frames, genres, participatory structures, and other dimensions of performance draw attention to the status of speech as social action' (Bauman and Briggs, 1996, p. 65). Rap and hip-hop, I want to suggest, play a very important role here: as language and embodied performances, they draw attention to language as social action.

A view of language performance as more than the incompetencies of the real world, furthermore, helps relate language use to performance studies. Originally dealing with theatre, performance studies have now grown to encompass a broader concept of performance, including ritual, dance, music and so on (see, e.g., Butler, 1990b; Case, 1990). This expansion of the notion of performance can open up our understanding of language as public display, whether performing live (Shusterman, 2000) or through digital media, shifting the Butlerian sense of the performative (which is less dependent on an audience) into a public space. It also opens up performance to a view of transmodality (see Chapter 3). Here the somatic turn takes us beyond a logocentric interest in discourse, and instead focuses on language use integrated with ritual, dance, music, graffiti, beat-boxing, clothing, gestures, posture, ways of walking and talking. This is a move to overcome a segregationist approach to language as an autonomous system (see Chapters 2 and 3) not merely through the addition of pragmatics, sociolinguistics or paralinguistics, but rather through an integrated understanding of the body as interlinked with other social and semiotic practices.

A focus on performance also emphasizes the notion of activity, of acts of identity. While this is not intended to imply false acts – acting out what one is not – it may also need to include such possibilities. As Walcott (1997) observes in his discussion of black diasporic language and culture, in the face of the extraordinary oppressions of slavery, it became necessary to be able to act out identities:

> Black people in the Americas have had an immediate relationship to identity and identification as twin acts which constitute performativity. This stems from the ways in which slavery produced spaces for particular forms of identity, identifications and disidentifications. Being forced to perform for the master in a number of different ways meant that a relationship to identity for diasporic black people manifested itself as something that could be invented, revised and discarded when no longer useful.
>
> (Walcott, 1997, p. 98)

This understanding of identity performances as a form of resistance ties in with James Scott's (1985, 1990) discussions of the 'weapons of the weak', the 'hidden transcripts' that underlie the many local acts of resistance to domination. From poaching, squatting and desertion to gossip, rumour, carnival, social myth and dissident subcultures, the arts of resistance are often hidden and subversive. These 'weapons of the weak … these simple acts of false compliance, parody, pretence, and mimicking are the strategies by which the marginalized detach themselves from the ideologies of the powerful, retain a measure of critical thinking, and gain some measure of control over their life in an oppressive situation' (Canagarajah, 2000, p. 122).

At this point we are confronted by the issue of choice and agency. If we view performativity along the lines of false compliances, parodies and pretences, as identity performances that can be invented, revised and discarded when no longer useful, on the one hand we run the danger of overlooking the effects of performativity, while on the other hand we open up the possibility for seeing how we may refashion futures through language. Central to Butler's caution not to view performativity as the casual pulling-on and taking-off of identity is the argument that these assumed identities are not so easily discarded; they become performatively realized. Thus, even if we assume a form of conscious identity-wearing as part of performativity – a less common case than our sedimented everyday performing of identity –

this can still make us into something new. As with the challenges to Butler's view of the performativity of gender, which suggested that she regarded gender as too easily pulled on and taken off – as if gender were something we performed like a play – so we need to be cautious not to suggest that language is merely a site of identity performance as a form of play-acting. Thus, while it is useful to view language and identity as interrelated acts, we should be cautious not to adopt a position which suggests they are acts that we freely choose. To paraphrase Butler's (1990a, b) discussion of gender, fashioning language and identity implies a set of repeated acts within a highly rigid regulatory frame that congeal over time to produce the appearance of substance.

The relation between performance and performativity, however, does allow for a sense of performance as refashioning. As Walcott goes on to argue, we can understand performativity as a form of the '(re)writing of English, Spanish, Dutch, French and Portuguese ... the (re)invention of musical sound; and a plethora of other act(ion)s that make clear a notion of fashioning and invention of the self' (p. 99). In the process of rewriting, reinventing and reclaiming, languages and identities are remade. 'Black folks', says Walcott, 'do not only perform language, but their language is made to perform, to work in the service of revising and altering the wor(l)d' (1997, p. 104). Performance and performativity here provide ways of understanding the refashioning of the self, going beyond a notion of the original and mimicry to include parody and appropriation: 'Black postmodern speech acts and language performance play with the notion of the original (if there is an original English at all), questioning origins while revealing the traces of residue from the "original" as important for the new invention' (p. 106). It is this sense of how futures are refashioned (see Scott, 1999) in the transmodal performances of popular culture that is crucial for seeing how language and identity are constantly performed and remade. Hip-hop, at least in its local street-based manifestations, remains a weapon of the weak, a form of local subversion, a series of transgressive acts that disrupt forms of domination. In doing so it opens up the possibilities to refashion identities and languages; it puts language on display as a form of social action. And by performing language and identity transgressively it performatively creates new identities.

From performative to transformative

I have tried to present a case here for understanding language, identity and refashioning in terms of performativity. Performativity opens up a way of thinking about language use and identity that avoids foundationalist categories, suggesting that identities are formed in the linguistic performance rather than pregiven. This opens up a way of thinking about the effects of language not only in terms of world view, ideology or discourse but also in terms of what language does, what effects it brings about. Such a view of language identity also helps us to see how subjectivities are called into being and sedimented over time through regulated language acts. This position then provides the ground for considering languages themselves from an anti-foundationalist perspective, whereby language use is an act of identity which calls that language into being. And performativity, particularly in its relationship to notions of performance, opens up ways to understand how languages, identities and futures are refashioned. Yet this is not an easy, free-willed choice to remake an identity. While a notion of performance may emphasize the temporary, present and enacted moment, the notion of the performative in Butler (via Derrida's emphasis on iterability), as Culler (2000) notes, depends on a history of repetition, of sedimented effects. The performance, as Cameron and Kulick (2003) observe, depends on the performative. Thus, while the notion of performativity opens up many possibilities for questioning prior notions of identity, the transgressive performance only achieves its effects in relation to the sedimentations of performativity.

In order to have a usable notion of performativity here, therefore, we need, on the one hand, to avoid the pull towards performance as open-ended free display (we perform whatever identities we want to) and, on the other, the pull towards oversedimentation (we can only perform what has been prescribed): to some extent, the performative is always along lines that have already been laid down, and yet performativity can also be about refashioning futures. What both concepts have in common is a sense of the present, the real, the everyday, the notion that, as Dimitriadis puts it, in a similar vein to the discussion of transtextuality in Chapter 3, 'texts – whether symbol systems or lived experiences – are always in performance. They contain no essential or inherent meaning but are always given meaning by people, in particular times and in particular places' (2001, p. 11). According to bell hooks (1994), 'teaching is a performative act' (p. 11) by which she means that to 'embrace the performative aspect of teaching we are compelled to engage "audiences," to consider issues of reciprocity. Teachers are not performers in the traditional sense of the word in that our work is not meant to be a spectacle. Yet it is meant to serve as a catalyst that calls everyone to become active participants in learning' (p. 11). From this point of view, then, the importance of the notion of performance is not so much in the spectacle, the acting out in front of people, as it is in the interactions that performance calls forth. It is this sense of performance as interactive, most obvious when performing live, that opens up the circle of performance and performativity. This move from the performative to the transformative is crucial for our understanding here of performativity as neither merely the playing out of public roles nor the acting out of sedimented behaviour, but the refashioning of futures. How this view relates to popular culture and public performance will be the topic of the next chapter.

5   Taking the vernacular voices of the popular seriously

Through the preceding chapters I have been suggesting at various points the need to take hip-hop seriously, to use an understanding of hip-hop in relation to global Englishes in order to develop a better understanding of transcultural flows. But why take hip-hop seriously? Is not hip-hop, like most of popular culture, just a superficial, commercialized, shallow form of cultural consumption, frequently misogynist, often homophobic, commonly violent, designed to capture a market among the young with the goals of political acquiescence, public consumption and (sub)cultural conformity dressed up as nonconformity? Such critiques of hip-hop should not be casually dismissed since popular culture, by its very nature, is always more open to commercial exploitation than unpopular culture; and its status as an oppositional, nonconformist, resistant cultural formation is often romanticized by both practitioners and those interested in the study of popular culture. Neither, however, should such critiques be casually adopted since there are also strong reasons to take hip-hop and other forms of popular culture far more seriously than such dismissive declamations allow. This and the following chapters locate hip-hop within a broad philosophical, cultural, linguistic and pedagogical understanding of transcultural flows.

Pop culture, mass culture, vernacular voices

While a number of sociolinguists have taken up the challenge of exploring language use in relation to popular culture,[1] remarkably little attention has been paid to popular culture within the fields of language education and applied linguistics. Perhaps because of the long ties between English language education and the study of literature (e.g. Talib, 2002), or the culturally conservative climate in applied linguistics brought about by its colonial connections on the one hand and its appeals to science on the other (see Pennycook, 1994, 1998), there is far more likelihood to see references to Shakespeare and the literary canon than to popular culture (though for exceptions see Ibrahim, 1999, 2001; Norton and Vanderheyden, 2004; Rasolofondraosolo and Meinhof, 2003). If an appeal to science cannot be made to justify a claim, then an appeal to high culture may achieve the same effect. From a culturally conservative point of view, engagement with popular culture is seen as a failure to appreciate higher values and a tendency to wallow in the superficial and vulgar. Such a position has a long history in education, where the forms of culture and knowledge propagated in standard school curricula have been formed to raise the cultural levels of the population and to ensure that the transgressive pleasures of popular culture are left at the school gate. A well-known version of this argument was presented in Allan Bloom's (1987) *The Closing of the American Mind*, in which he decried decadent forms of popular culture such as rock music, with its 'three great lyrical themes: sex, hate, and a smarmy, hypocritical version of brotherly love. Such polluted sources issue in a muddy stream where only monsters can swim' (p. 74). Salvation, he insisted, was to be found only in a higher canon of knowledge, the Great Books, a study of Western Civilization.

While more liberal and critical perspectives have tended to acknowledge a broader diversity of cultural formations and to be suspicious of claims about a monocultural path to learning, they have also tended to venerate the traditional rather than the popular. Indeed, different positions on the political spectrum have often been strangely united in their denigration of the popular (see Brantlinger, 1983). A strong theme in Marxist-derived arguments equates popular culture with 'mass culture', and this in turn with ideological forms that subjugate working people. As Horkheimer and Adorno (1944/1986) argued in their key book *Dialectic of the Enlightenment*, the culture industry (*Kulturindustrie*) is responsible for the oppression of the working class: mass culture is part of the ideological superstructure that maintains the hegemony of dominant classes. Mass culture, from this point of view, 'is the prolongation of work. It is sought after as an escape from the mechanized work process, and to recruit strength in order to be able to cope with it again' (Horkheimer and Adorno, 1944/1986, p. 137). As Adorno (1975) later explained, the 'total effect of the culture industry is one of anti-enlightenment, in which ... enlightenment, that is the progressive technical domination of nature, becomes mass deception and is turned into a means for fettering consciousness' (p. 18). From this point of view, mass culture serves both to distract working-class consumers from the realities of oppression, and to refresh workers in their leisure time so that they are better able to participate in the workforce.

This intellectual heritage clearly informs the homogeny approach to studies of global English (see Chapter 2). Globalization from this point of view is seen 'in some gloomy Frankfurt School fashion, as the worldwide Americanization or standardization of culture, the destruction of local differences, the massification of all the peoples on the planet' (Jameson, 1998, p. 57). Language and globalization is therefore a process of *the homogenization of world culture* ... spearheaded by films, pop culture, CNN and fast-food chains' (Phillipson and Skutnabb-Kangas, 1996, p. 439; italics in original). Here, then, 'pop culture', in alliance with English, is part of the homogenization of world culture, a delusionary pleasure in cultural forms that is not in the interests of the participants. As Tollefson (2000) puts it, 'English is desirable because of its connections with popular culture – U.S. film and television, popular music and other forms of mass entertainment, even McDonald's. Thus learning English is a mechanism for participating in mass consumer culture' (p. 10). This view of 'mass culture', whereby popular culture is equated with passive consumerism, underpins views of cultural and linguistic imperialism: The global dominance of certain languages and cultures is seen to be a submissive acceptance of their domination by an uninformed periphery, and to take up English is indeed to be a consumer of mass culture. From this 'dystopic, neo- or post-Marxist, political economic critique that still tends to employ ... the metaphor of "penetrations"' (Jacquemet, 2005, p. 259), there has, as Phillipson (1994) puts it, 'already been a penetration of the language into most cultures and education systems' (p. 21). Salvation, meanwhile, is to be in the maintenance of local languages, cultures and traditions (guaranteed through linguistic and cultural rights) as the necessary safeguard to the penetrations of mass culture (see also Chapter 7 for further discussion of cultural maintenance and invention).

It is in part because these concerns have been discussed and thought through in far more complex ways in cultural studies than they have in language studies[2] that I have found it useful to look at relations between English and popular culture through the lens of cultural studies. What sense, then, has cultural studies made of the critique of mass culture as reproducing the subservience of working people, and of cultural imperialism as the imposition of cultural forms on unwitting populations? It was as part of an attempt to understand popular culture in more complex ways in relation to class that cultural studies developed in the 1970s, particularly through the work of the Centre for Contemporary Cultural Studies (based in Birmingham in the UK). A central premise of their early work was that emergent subcultures were part of a collective reaction by working-class youth to their class position within changing politics and economics in the UK. Willis's (1977) classic study of young 'lads'' resistance to schooling, for example, showed how both the school and resistance to school could lead working-class youth into working-class jobs. Consequently the study of popular culture developed a focus on subcultures (Hebdige, 1979; Macdonald, 2001; Mitchell, 1999, 2003c, d; Muggleton, 2000), lifestyles (Jenkins, 1983) and the ways in which young people engaged with local, class-based, often oppositional cultural practices.

Thus the study of popular culture emerged as a sociological endeavour to understand class and culture. Just as the philosophy and sociology of science are not so much interested in good or bad science as in how science operates in epistemological or social terms, so an important part of the focus on popular culture has been concerned not necessarily with the aesthetic evaluation of cultural practices so much as with the social role such cultural adherences play, and the obvious concern that popular culture, by its very popularity, cannot be ignored. Thus Larry Grossberg (1992) sees popular culture as 'a significant and effective part of the material reality of history, effectively shaping the possibilities of our existence. It is this challenge – to understand what it means to "live in popular culture" – that confronts contemporary cultural analysis' (p. 69). As Grossberg (1989) explains elsewhere, popular culture is implicated in the 'multilayered, fragmented collection of meanings, values, and ideas that we both inherit and construct and which largely define our taken-for-granted interpretations of the world'. It plays a key role in the ways 'desires and pleasures, joys and pains, emotions and moods are rapidly constructed and deconstructed, promised and withdrawn, celebrated and realized'. And it is central to the production of 'our identities and experiences': 'Caught between the varieties of discourses we speak and the ultrarapid shifts of mood we inhabit, we are offered possibilities for experiencing the world and locating ourselves within it' (1989, p. 94).

If we accept this view of popular culture as a crucial site of identity and desire (Frith, 1996), it is hard to see how we can proceed with any study of language, culture, globalization and engagement without dealing comprehensively with popular culture. Thus while there is doubtless an argument in terms of scale – if popular culture is indeed so popular and, moreover, closely bound up with English and globalization, we would be foolish to ignore it or to reduce it to dismissive comments about 'pop culture' or 'mass culture' – there is also an argument that has more to do with its role in constructing desires and identities. As David Scott (1999) argues, the 'real question before us is whether or not we take the vernacular voices of the popular and their modes of self-fashioning seriously, and if we do, how we think through their implications' (p. 215). It is to issues of identity, desire and locality that I wish to draw particular attention here since a focus on hip-hop within processes of globalization requires an understanding of how and why people identify in particular locations with particular cultural forms. For some, this still may not justify taking popular culture, or more specifically hip-hop, as seriously as I intend to here. Several other reasons for doing so can be put forward, including aesthetic, cultural and political arguments.

One concern has to do with dealing with popular culture as culture, rather than as a social phenomenon, which is to raise the spectre of cultural relativism, not in the sense of different cultures having incommensurable world views but rather in the sense of different cultural practices being of equal value. Shusterman (2000), however, mounts a strong argument for an understanding of the aesthetics of popular culture, including hip-hop: 'Intellectualist critics typically fail to recognize the multilayered and nuanced meanings of popular art either because they are "turned off" from the outset and unwilling to give these works the sympathetic attention needed to tease out such complexities, or more simply because they just can't understand the works in question' (p. 49). For Shusterman, to argue 'for the aesthetic legitimacy and potential of popular art is not to advocate its dominance

or the obliteration of the high art tradition' but rather to challenge 'its exclusionary claim to value' (p. 59). As he argues, the rejection of popular culture
as 'mass culture' is to wrongly assume a mass product and a mass audience
of impossible shallowness, since

> the very idea that the popular art audience is psychologically too naïve
> and one-dimensional to entertain and be entertained by conflicting
> ideas and ambiguity of value is clearly refuted by the baffling experience
> of postmodern living, where everyday coping frequently requires the
> simultaneous inhabiting of contradictory roles and conflicting language
> games.
>
> (Shusterman, 2000, p. 53)

The rejection and denigration of popular culture is largely premised on
the continued elevation of some supposedly higher realm of disembodied
intellectual experience, and the denigration of the embodied, affective, experiential domain. Thus, while Bourdieu (1984) usefully argues on the one
hand that supposedly aesthetic judgements have more to do with a form
of aesthetic capital – our judgements of good and bad taste are more about
positioning ourselves socially than about aesthetic preferences – on the
other hand, he also, less usefully, denigrates popular culture as too embedded in the everyday. This argument, going back to Plato's rejection of art,
'has been sustained by a philosophical tradition that was always eager, even
in defending art, to endorse its distance from the real so as to ensure philosophy's sovereignty in determining reality, including the real nature of art'
(Shusterman, 2000, p. 56). Thus, just as Bloom (1987) denigrates popular culture as superficial and banal, so he also attacks what he sees as an
overconcern with the everyday and pursuit of individual concerns, coupled
with a form of relativism which suggests that every person's values should
be equally respected. As I shall argue in Chapter 6, by contrast, following
Charles Taylor's (1991) discussion of popular understandings of being true
to oneself, the issues of authenticity raised by hip-hop's take on the real – its
insistence on staying true to the local – open up a far more complex understanding of language, reality and the everyday.

A constant theme in discussions of popular culture has to do with its commercialization. In noting its role in the formation of identity, its connections
to desire, its localities, we may overlook the forces of commercialization that
drive sales, or romanticize the authentic, pre-commercialized forms of popular expression as a true originary voice form the margins. Popular culture
may indeed be racist, homophobic or misogynist: its frequent articulations
of heteronormative sexuality constantly position other sexualities as other. It
can be crass, maudlin, simplistic, dull, tedious, overmarketed and reactionary. It would be foolish to overlook the pernicious ways in which popular
culture is taken up and marketed: We need to take seriously the common
equation between becoming 'popular' and 'selling out'. As Wermuth (2001)

argues, however, the struggles over authenticity as hip-hop becomes localized are indeed struggles over all these concerns. As the *Nederhopper* community developed in Holland, there was a constant struggle over commercial versus independent, authentic versus artificial, local versus global, male versus female and white versus black themes in hip-hop. Rather than commercialization, imitation, globalization, male dominance and white appropriation being grounds to dismiss hip-hop, therefore, they are in fact the very terrain of struggle.

A further problem with dismissing 'pop culture' as superficially commercial is that it overlooks the role of popular music as part of political protest. While this may be overplayed and romanticized within some circles, it also needs to be recognized. There is a long tradition around the world of using popular music (as well as, of course, drama, poetry, painting, graffiti, novels and so forth) for political protest. On the one hand, musicians have been able to mobilize huge audiences and raise significant amounts of money for causes such as BandAid, or more recently Band 8. On the other hand, popular music, because of its very popularity, its ease of travel and its catchiness, has been a potent site of protest itself. The 1970s were a time of peace lyrics and politics, with songs by John Lennon ('Imagine'), Yusuf Islam (the former Cat Stevens) ('Peace Train'), Bob Dylan and Joan Baez, among many others. Alongside these were the 'black pride' songs of Nina Simone ('To Be Young, Gifted and Black') or James Brown ('Say it Loud, I'm Black and I'm Proud). From Algeria *raï* music emerged in the 1920s and, in such singers as Remitti and later Cheb Khaled, found an anti-colonial voice as well as a voice for women and freedom. From Chile came Victor Jara, killed by Pinochet's troops after the 1973 coup. The Nigerian poor found a voice in Fela Kuti; and the disenfranchised in South Africa had Miriam Makeba singing for them. The growth of aboriginal rock bands, such as *Yothu Yindi*, in Australia in the 1980s, with their emphasis on politics and indigenous culture, was a significant factor in the development of indigenous land rights movements and white Australian awareness of indigenous concerns (Lawe Davies, 1993).

From Jamaica came Bob Marley, with his Third World and Rastafarian politics, singing of revolution ('Redemption Song'), slavery ('Slave Driver'), hunger ('Them Belly Full (But We Hungry)') and peace ('One World, One Love'). While the reggae styles he brought to the world have had lasting effects on music across the world, his politics have also lived on, so that in a new globalized era, Senegalese rappers such as Daara J (see Chapter 7) see clear ties between their music and the legacy of Bob Marley. Taking dissonant voices seriously means recognizing the popular resistance to being integrated into the available middle-class forms of identification. As Bob Marley and the Wailers (1979) put it in 'Babylon System':

Wi refuz to bii wat yu wantid us to be
wii ar wat wii ai ar

dat's di wie its gweng to bii
(ef yu doan kno)
Yuu kya edikiat us far no eekwal opatuuniti
Taakin bout ma friidom
Piipl, friidom an libertii[3]

As Scott goes on to argue, 'taking the popular seriously entails thinking through the ethical-political from within the field defined by Marley's oppositional claims, from within the field defined by his *ruud bwai*[4] refusal' (1999, p. 216). Hip-hop has also played a significant role in political protest and awareness (Stapleton, 1998). In Kenya, for example, the track 'Unbwogable (unbreakable)' by Gidi Gidi Maji Maji, which was adopted by the opposition coalition in 2002, is attributed with helping to bring down the government of Daniel Arap Moi after twenty-four years (Lynskey, 2004).

It is not only the forms of popular culture themselves that we need to look at but also the take-up and reaction to these forms. Studies of 'high culture' often make the same error as critical discourse analysis (CDA) (e.g. Fairclough, 1995) by assuming that an understanding of a text and the ideologies to which it subscribes can be derived through an internal investigation of that text. As the transtextual framework for understanding meaning (Chapter 3) suggests, while much can be derived from pretextual, subtextual and intertextual interpretations, the meaning of a text cannot be reduced to the readings of the text analyst outside the context of its social (post-textual) take-up. It is one thing to analyse the ideologies that apparently underlie forms of popular culture, but another to impute necessary implications of those ideologies. What is done with a text is of equal importance. As Sunderland *et al.* (2000) note, the effects of a text may be less a product of a particular reading of that text than the result of talk around the text. Moffatt and Norton's (2005) re-examination of an *Archie* comic text, for example, suggests that 'even a text that appears to be a simple mechanism for the reproduction of dominant ideas of gender relations may contain radical possibilities for investigating these very same relations' (p. 10).

Given the intensive scholarly interest in hip-hop, furthermore, we cannot ignore the level of academic uptake. The sophisticated and complex discussions of hip-hop philosophy, politics and poetics that abound, particularly in the US, suggest that the debate is not so much about whether we should take it seriously as how we should do so. In a discussion over the political philosophy of US rap, for example, Lawson (2005) argues that 'some rap represents a fundamental challenge to liberal political philosophy' (p. 161), concluding that the challenges to the supposed social contract between African Americans and the State posed by some rap lyrics need to be seen in a different light from the earlier Civil Rights movements: 'Hip-hop culture, at least the political segment, speaks to the unfinished business of social justice but in a post-civil rights voice' (p. 172). McPherson (2005) challenges this proposition, however, suggesting instead that political rap in the US is still very much part of the broader American culture and as such tends towards versions of benevolent capitalism rather than a vision of revolutionary change: 'Political rap is the soundtrack to the hip-hop generation's disaffection over being left out of the American dream' (p. 182). On one level, then, there is certainly a case to take hip-hop (or other popular culture) seriously from a sociological or anthropological/cultural studies point of view because of the major effects this cultural formation has on people's lives. On another level, however, the question concerns whether we should take hip-hop seriously on its own terms, as a culture whose ideas about itself need to be taken seriously.

A more particular concern with hip-hop has to do with its perceived relations to violence, particularly when for many people rap is predominantly associated with US gangsta rap, whose lyrics are often violent, sexist and homophobic, and which seems indelibly linked to a cultural of violence that has seen the death of Jam Master Jay (2002), Tupac Shakur (1996) and Notorious B.I.G. (1997) among many others. To the extent that hip-hop has emerged from the inner city ghettos of the US (for further discussion, see below), and has then been fuelled by large amounts of money and a culture of weaponry, it is by no means surprising that aspects of its authenticity should lie in violence, but this does not render hip-hop itself inherently violent. Several points need to be made here: First, there are many varieties of rap, gangsta rap being only one. Krims (2000), for example, outlines four rap genres based on musical style, MC flows and topics of lyrics: party rap, mack rap, jazz/bohemian rap and reality rap (which includes gangsta). Thus, not only are there several styles of rap but there are also different realities within reality rap. We might add to this list 'message rap' or 'conscience rap' which takes overt political stances against racism, violence and so on.

Second, as Riley (2005) argues, if we take into account the audiences of gangsta rap in the US – 'non-urban and suburban middle-class youth (of all races, but predominantly white)' (p. 299) – we are compelled to reinterpret the effects of gangsta rap not so much in terms of a black urban culture but rather in terms of a white fascination with violence. And third, and most importantly for the arguments of this book, rap becomes something very different in the global context. While hip-hop around the world may draw on aspects and styles of US hip-hop, the localization of hip-hop as well as overt opposition to violence and 'bling bling' culture make rap in different contexts explicitly non-violent. The culture of authenticity in hip-hop means that to be real must involve the rejection of imitated wealth and violence. Indeed, the appeal of some rappers is precisely in their non-violent, non-gangsta position. When Malaysian rappers Too Phat, for example, signed a contract with German record label ProperGamble Records in August 2002, part of their appeal, according to Danny Ansari, CEO of ProperGamble, was in Too Phat's 'healthy' version of hip-hop. Ansari 'marvelled that Too Phat is a hip-hop band that does not advocate violence, gangsterism or drugs' (Too Phat for Germany, 2002). Indeed, as we shall see, many hip-hoppers round the world take a stance directly against what they see as the negative forms of US hip-hop. It is to issues of origins and appropriations of hip-hop that I now turn.

Hip-hop: elements, origins, spread

The *Hip Hoptionary* (Westbrook, 2002) defines hip-hop as 'the artistic response to oppression …. As a musical art form it is stories of inner-city life, often with a message, spoken over beats of music. The culture includes rap and any other venture spawned from the hip-hop style and culture' (p. 64). Hip-hop is often defined in terms of its four elements: MC-ing (rapping), DJ-ing, break-dancing and graffiti. According to Wikipedia (2005), beat-boxing (vocal percussion, using the mouth to imitate drums and other sound effects) is sometimes seen as a fifth element, along with other possible contenders such as hip-hop fashion or hip-hop slang. Others argue that it needs to be defined more broadly in terms of its underlying philosophy or style. For Shusterman (2005), hip-hop 'captures its fans not simply as music, but as a whole philosophy of life, an ethos that involves clothes, a style of talk and walk, a political attitude, and often a philosophical posture of asking hard questions and critically challenging established views and values' (p. 61). Alim's (2004) discussion of the term *steez* captures this well: 'Yo steez not only refers to how you talk or how you walk, but more generally, it's how you do yo thang, how you let it hang – how you let it swang' (p. 5). As Altimet from Malaysian rap group Teh Tarik Crew[5] explains, hip-hop culture should not be reduced to the four elements but rather should be seen as a broader cultural formation:

> Altimet: It is not just about being an MC, being a DJ, being a graffiti writer, being a b-boy. There are other things. He [DJ Fuzz] teaches people … how to scratch, how to mix, she [Mz Nina] has the radio show. You don't have to be one of these four to contribute to hip hop. He is on the technical side. He makes the beats, he makes sure the mixes are right, you know the mastering is right. And there are people who are photographers. They are also contributing to the scene. And also there are people who just listen. They contribute to the scene as well. It is not just about being a b-boy or ….
>
> (TTC, 13 December 2003)

The struggle over what constitutes the elusive fifth element is itself one of the more revealing ways of opening up different understandings of hip-hop. For Afrika Bambaataa and Zulu Nation (Bambaataa, 2005), the crucial fifth element is *Knowledge*: knowledge and awareness through hip-hop, a definition now enshrined in the new (2005) *Journal of Hip Hop*, where hip-hop is described as 'consisting of at least 5 elements: bombing, b-boying, dee-jaying, emceeing, and knowledge (of self and culture)' (p. 4) Likewise, Darby and Shelby (2005) express the importance of highlighting 'the often suppressed fifth element of hip hop – knowledge – to represent the funky-ass ways that philosophy is carried out in everyday life, often in unexpected places and using unconventional means' (p. xvii). Given that much of this focus on knowledge is about the passing on and learning of knowledge – Hip Hop Matters, who produce the *Journal of Hip Hop,* for example, emphasize youth advocacy, urban policy analysis and educational publishing and consulting, and the *Journal of Hip Hop* logo itself, representing the five elements, uses figures in college/university mortar boards to represent knowledge, describing this fifth element as 'knowledge, which educates the masses on the history and responsibilities of Hip-hop' – a good case might be made to talk of education as the fifth element. I shall return to this issue in the final chapter.

Much has been written about the development of hip-hop (Baker, 1993; Chang, 2005; Forman, 2002b; Kitwana, 2002; Lipsitz, 1994; Perry, 2004; Rose, 1994; Toop, 1991), and there is both agreement and controversy over its origins, with arguments on the one hand for seeing both its origins and contemporary manifestations as ineluctably expressions of African American culture, and arguments on the other hand for a view of multiple origins and contemporary diversity. While one side of this debate – to do with the influences on the development of hip-hop in New York in the 1970s – is of no great concern for this book, the broader issue of whether the global spread of hip-hop is a global spread of African American culture is far more significant. The issue is in part captured by Perry's (2004) recent intervention in this debate when she argues that hip-hop is 'situationally black, that is to say that the role it occupies in our society is black both in terms of its relationship to other segments of the black community and of its relationship to the larger white segment of the country and of the "global village"' (p. 29). Here then is the point that, at least so far as the United States is concerned, hip-hop needs to be understood as 'situationally black'. But when Perry goes on to suggest that this also applies to the 'global village', representing 'that strange blend of voices of resistance and otherness marketed through the channels of American imperialism' (p. 29), she appears to take up a view of imperialism that does not allow for the many reactions, appropriations and transformations that occur within cultural spread, and overlooks the point that while being 'situationally black' may mean one thing in the United States, it has very different meanings elsewhere.

From one perspective, then, there are very good reasons for placing African American culture and experience at the heart of hip-hop. Rose describes hip-hop as

> a cultural form that attempts to negotiate experiences of marginalization, brutally truncated opportunity, and oppression within the cultural imperatives of African-American and Caribbean history, identity and community. It is the tension between the cultural fractures produced

by postindustrial oppression and the binding ties of black cultural expressivity that sets the critical frame for the development of hip hop.

(Rose, 1994, p. 21)

Likewise, Smitherman (2000) describes rap as 'rooted in the Black Oral Tradition' that includes tonal semantics, narrativizing, and a range of features of African American speech. While she acknowledges that 'Rap has its violence, its raw language, and its misogynistic lyrics', she stresses its authenticity as a voice of opposition from the ghetto, as a 'a resisting discourse, a set of communicative practices that constitute a text of resistance against White America's racism and its Euro-centric cultural dominance' (p. 271). While the origins of rap 'stretch far into the orally influenced traditions of African-American culture', and may be traced back through African American history to West African *griots* (travelling singers and poets whose traditions were carried on the slave ships), Rose (1994, p. 95) warns that rap needs to be understood as a 'technologically sophisticated and complex urban sound'. Rap, she argues, is 'fundamentally literate and deeply technological. To interpret rap as a direct or natural outgrowth of oral African-American forms is to romanticize and decontextualize rap as a cultural form.' Ultimately, the 'lyrical and musical texts in rap are a dynamic hybrid of oral traditions, postliterate orality, and advanced technology'. This point is significant not only as a warning against the tendencies to trace a particular romanticized lineage for rap, but also both to understand its connections to literacy practices and modern technologies (and see Chapter 8), and in terms of the different cultural practices it encounters as it spreads globally.

While a major focus of this book is to follow the diasporic journey of hip-hop away from the US, and to suggest that the African American origins of hip-hop are at times only peripherally relevant to performers globally, it is important to acknowledge the significance of these material and cultural origins. Not only is hip-hop part of the ongoing battle against the deep-seated racism of the US, a battle which includes the constant need to show how African American language use is a different, not a degraded, form of English, that 'there are numerous Black linguistic practices that are misunderstood and misinterpreted in White public space' (Alim, 2004, p. 240), but the power and lyricism of rap across the world surely still carry the traces of the oral expressivity of African American cultures. Thus, when Smitherman argues, for example, that 'the language of Hip Hop is African American Language' (p. 271), this needs to be seen primarily as an argument about language in the US, but also as a recognition that African American Language echoes through global hip-hop.

Any attempt to trace too pure a lineage for hip-hop, however, faces various problems. In a number of ways this runs counter to aspects of hip-hop culture itself, which places great emphasis on borrowing, sampling and multiple origins, rather than lineage and fixity. As Potter (1995) points out, one of the three fundamental aspects of hip-hop[6] is 'the relentless sampling of sonic and verbal archives' (p. 53). In addition to being a highly skilled form of postliterate orality, then, rap and DJ-ing are also complex forms of intertextuality. According to Rose, 'Sampling in rap is a process of cultural literacy and intertextual reference' (1994, p. 89). This use of sounds from elsewhere also has great significance for an understanding of hip-hop as a contemporary cultural practice, as an intertextual forum for cultural exchange. Thus, as Potter (1995) notes, hip-hop built on and sampled many other forms, including not just music but also sound bites from many sources: hip-hop 'draws not only upon African-American traditions, but upon its dense interconnections with black diasporic music, from dancehall to Afro-pop, from soca to UK funk' (p. 26). As suggested at the beginning of Chapter 2, if we take a cultural form such as break-dancing, it is hard to separate its development from a range of other contemporary influences, from Brazilian *capoeira* (which also, of course, traces its roots back through the African diaspora) to martial arts movies. It is evident that hip-hop emerged from the inevitable cultural mixture of the poor inner city spaces of the USA, a mixture that at the very least included Puerto Rican and Jamaican influences. According to Rivera (2003), 'New York Puerto Ricans have been an integral part of hip hop culture since the creative movement's first stirrings in New York City during the early 1970s'. Indeed, she goes on to argue, 'hip hop is as vernacular (or "native") to a great many New York Puerto Ricans as the culture of their parents and grandparents' (p. 1).

A broader argument around origins emerges in Gilroy's critique of the 'ontological essentialist standpoint' (1993, p. 34) which mobilizes the very discourses about race and culture that it seeks to oppose: a version of some pure African American origin that becomes all too easily tied to a version of racial authenticity. Gilroy (1993) argues that 'hip hop culture grew out of the cross-fertilisation of African-American vernacular cultures with their Caribbean equivalents rather than springing fully formed from the entrails of the blues' (p. 103). For Gilroy, we need at the very least to understand the notion of the *black Atlantic*: 'the transnational structures which brought the black Atlantic world into being have themselves developed and now articulate its myriad forms into a system of global communication constituted by flows' (p. 80). From this point of view, looking at hip-hop in the UK, Hesmondhalgh and Melville (2001) argue that rather than 'seeing U.S. hip-hop as a point of origin ... we argue for a view that sees black cultures in Britain, the Caribbean, and the United States as linked in a complex network of cultural flows' (p. 87). Connell and Gibson (2003) expand this notion to a broader vision of 'transnational networks of affiliation, and of material and symbolic interdependence, well evident in the diasporic ties across the "Black Atlantic", and across all other oceans .... Music nourishes imagined communities, traces links to distant and past places, and emphasizes that all human cultures have musical traditions, however differently these have been valued' (p. 271). As I suggest in Chapter 7, these 'transnational networks of affiliation' or circuits of flow operate in many different ways in many parts of the world.

While acknowledging hip-hop's *créolité*, its mixed urban origins, its Caribbean influences, however, Perry (2004) critiques this 'romantic Afro-Atlanticism' (p. 17). Although African American culture is exported globally, 'Black Americans as a community do not consume imported music from other cultures in large numbers', and thus ultimately the 'postcolonial Afro-Atlantic hip hop community is ... a fantastic aspiration rather than a reality' (p. 19). Korean DJ Jun attests to this lack of interest in music from elsewhere: during his time in New York he felt that 'they don't really respect about Korean hip hop at all and Asian hip hop at all. They think, "Oh OK so your guys' music is kind of wack"' (DJJ, 2 November 2003). Perry has a good point here about the isolation of the US, which perhaps undermines some of the force of the Black Atlantic. As I argue in Chapter 7, however, the multiple circuits of flow around the world, from the French-language-oriented circle to the Pacific Islander circuit, render this a more complex question than one of US isolationism. Whatever the origins of hip-hop may be, it is now clear that it has spread widely across the globe. 'From very modest beginnings', suggest Richardson and Lewis (2000, p. 251), hip-hop 'has grown into a cultural phenomenon that has transcended boundaries, such as race, class, gender, and geography.' Young people across the globe have 'embraced various elements of the culture. They listen to and enjoy the intricate rhymes and rhythms or rap music, and make up their own; they pop and glide in breakdance; they pop open a spraycan and create public works of art in graffiti; and they mix and scratch their way into the art of DJing.' The important concern for this book is how we understand this spread.

From one perspective, the global spread of hip-hop is the global spread of African American culture: 'Hip-hop is and always will be a culture of the African-American minority. But it has become an international language, a style that connects and defines the self-image of countless teenagers' (Bozza, 2003, p. 130). Osumare (2001) draws a slightly more complex picture, seeing the spread as one of 'connective marginalities ... social resonances between black expressive culture within its contextual political history and similar dynamics in other nations' (p. 172). For Osumare, this 'US subculture truly has a diaspora that is, in fact, shifting the global center and the margins through youth's participation in popular culture. Hip hop, as an extension of African American popular culture, then, becomes a global signifier for many forms of marginalizations' (p. 173). Perry (2004) makes a similar connection when she suggests that 'Black American music, as a commercial American product, is exported globally. Its signifying creates a subaltern voice in the midst of the imperialist exportation of culture' (p. 19). All these positions seem to have in common a view that while hip-hop has spread globally, it is still (African) American culture that is spreading and being taken up, it is still the marginalized or subcultural aspects of hip-hop in the US with which youth around the world identify.

Yet we need to be cautious here in suggesting that global hip-hop identifications are always with either African American cultural forms or forms of marginality. For many, the identification with 'a subaltern voice' within an 'imperialist exportation of culture', as Perry (2004, p. 19) puts it, is a highly conflictual space. When hip-hop is seen as part of the dominance of US culture, the fact that it may be a marginalized cultural form within the US is less relevant on the world stage. The identifications with American and African American culture by hip-hop artists around the world are embedded in local histories of difference, oppression, class and culture, often rejecting aspects of American dominance while identifying with forms of local struggle. For a Brazilian *favela* dweller of African background, an identification with hip-hop may indeed be centrally an identification with urban poverty, racism, drugs and violence, though this will always also be about local issues, conditions and themes, and will contain local musical and lyrical influences. For a Pacific Islander, the forms such an identification takes depend on the dominant language (English or French), the state of struggle for independence, the rural/urban relations on particular islands, employment and migratory possibilities, and the deeply criss-crossed influences of local music. For Hong Kong or Singaporean rap artists, an identification with African American culture becomes something different again, linked to the complex roles of class and English. As we shall see in Chapter 6, the relation between different languages – either widely used languages such as English, French or Spanish, or more locally used languages such as Swahili, German or Maori – and questions of class, culture and locality has major implications for the adoption and adaptation of hip-hop. As argued in Chapter 7, the transcultural circuits of flow render the United States a peripheral rather than a major influence on hip-hop adaptations.

The vital question, then, concerns the ways we understand the notion of cultural spread, since this goes to the heart of one of the themes of this book. As Androutsopoulos (2003) suggests, since 'hip-hop is a globally dispersed network of everyday cultural practices which are productively appropriated in very different local contexts, it can be seen as paradigmatic of the dialectic of cultural globalization and localization' (p. 11).[7] Once cultural forms are taken up within local cultural contexts, any search for origins and influences becomes not so much a project of tracing back a clear lineage as one of understanding the convoluted interplay of different cultural forms. As we shall see in Chapter 7, once hip-hop goes global, its origins can be anything from British TV programmes aimed at new immigrants to fourteenth-century Turkish minstrels, from traditional Malaysian song to diverse Fijian cultural practices. When Potter (1995) laments the 'danger that it will be appropriated in such a way that its histories are obscured and its message replaced by others' (p. 146), he appears caught in a nostalgic hope for purity. Just as native speakers of English in the English-dominant countries have been urged to give up a notion of the ownership of English, so African Americans may need to let go of this sense of a true history and message that is being corrupted. Once cultural forms become transcultural forms (if indeed all cultural forms are not transcultural to start with), we have moved beyond questions of ownership and origins.

Mitchell (2001) makes a strong case against any view that rap and hip-hop are essentially expressions of African American culture, and that all forms of rap and hip-hop elsewhere are therefore derivative of these origins. Rather, he suggests, hip-hop has become a vehicle through which local identity is reworked. Mitchell's argument goes one step further than this, however, suggesting not only that hip-hop and rap have become local forms of popular culture and identification, but also that it is in these different contexts around the world that more exciting developments may be found: 'For a sense of innovation, surprise, and musical substance in hip-hop culture and rap music, it is becoming increasingly necessary to look outside the USA to countries such as France, England, Germany, Italy, and Japan, where strong local currents of hip-hop indigenization have taken place' (p. 3). While at one level the local development of hip-hop may still involve the appropriation of African American cultural forms in anything from the use of African American speech styles to more complex forms of identification with African American identities and politics, at another level the local context in which it evolves may engage a quite different range of cultural, musical and linguistic forms while mobilizing a quite different politics that can include opposition to forms of US hip-hop. Scholz (2003) makes a similar point in relation to rap: 'If one looks at the history of the reception of rap in different target cultures, it becomes clear that the globalization of American rap albums does not so much engender passive consumption as it releases cultural activity' (pp. 151–152). Thus, as Connell and Gibson (2003) suggest, while the global spread of music may on the one hand be part of the global hegemony of particular cultural forms, it also enables resistance to globalizing trends.

While the appropriation of cultural forms around the world is commonplace, Androutsopoulos (2003) suggests that the extent and durability of hip-hop appropriations are somewhat unique. This, he argues, is a result of five particular features of hip-hop. First, the *accessibility* of the culture: there is no particular training, technology or equipment – except possibly with DJ-ing – required to participate in dance, rap or graffiti. Second, what Androutsopoulos calls the *performative character* of hip-hop (and see Chapter 4), by which he means the way in which community is produced through participation: a sense of belonging and gaining local recognition are dependent on participation. Third, the importance of *style*: the forms of artistic expression in hip-hop offer a context to develop individual creativity with limited resources. Fourth, the *principle of competition*: participants develop their style and abilities through a constant and open form of 'battle'. And fifth, the use of the four elements, but particularly rap, to represent local experience. As I suggested above, and will discuss further in Chapter 8, if we take the fifth element of hip-hop to be education, we can see another reason why it has spread so readily.

This representation of local experience, this emphasis on authenticity or keeping it real, is crucial for hip-hop and the arguments of this book. As Forman (2002a) points out, 'claiming one's place within Hip Hop culture involves more than simply exhibiting particular consumption patterns, sartorial tastes, or other surface gestures; it also encompasses the demonstration of deeply invested affinities or attitudinal allegiances that shape one's modes of expression and inform the core of both self and group identity simultaneously' (p. 102). Central to this identity, he goes on, are 'values of authenticity, or, in the contemporary parlance of Hip hop-identified youth, "the real"'. Reality, he suggests, has 'emerged as a central site of conjecture'. I shall return to issues of authenticity and the real, particularly in relation to language, in Chapter 6. Here it is worth noting that the culture of authenticity, which indeed is one aspect of hip-hop culture that has spread globally, becomes, by its very nature, something different in each context in which it is taken up. It is played out in very different ways in different parts of the world, sometimes in opposition to what is seen as an imposed reality from US hip-hop, and more particularly in relation to local conditions of language, culture and politics.

The politics of language and the ordinariness of diversity

This understanding of the local is of particular importance when we return to the debates around cultural and linguistic imperialism (see Chapter 2). While the observation that Western and often English-language media dominate the global scene has led to many accusations of cultural imperialism (and the belated focus on linguistic imperialism in language studies), the limitations of this view became increasingly apparent since the 'validity of the local/authentic versus imported/commercial dichotomy is difficult to sustain with reference to specific examples, while media effects are assumed in a too one-dimensional fashion, underestimating the mediated nature of audience reception and use of media products' (Shuker, 2001, p. 71). Thus, just as it has been hard to maintain the notion of linguistic imperialism (Phillipson, 1992) as imported/commercial English in relation to local/authentic mother tongues (see, e.g., Makoni and Pennycook, 2005), so it is ultimately difficult to sustain a version of culture as imposition. This is not, of course, to deny that global media are dominated in particular ways, or that popular culture is highly commercialized, but it *is* to deny the vision that casts those who partake in this transcultural flow as mere passive recipients of culture. As Gurnah (1997) points out in his discussion of 'Elvis in Zanzibar', neither a model of sharing (as if cultures were just passed around and handed out) nor a model of imperialism (as if cultures are imposed upon people) will work, since 'the export and import of culture cannot uncomplicatedly depend on "exchange" or "sharing," "domination" or "imperialism". Both sets of processes presume for their possibility, the pre-existence of profound social, cultural and especially linguistic common denominators' (p. 122).

Shuker (2001) also draws attention to the problem raised in Chapter 2 that the 'cultural imperialism thesis is predicated on accepting the "national" as a given, with distinctive national musical identities its logical corollary' (p. 71). Likewise, both the world Englishes and the linguistic imperialism frameworks are predicated on distinctive national linguistic identities. If we are to take globalization seriously, we have to think beyond these frameworks of national or local identity as fixed. As I discussed in chapters 1 and 2, a focus on 'place and movement, of proud heritages and dynamic, fluid soundscapes' (Connell and Gibson, 2003, p. 2) starts to open up more useful ways of thinking about transcultural flows and localities. Thus by looking not only at *fixity* – referring to ways in which music is about location, tradition and cultural expression – but also at both *fluidity* – referring to the movement and flows of music across time and space – and *flux* – referring to the constant changes that are part of a process of identity refashioning – we can avoid the juxtaposition of a fluid global movement of culture with a fixed, static, local tradition. Rather, the point is to draw attention to the ways in which locality and globality, worldliness and globalization are always pushing and pulling in different directions. As a global form becomes localized, the local and the global are changed. As Connell and Gibson (2003) point out, 'transnational cultural products, in whatever direction they appear to be travelling, do not simply replace local ones, but are refashioned and given new meaning' (p. 191). This can take us beyond the global/local dialectic by opening up more dynamic relations between transcultural flows and local materialities.

Thus, while the focus on globalization has also highlighted the need to focus on the local, it is important not to see the local as some static, traditional, unchanging place of cultural security. Rather 'in referring to the "local", we are in effect speaking about a space that is crossed by a variety of different collective sensibilities each of which imposes a different set of expectations and cultural needs upon that space' (Bennett, 2000, p. 66). Looking, for example, at popular music and what it means to be British, particularly in an era in which notions of 'Englishness' or 'Britishness' are under contestation from an array of Asian and Caribbean diasporic identities which themselves borrow and mix from multiple sources, Zuberi (2001) suggests that 'recorded music culture has a significant role in private and public memory' (p. 3). Popular music, he argues, creates (rather than just reflects) national identity: 'words, music, audio samples, and video and photographic images in popular music culture contribute to the construction of historical knowledge, activating memory and bringing the past into dialogue with the present' (p. 4). And thus in Massive Attack's mix of rap with reggae base lines and Jamaican samples from the 1970s, for example, or Fun-da-mental's mix of Malcolm X speech fragments, Louis Farrakhan, Bollywood samples and hip-hop rhythms, 'Nation of Islam militancy rubs against post-Rushdie British Islam in Bradford and London' which 'tells us something about the history of cultural exchange and *digitally enabled diasporic consciousness'* (pp. 4–5; italics added). As we shall see in the following chapters, popular culture is often at the forefront of this redefining of identity and reimagining of community. As Connell and Gibson (2003) put it, 'Music remains an important cultural sphere in which identities are affirmed, challenged, taken apart and reconstructed' (p. 117).

In the following chapters I will be looking at language in relation to hip-hop in a number of different ways. As Bennett (2000, 2003, 2004) points out in his discussion of the tensions between English, German and Turkish lyrics in the hip-hop scene in Frankfurt, while a great deal has been written about the cultural and political significance of the lyrics of popular music, less attention has been paid to the language or varieties of language in which the lyrics occur. It is to draw attention to this need for a form of sociolinguistic analysis of hip-hop that I have been using – somewhat tongue in cheek – the term *socioblinguistics*. This is also intended to avoid two common pitfalls in the analysis of popular music. The first is the tendency to work from an unacknowledged normative position, namely the bourgeois-leftist politics common in cultural studies; thus bands that convey an anti-capitalist, anti-globalist, anti-racist, environmentally friendly pro-feminist message may be seized upon, praised and held up as examples of the 'progressive' aspects of popular culture, while those that rage too violently, or take up unacceptable cultural and political positions are carefully avoided. The second pitfall is the tendency to indulge in what Hutnyk (2000) criticizes as the 'liberal exoticist enthusiasm' for hybridity. As he suggests, the constant interest in hybridity has become a goal in itself and, as Zuberi (2001) cautions, 'the notion of the "hybrid" can become as fixed a category as its essentialist nemesis' (pp. 239–240; and see Young, 1995).

To work socioblinguistically, then, I intend to take seriously the politics of language and the ordinariness of diversity. Thus, I am not so much interested in the analysis of lyrics for their political stance as in the political implications of linguistic and cultural choices. And I want to take seriously here Higgins's and Coen's (2000) argument about 'the ordinariness of diversity' (p. 14). Difference and diversity, multilingualism and hybridity are not rare and exotic conditions to be sought out and celebrated but the quotidian ordinariness of everyday life. In accord with Higgins and Coen, I 'do not think that as humans we have anything in common but our differences; there is no general human nature to be found, nor will the deconstructing of social or cultural practices reveal some kind of common human core' (pp. 14–15). And thus, while it is of course true that 'consumer capitalism subverts differences into lifestyles as commodities', it is also the case that 'diversity is the given reality of human social action' (p. 15). To dwell on forms of diversity in the following chapters, then, is to draw attention to the everyday practices of difference that imbue much of daily life in the face of what are often seen as the homogenizing forces of English and popular culture. In the next chapter I will look in greater depth at issues of English use and authenticity; I will explore language mixing and identity creation in Chapter 7.

6   English and the global spread of authenticity

In the example below, from the track 'Bring Your Style' by Japanese rap group Rip Slyme, one line of African American-influenced rap – with its indexical 'yo' – is juxtaposed with a line of Japanese, albeit Japanese which contains a constructed word – freaky side – in katakana (the script generally for non-Japanese items). How can we go about understanding this use of English, this incorporation of African American-influenced lyrics in a Japanese track? Is this yet another example of the steady creep of English into other cultures, invading, homogenizing, destroying? Is the use of English a reflex of the global music industry where an English word or phrase may signal the international over the local, dollars over yen? Does the English reflect a will to global communication and the Japanese a will to local identity? Is the English here possibly also part of Japanese culture? What does it mean to imitate American language and music in this way? Does such copying mean only slavish duplication or is there something else to be understood in the process of such mimicry, such 'styling the Other', as Rampton (1999) puts it? These are some of the questions that inform this chapter, which will look particularly at issues of English and authenticity.

Lyrics	Transliteration and translation
Yo Bringing That, Yo Bring Your Style	*Yo Bringing that, Yo Bring your style*
人類最後のフリーキーサイド	*Jinrui saigo no furikiisaido*
Rip Slyme	Yo Bringing That, Yo Bring Your Style
'Bring Your Style'	The last freaky side of the human race
'Tokyo Classic'	

That both English and hip-hop have spread on a global scale is an uncontroversial claim. As the previous chapters have suggested, however, quite what this means is not so straightforward. As discussed in Chapter 2, the global spread of English is sometimes tied to visions of global homogenization (see, e.g., Phillipson, 1999). And when we see English being used by the vast majority of singers in the Eurovision Song Contest, for example, we may be very tempted to accept this vision. Here in this competition that might be used to emphasize a multilingual and multicultural Europe, with varying styles of music and a range of national or regional languages putting European diversity on display, we find instead remarkably similar performances, the majority of which are in English. The Eurovision Song Contest, then, may well be taken to be an example of this apocalyptic vision of European homogenization that Phillipson (2003) envisages for the European Union (EU), where the adoption of English as 'the sole in-house working language' is leading to 'a limiting, technocratic dumbing-down process, and evolution of a simplified, pidginized but unstable "Euro-English" that inhibits creativity and expressiveness, whether English is used as a mother tongue or as a foreign language, a language that is spoken with so much imprecision that communication difficulties and breakdowns multiply' (p. 176). If nothing is done to prevent this downward slide into communicational mediocrity, Phillipson warns, 'we may be heading for an American-English only Europe' (p. 192). And on a wider level, if we accept this vision, we may be heading towards a pidginized but unstable global English that inhibits creativity and expressiveness, where '*Yo Bring Your Style*' is the common parlance of the globe.

There are, however, good reasons to question such visions of cultural and linguistic imperialism whereby the English language and American popular culture are homogenizing the world as they are thrust on to local populations. While it is evident that there are very unequal structures of production and distribution of both English and popular music, it is equally evident that we need to explore, as I suggested in Chapter 2, not only processes of Christianizing and discovering, civilizing and enlightening, conceptualizing and developing, capitalizing and universalizing, and corporatizing and globalizing, but also processes of transgression and resistance, translation and rearticulation, transformation and reconstitution, translocalization and appropriation, and transculturation and hybridization. When and how do English and hip-hop become local? As I suggested in Chapter 2, the world Englishes framework can take us some way towards an understanding of processes of localization, though its focus on emergent national varieties in the 'outer circle' limits and excludes the possibilities of dealing with Other Englishes. From this point of view, while English use in countries that fulfil certain criteria – the use of English in media and education, the codification of local norms in dictionaries, grammar and literature – constitutes a localization of English, for the majority world, to use English is always to be dependent on central norms, and thus English 'will probably never be used within the Japanese community and form part of the speaker's identity repertoire. There will not be a distinctly local model of English, established and recognizable as Japanese English, reflecting the Japanese culture and language' (Yano, 2001, p. 127). Rip Slyme's use of English, therefore, can never be Japanese; this can never be part of Japanese culture; this is always imitative English added to Japanese.

This chapter aims to explore many of the assumptions that underlie such views. By looking not only at the parallel spread of English and hip-hop but also at the interconnectedness of this spread, a range of concerns come to the fore. Central to hip-hop culture is the mantra of authenticity, of 'keepin' it real'. If, on the one hand, we have the global spread of a culture of being true to the local, of telling it like it is, this always implies a parallel localization, a compulsion not only to make hip-hop locally relevant but also to define locally what authenticity means. Taken in conjunction with frameworks of translation and transculturation (which suggest that the use of different languages and codes simultaneously in a range of channels is best seen in terms of transidiomatic practices), theories of performativity (which suggest that both language and identity are products of sedimented performance rather than pregiven categories), transmodality (which shows how language is always embedded within other semiotic systems, particularly music and dance) and mimesis (the ways in which reiteration implies a new context rather than mere copying), we can start to open up alternative ways of viewing the localization of language within the globalization of hip-hop.

Language, authenticity and the real

Localization inevitably involves complex relations of class, race/ethnicity and language use. Although a local 'Nederhop' movement of Dutch language rap has emerged in the Netherlands, for example, it features almost exclusively white Dutch youth. While this Nederhop movement can claim greater Dutch linguistic and cultural 'authenticity', it also struggles against a more American/English oriented rap movement by non-white youth (largely of Surinamese origin), who can claim greater global authenticity in terms of the discourses of marginalization and racial identification within hip-hop. The Surinamese-Dutch hip-hoppers, on the other hand, face challenges to their authenticity both in terms of their relation to local language use and in relation to the dominance of African American English as the true language of rap (see Krims, 2000; Wermuth, 2001). One of the most fascinating elements of the global/local relations in hip-hop, then, is what we might call *the global spread of authenticity*. Here is a perfect example of a tension between, on the one hand, the spread of a cultural dictate to adhere to certain principles of what it means to be authentic, and on the other, a process of localization that makes such an expression of staying true to oneself dependent on local contexts, languages, cultures and understandings of the real. This tension opens up some significant issues for our understanding of language use and localization.

The notion of authenticity in global popular music, as Timothy Taylor (1997) notes, takes many forms, though it is most often associated with not 'selling out' and staying true to one's roots. Within global cultural industries, this discourse of authenticity insidiously insists on world music artists staying true to tradition, remaining within an external definition of their cultural sphere and not adopting metropolitan styles, instruments, rhythms or languages. While popular musicians around the world 'face constant pressure from westerners to remain musically and otherwise premodern –

that is, culturally "natural" – because of racism and western demands for authenticity', Taylor argues that musicians such as Youssou N'Dour and Angélique Kidjo[1] also find a means to subvert such demands by adopting a form of 'strategic inauthenticity' (p. 126), integrating a wide range of musical forms, styles and languages into their performances. By contrast with Spivak's (1993) *strategic essentialism* – the adoption of essentialist categories for strategic purposes – or James Scott's (1985) *weapons of the weak* – acts of mimicry, and false compliance (see Chapter 4) – such strategic inauthenticity is a deliberate move to defy imposed categories of what should count as real by adopting and adapting from as wide a set of sources as possible while still claiming a particular locality of identity.

The particular take on the real within hip-hop culture is often derided as an obsession with a particular story about violence, drugs and life in the 'hood, or a naïve belief that there is something essentially authentic to life lived on the edge. But the implications of an emphasis on the real need to be taken far more seriously than this. As Morgan (2005) suggests, 'the hip-hop mantra "keepin' it real" represents the quest for the coalescence and interface of ever-shifting art, politics, representation, performance and individual accountability that reflects all aspects of youth experience' (p. 211). Perry (2004) outlines some of the different possible meanings of keeping it real, from 'celebrations of the social effects of urban decay and poverty' to 'assertions of a paranoid vigilance in protecting one's dignity' (p. 87). It is also an 'authenticating device responding to the removal of rap music from the organic relationship with the communities creating it' and 'an explicitly ideological stand against selling one's soul to the devils of capitalism or assimilation' (p. 87). For some, it is a rejection of sanitized Hollywood versions of reality; for others, it is about not selling out and succumbing to the commercial pressures of the music industry, or crossing over and appealing to white audiences; others focus on the 'artistry, craft, and sense of community that hip hop has at its best' while for some it means 'telling a story of how life in the hood is, in any number of ways, for good or bad' (p. 95).

One might nevertheless view this emphasis on authenticity as the global spread of a particular individualist take on what counts as real. Charles Taylor's (1991) exploration of authenticity in terms of current ways of thinking about 'being true to oneself' (p. 15), however, opens up some useful perspectives here. This common ideology is much derided by cultural critics (from both the Right and the Left) such as Bloom (1987; see Chapter 5), who argue that this is a form of relativistic individualism that is concerned only with self-gratification. Meanwhile, the notion of being true to oneself has also received short shrift from a poststructuralist perspective which views such notions as hopelessly caught in a modernist and humanist dream of a unitary subject (you cannot be true to yourself, the argument goes, if truth is contingent and the self is multiple). And yet, as the arguments in Chapter 5 suggest, we should be cautious of dismissing such popular views.

As Taylor argues, we need to appreciate the fundamentally *dialogical* nature of human life, and thus, as Bakhtin (1981, 1986) and Vygotsky (1986) have argued, we cannot understand language or psychology without seeing them as always developed in dialogue with others. Authenticity, then, cannot be defined without relation to social contexts and what Taylor terms 'horizons of significance' (p. 39), the fact that what matters can only be defined in relationship to what is deemed to matter more broadly. Authenticity demands an account of matters beyond the self: 'If authenticity is being true to ourselves, is recovering our own "sentiment de l'existence²," then perhaps we can only achieve it integrally if we recognize that this sentiment connects us to a wider whole' (p. 91). From this point of view, then, while statements about being true to oneself may seem to draw excessive attention to the individual, Taylor suggests that this sense of authenticity can only operate according to the local horizons of significance that connect to a wider world.

Likewise, from an existentialist perspective on authenticity – often misrepresented as unbridled individualism and agency – the issue, as developed by Jean-Paul Sartre (2003) (drawing on Heidegger), is about the condition of self-making. A person who lives an inauthentic life – in bad faith (*mauvaise foi*), in Sartre's terms – is one who is bound only by the facticity of life, who is unable to develop a sense of personal choice in life. An authentic life, by contrast, is one that transcends the confines of the everyday and follows a trajectory of specific choices. Existential authenticity may therefore be seen as individualist to the extent that it eschews philosophical, religious or cultural claims to be able to dictate a standard of moral and social standards, instead placing the emphasis on being true to oneself. Yet it also presents a much broader vision to the extent that it deals centrally with the tension between facticity and freedom, providing a sense of how we live in a space of limitations and possibilities. Albeit from a different perspective, this links back to the discussion of a critical philosophy of transgression (Chapter 3), and Foucault's (1984) contention that a profound and methodical investigation of how to understand ourselves, our histories and how the boundaries of thought may be traversed gives new impetus to 'the undefined work of freedom' (p. 46).

My contention here, then, is that the emphasis on authenticity presents neither an insistence on a particular form of identification (an insistence that authentic hip-hop needs to follow certain narrow forms) nor the globalization of an individualist philosophy (keeping it real is being true to oneself without other considerations), but rather an insistence on exploring different horizons of significance in order to make things local. In his discussion of 'reality rap' Krims (2000) refers to 'any rap that undertakes the project of realism, in the classical sense, which in this context would amount to an epistemological/ontological project to map the realities of (usually black) inner-city life' (p. 70). Once we move outside the North American context, the question becomes how such a *project of realism* is enacted. Given the problematic status of 'the real', and particularly its uncomfortable position within the social sciences, a few comments on realism may be useful here. Various attempts have been made to reclaim realism from a postpositivist (e.g. Mohanty, 1997) or critical realist stance by avoiding both the unmediated realist position – the real world is simply there, irrespective of the languages, cultures and discourses through which we interpret it – and the phenomenological dilemma of taking only people's perceptions of the world as possible data.[3]

Roy Bhaskar's (1989) 'scientific, transcendental and critical realism', which is 'opposed to empiricism, pragmatism and idealism alike' (p. 2), has also served as a possible way forward for applied linguistics. Critical realists, Bhaskar argues, 'do not deny the reality of events and discourses; on the contrary, they insist upon them. But they hold that we will only be able to understand – and so change – the social world if we identify the structures at work that generate those events or discourses' (p. 2).[4] As David Corson explains, Bhaskar's theory of being (ontology) includes the properties of the social world – including beliefs, and accounts of why people behave in certain ways – as real entities. In order to develop an 'emancipatory social practice' the world must be adequately interpreted, and this is best done by 'starting with the reasons and accounts of relevant actors in that world, whether or not their reasons and accounts seem rational, mentalistic, or irrational to those doing the interpreting. People's reasons and accounts are emergent phenomena: that is they really exist' (Corson, 1997, p. 169). Fairclough (2003), from a slightly different perspective, also draws on Bhaskar's critical realism, explaining that 'Reality (the potential, the actual) cannot be reduced to our knowledge of reality, which is contingent, shifting, and partial' (p. 14). Rather than the poststructuralist claim that there is no unmediated access to reality (often misunderstood as being a complete denial of reality) and that we may as well therefore deal only with the forms of mediation (discourse), this position separates reality from accounts of reality (and epistemic relativity from judgemental relativism) and insists on the reality of both. While this may help us out of the trap of trying to mediate between raw realism and pure phenomenology, or dealing only with the mediating effects of discourse, it does not, it seems to me, provide us with a sufficiently complex understanding of the mediating role of language.

A similar shortcoming may be found in Latour's (1999) discussion of the 'modernist settlement'. Relating his reactions to being asked if he believes in reality, Latour assures his interlocutor that it would be hard not to. The question, however, comes down to what we mean by reality, or rather the ways in which reality has been limited to an isolated domain of knowing as a result of the modernist settlement, which

> has sealed off into incommensurable problems questions that cannot be solved separately and have to be tackled all at once: the epistemological question of how we can know the outside world, the psychological

question of how a mind can maintain a connection with an outside world, the political question of how we can keep order in society, and the moral question of how we can live a good life – to sum up, 'out there' [nature], 'in there' [the mind], 'down there' [the social], and 'up there' [God].

(Latour, 1999, p. 310)

Reality, he suggests, is 'an object of belief only for those who have started down this impossible cascade of settlements, always tumbling into a worse and more radical solution' (p. 14). When we say there is no outside world, he argues, 'this does not mean that we deny its existence, but, on the contrary, that we refuse to grant it the ahistorical, isolated, inhuman, cold, objective existence that it was given *only* to combat the crowd' (Latour, 1999, p. 15). Like Bhaskar's critical realism, this view refuses to separate the world and people's knowledge of the world. And yet, as Bauman and Briggs (2003) point out (see Chapter 2), Latour also misses the role of language here as the fifth domain of autonomous construction.

This, then, ties in to the point made earlier (Chapter 3) about the separability of language from other domains of life, and the significance of the attempts to achieve such separability in the project of modernity (Makoni and Pennycook, 2005, 2006). Latour's modernist settlement that we need to unravel in order to have a workable notion of reality and authenticity needs also to address the separation of language from the world; and thus a reworking of this relationship may be best achieved through a domain that takes both language and reality seriously. As Shusterman (2000) argues, 'the realities and truths which hip hop reveals are not the transcendental eternal verities of traditional philosophy, but rather mutable but coercive facts and patterns of the material, sociohistorical world' (p. 73). Hip-hop, I am therefore suggesting, presents a position on language and reality, which, while easily glossed as keepin it real, or as 'living honestly' Westbrook (2002, p. 81), has always been concerned not so much with an inner sense of 'being true to oneself' as with a vision of using language to present particular local visions of the real. The ways in which local realities are defined and understood cannot be removed from the discourses that construct them, and thus while 'staying true to oneself' may look from one perspective like the global spread of an ideology of self-gratification, it is far more interesting to look at this in terms of a global ideology that is always pulled into local ways of being. By looking at authenticity in this way, we are therefore able to rescue the notion from an individualistic ideology, or an overly humanist one that posits a true self and unmediated inner access to such a self, and instead to understand the hip-hop ideology of keepin' it real as a discursively and culturally mediated mode of representing the local. In his discussion of hip-hop in Brazil, Pardue (2004) suggests that hip-hoppers 'view themselves as social agents who force the Brazilian public to be more inclusive about what constitutes knowledge and legitimate perspectives on reality' (p. 412).

This is why the project of realism is crucial: hip-hop is pushing people to understand reality differently.

The questions I want to try to open up here concern the relationship between this call for authenticity, its relocalization in other contexts, and the use of English. Hip-hop forces us to confront some of the conflictual discourses about authenticity: those who insist that African American hip-hop is the real variety and that all other forms are inauthentic deviations; those who insist that hip-hop must be a culture of the streets and to become popular, to become a commercial success, is to sell out, to lose authenticity; those who insist that to be authentic one needs to stick to one's 'own' cultural and linguistic domain, to draw on one's 'own' traditions, to be overtly local; those who suggest that to be authentically local is a question of using a true local variety of a language, be that a local English, a creole, or any language of the streets; those who insist that being authentic is a matter of telling people how one feels, that the expression of one's feelings is an inherently authentic activity; those who claim that authenticity is a question of style and genre, of finding ways to tell a story that resonates with an audience, of achieving agreement about what matters; those who suggest that any recontextualization of language and culture renders it authentic anew. These are the multiple realities that hip-hop presents us with. According to Shusterman, 'the notion that reality is fundamentally mixed and multiple rather than pure and uniform provides a contrast to Plato's view of reality as pure, ideal, permanent, and changeless Forms. If rap has an underlying metaphysics, it is that reality is a field of change and flow rather than static permanence' (Shusterman, 2005, p. 55). The question therefore is how is this *project of realism* carried out as *a field of change and flow* in relationship to language choice?

The project of localism: 'they are trying to be Malay boys doing rap'

To use English in popular music is of course very common, suggesting anything from a commercially oriented choice to a belief that English is better suited to carry particular meanings or to perform particular genres. English-language popular music carries both images of modernity and possibilities of economic success. Yet it would be a mistake to fall into the trap of the easy belief that English is for global communication, financial gain and international identity while local languages are for local audiences and identities. This vision of complementarity between English and local languages, the former allowing communication across boundaries, the latter maintaining local identities and traditions, is widely held, supporting both the benefits of English as a global means of communication ('international intelligibility') and the importance of multilingualism ('historical identity') (see Crystal, 1997). As Hogben (1963) proposed, English can serve people around the world as a universal second language 'for informative communication across their own frontiers about issues of common interest to themselves and others' (p. 20), while other languages play a role as 'a home tongue for love-making, religion, verse-craft, back chat and inexact topics in general' (p. 20). This categorization of global and local languages whereby English serves people as a language of international communication while local languages help maintain culture, tradition and identity underlies many current positions on TESOL (strengthening the effective teaching and learning of English around the world while respecting individuals' language rights), bilingualism and language rights. By relegating vernacular languages only to local expression, however, and by elevating English only to the role of international communication, such a view ignores the many complexities of local and global language use.

To assume that using English automatically implies global communication overlooks several issues. Returning to the lyrics from Too Phat's *360°* discussed in Chapter 1, for example, the first set of lyrics – 'Hip hop be connectin' Kuala Lumpur with LB' ('Just a lil' bit') – we have an image of global hip-hop connecting rappers across the world. And yet, at the same time that these Malaysian MCs adopt aspects of African American English (hip hop be connectin'), show their knowledge of global cultural fashions (laced wit' LV/ice rimmed M3s), and appear to be overtly addressing an external audience (the more common 'KL' for Kuala Lumpur is spelled out in full, while Long Beach is LB), they are also rejecting aspects of American 'bling' culture: they don't have to accept features of American hip-hop culture to participate in global hip-hop. At the same time that they are using English, furthermore, connecting across the world, the hip-hop register they use, with its inside cultural references, is both inclusive and exclusive. This may be a global language, but its use is always in terms of particular registers that are also local, generational, cultural and distinctive.

The rejection of aspects of American hip-hop culture and the move towards forms of localization can take a number of forms. While the take-up of rap by Tanzanians, for example, initially involved wholesale adoption of American idioms, from clothes and names to language and musical style, English-language Tanzanian hip-hop was soon distancing itself from various North American elements since 'expression of themes such as violence and vulgar language was frowned upon by Tanzanians and considered disrespectful, while the topic of male/female relations was more appropriate and found in most Tanzanian music' (Perullo and Fenn, 2003, p. 27). Elsewhere, Lockard (1998) notes a similar set of rejections since the 'profane bitterness, antisystemic radicalism, and overt sexual warfare' of some forms of rap, particularly from the US, would be 'considered excessive by most Southeast Asians' (p. 263). As Singaporean producer and rap artist Shaheed explains, 'We don't want to promote anything that is morally incorrect. That is my principle to me and to them. For me if I find smoking and drinking is morally incorrect then I won't include it in my song' (Shaheed, 13 December 2003). Korean DJ Jun also talks of the move away from American hip-hop themes to deal with 'the Korean problem': 'It is like, every young Korean man has to join the army, so they are rapping about it' (DJJ, 2 November 2003). One form of localization, then, concerns the introduction, irrespective of language, of local themes and references.

Similar issues concern Joe Flizzow of Too Phat: 'If suddenly I start rapping about pushing cocaine or rocking bling bling, then ... that wouldn't be keeping it real, but what we rap about is related to stuff that is related to – that we go through. I mean we don't rap about violence. But we talk about issues that are relevant to the Malaysian scene' (TP, 12 December 2003). In Senegal, Daara J note a similar move away from American themes towards more local elements. According to Faada Freddy, the hip-hop movement in Senegal was at first just imitating US rap: 'carry a gun, go down to the streets and try to show that you are someone that you can express yourself with violence'. But eventually they realized that

> we should care more about our hunger problems ... we live in a country where we have poverty, power, race ... you know ethnic wars and stuff like that. So we couldn't afford to go like Americans, talking about 'Bling Bling', calling our pretty women 'Hoes' or stuff like that. So we couldn't afford that! So that's why we went out at a point where we begin to realize ... you know ... that rap music was about the reality and therefore we went back to our background and see that ... OK ... and not only rap music is a music that could help people ... you know ... solve their problems, but this music is ours! It is a part of our culture!
> (Daara J/1)

Daara J, it is also important to note, while very conscious of the American hip-hop world, are also part of the broad French-language hip-hop circuit, which is discussed further in Chapter 7.

For many hip-hop artists, then, the first move towards localization is a rejection of aspects of rap from the US and a turn towards overtly local themes. The penalties for not doing so can at the very least be mockery by one's peers. Australian rappers Two Up (2002) ('Why Do I Try So Hard?') lay into local hip-hoppers trying to be American: 'Could someone tell me what's up with these try-hard homies?/Their caps are back to front but I think they're phonies.' They are lambasted for their clothes and ways of walking: 'The triple extra large pants so big they're saggin'/With the pimp limp their leg they be draggin''; for the places they hang out, the pretence at gangsterhood and the imitation of all that is American: 'The local shopping centre is the place you hang/Chillin' with your bitch and the rest of the gang/Comparing knives, shooting dice and working on your plan/To become an Aussie version of the Wu Tang Clan'; and above all for being young middle class kids hanging round stores such as Grace Brothers (a department store in Sydney): 'The gangs are gathered round the front of Grace Brothers/Some too young to drive, so they're waiting on their mothers/To come and pick them up and take them home/That's why they've got that flashy new mobile phone.' Accused of being 'cutesy-wootsy little gangsta Gs' and 'wiggers' (White, wannabe niggers) in their 'Tommy Hilfiger' outfits, these local hip-hoppers who haven't localized what they do may be much derided.

Localization may also be accompanied by a move into local languages. Alongside an English-language style that was oriented predominantly towards a particular urban middle-class lifestyle, a Swahili style of rap gradually emerged in Tanzania that typically dealt with more local concerns. As Perullo and Fenn (2003) remark, Tanzanian rapper Mr II mirrors Julius Nyerere's use of Swahili during Tanganyika's struggle for independence, 'to connect to the country's youth, hoping they will take action to address their problems' (p. 26). While many rappers had initially used English in the belief that this would give them more radio play, by the end of the 1990s 'local attitudes had changed, and fans and artists pushed Swahili rap onto the airwaves' (p. 32). Eventually 'swarap' became the more significant style: 'Swahili became the more powerful language choice within the hip hop scene because of a desire among youth to build a national hip hop culture that promoted local rather than foreign values, ideas and language' (p. 33). In Tanzania's case, therefore, while hip-hoppers continued to adopt and adapt American styles and lyrics into their music and identity, the meanings of these appropriations changed as they were re-embedded in swarap with different cultural references, social concerns and musical styles.

As Mitchell (2003a) observes in his discussion of local language use in hip-hop in Zimbabwe, Italy, Greenland and Aotearoa/New Zealand, 'the rhizomic globalization of rap is not a simple instance of the appropriation of a U.S./African-American cultural form; rather, it is a linguistically, socially, and politically dynamic process which results in complex modes of indigenization and syncreticism' (pp. 14–15). The move from English to German in cities such as Frankfurt, Bennett (2000) argues, had numerous implications, even though substantial numbers of German hip-hop artists of Turkish background use German as a second language. In German 'a new measure of accuracy was made possible between localised social experience and linguistic representation'. But this was not only a question of linguistic facility, but also of more ideological concerns: 'only when local rappers started to write and perform texts in the German language did their songs begin to work as an authentic form of communication with the audience' (p. 141). As I argued at the end of Chapter 5, this is why we need to take the politics of language and the ordinariness of diversity seriously. The choices around moves into particular languages may be on pragmatic, aesthetic or commercial grounds, but they are also political decisions to do with language, identity, authenticity and diversity.

It might be tempting to conclude, therefore, that the greater the use of English (or other metropolitan languages), the greater the identification with a global, commercial, imported version of rap, while the greater the use of local languages, the greater the identification with local politics, music, culture. Such a formulation, however, misses several layers of complexity that need to be considered. In particular, we need to understand here local language politics and modes of localization other than along the lines of language codes. While it might be assumed that to choose between Swahili and English in Tanzania, or Chichewa and English in Malawi, for example, is to choose between the local and the global, there is much more at stake here, including the history of language use and colonialism, commercial and aesthetic considerations, and local language ideologies (Fenn and Perullo, 2000, Perullo and Fenn, 2003). As Androutsopoulos and Scholz (2003, p. 476) put it, 'the importance of English for reterritorialized rap discourse is at once referential, sociosymbolic, and aesthetic'. While Malawi shares some similarities with Tanzania in its colonial past, the linguascape of Malawi is different. A less successfully imposed 'national language', Chichewa struggles for ascendancy over other languages and English. A weaker economy and less developed infrastructure, meanwhile, make recording in languages other than English more difficult, an important issue in a number of contexts where access to recording industry infrastructure is tied to other forms of linguistic, cultural and economic capital. While some Malawian rappers push the use of Chichewa for its greater accessibility to a wider audience, English has tended to dominate.

In contexts where English is widely used, it may also already be seen as a local language. Malaysia is an obvious example here, and indeed the language shift in Malaysia appears, at least to some extent, to have been in the opposite direction. Despite a ban on radio or television performances, 4U2C and KRU (1999) gained reasonably wide support in the 1990s with their Malay-language lyrics attacking pollution, abandoned children, alcoholism and other significant but safe social concerns (Lockard, 1998). Since then, rappers such as Too Phat, using predominantly English, have come to the fore. As Pietro Felix from Positive Tone explains,

> once KRU did it people started to go 'oh OK it can be done in Malay also but look there is an English version. That is quite cool' ... and once Too Phat came out – they came out with one song called Anak Ayam and ... there was a layer of traditional music in the background. Everybody knows that song. So immediately the masses said 'we can relate to this song. This is cool and it is two Malay guys singing rap – they are not trying to be American, they are not trying to be black, they are trying to be Malay boys doing rap. So everybody really took to them.'
>
> (PF, 12 December 2003)

This does not mean that all rap in Malaysia is moving towards English – local rap artists are using a range of languages, and Poetic Ammo's 1998 CD, *It's a Nice Day to be Alive*, has tracks not only in English but also in Bahasa Malaysia, Tamil and Cantonese – but it does suggest that the use of English or other languages engages a far more complex and dynamic set of concerns than is suggested by a dichotomy between the local and the global.

It is perhaps surprising that the multilingual code-mixing so commonly found in Malaysia is not represented in Too Phat's separation of English and Malay. This is, however, more a product of official attitudes to language in Malaysia than of local language use. As reported in the *Star* (Sunday, 25 April, 2004), following a report that several tracks such as KRU's 'Babe', Ruffedge's 'Tipah Tertipu' and Too Phat's 'Alhamdulillah' were to be taken off the air, due to the Ministry of Information's proposed ban on Malay songs containing English words, the Deputy Minister Datuk Zainuddin Maidin, was quoted as saying: 'The ministry disallows Malay songs that incorporate English lyrics. We are following the guidelines given by Dewan Bahasa dan Pustaka (DBP) [the Agency for Language and Literature] which state that songs with inaccurate translations or improper language should be banned.' The use of what is commonly called *rojak* English or *rojak* language[5] (referring to the mixed, salad-like make-up of multicultural Malaysia) has long been a point of contention. As the DBP Director-General Datuk Abdul Aziz Deraman said, 'Inappropriate usage of Bahasa Malaysia could corrupt the national language. The usage of rojak language could also lower the status of the national language and make the Malaysian race lose its identity and culture' (*Star*). As Pietro Felix of Positive Tone explained, using Malaysian English 'would count as slang ... Let's say you say something like – you start off with one verse in English and another verse in Malay, the song will get banned. You cannot have a bilingual song....A lot of Malaysians use the word "lah": "Come on lah", "let's go lah". When we say something like that, they will ban that song because it is grammatically wrong' (PF, 12 December 2003).

Clearly, then, the use of one language or another depends very much on the local configuration of culture, language and politics. It also depends on particular identifications with English in relationship to a musical idiom. As Connell and Gibson (2003) observe, English music was popular in the former European Eastern Bloc countries, in part because of the political implications of listening to English/Western music. The use of English by rock groups in the DDR (East Germany), as in Russia and other communist states, was a highly political act (Larkey, 2003; Pennay, 2001). While, as suggested above, the move from English to German allows for a more local form of expression, the use of English was initially an act of political critique rather than of commercial acquiescence. In a very different context, underground musicians in Indonesia 'switched to Indonesian not out of a desire to "indigenize" the music but with the aim of making their music resemble more closely underground music in the West, which they viewed as using everyday language to convey urgent and powerful messages to its listeners' (Wallach, 2003, p. 54).[6] In this context, then, the use of Indonesian is a form of translocal identification with the use of English elsewhere.

Transmodality and local enactment: when do a pair of Jordans become local?

As I suggested in Chapters 2 and 3, it is important here that we do not fall into the trap of looking at languages as if they were separate, disembodied entities that people choose to use for various communicative purposes. Language use as transmodal and transidiomatic practice involves modes, codes and bodies. A good example of this may be seen in the way cultural formations such as hip-hop enter a cultural sphere. Because of the emphasis on Russian and the suspicion of English within Eastern Europe, the levels of English knowledge in the German Democratic Republic were relatively low, especially when compared with West Germany, and thus the flow of English-language-influenced culture was slower in the East than in the West (Pennay, 2001). And yet, with a transmodal cultural form such as hip-hop, it is possible for cultural practices to enter domains where the language may be inaccessible. In a number of contexts where English is not the first language, break-dancing first gained people's attention – in part because of the cultural and linguistic difficulties in understanding rap, in part because of the more immediate appeal of the physical.

As Condry (2001) comments, 'A striking feature of global flows of popular culture ... is that dance – movement of the body – moves easily across linguistic and cultural boundaries, and that movies and videos are a primary channel for this exchange' (p. 229). He goes on to argue that language 'is a key variable for understanding Japanese hip-hop and for transnational exchanges more generally. When we consider cultural globalization, we need to examine what actually moves across the cultural divide, because that is how to get a sense of what kind of divide it is' (p. 231). With clothes, style, dance, graffiti, DJing, and beat-boxing, hip-hop is less dependent on language as a means of communication. Korean DJ Jun talks of a similar effect when he started to move into the Melbourne scene. When he first arrived, his English was limited but 'some Asian dudes came down to the club and they do breakdancing there'. As he entered the scene, people started asking 'oh who is that dude?', and when he explained he was listening to Korean hip hop, 'and they feel kind of fresh. Kind of new to different culture. People does hip hop thing like that.' And from there he moved into the local hip-hop scene (DJJ, 2 November 2003).

Music is also of course crucial here. As Pietro Felix noted above, Too Phat's track 'Anak Ayam', from their CD *Plan B*, raises a further question about how we understand localization. As Joe Flizzow explains: 'Well I think the way we rap ... we don't try to sound American, we just try to sound, well that is just how we sound, you know? But we do like Malaysian traditional instrumentations and elements of Malaysian music, so that is what makes us different, I would say, from other hip hop' (TP, 12 December 2003). Malique explains further:

It's not just the language, it's also the instruments involved .... We're known for our fusion of traditional elements and we use old folk songs and we add a break beat to it and we rap on top of it .... Like if you listen to a rap act rapping in a normal beat they would be like 'oh, that's another rap act' right. But if you hear a rap like us on Anak Ayam you will be like 'hey, how come they are rapping in English but the background is, you know, is Malay'. So like something they can relate to. Like in Indonesia Anak Ayam was pretty big.

(TP, 12 December 2003)

From this perspective, it is not so much a local language, a local variety of English or references to local contexts that place this track in its particular context, but rather the instantly recognizable melody in the background.

Within the sampling culture of hip-hop it is very common to include music of many different types: the opening track from Senegalese Daara J's *Boomerang*, for example, starts with a Mandinka traditional melody sung by Malian singer Rokia Traoré. But this role of music as a form of localization raises some issues for further consideration. Another Malaysian group, Teh Tarik Crew, reject the option of local instruments, however, suggesting that what makes their music Malaysian is, as Altimet puts it, 'The fact that it is made by us. You see when we were recording our first album a lot of people were telling us ... we had great pressure to put in traditional elements. Like sounds, whatever. But we don't feel that it is necessary. You don't have to put in traditional sounds to sound Malaysian' (TTC, 13 December 2003). For them, the use of traditional instruments is to buy into a somewhat stereotypical view of cultural identity. As they point out, if a European or North American band used samples of Asian music, it does not make them Asian. Localization, by contrast, is about talking about local conditions.[7] This raises some important questions for the studies of the localization of English. For too long, the focus on world Englishes has looked within languages – syntax, pronunciation, pragmatics – to find aspects of localization: a local English has emerged when it bears significant and regular differences from other varieties. Yet the discussion here raises other issues: language may become local by dint of background music or local themes. Localization may be as much about a language being in the world in particular ways as about changes to that language.

Once we start to think about languages being in the world, the question of language use as enactment and performance also emerges. As we saw in the discussion of performativity in Chapter 4, the idea that both language and identity are the products rather than the precursors of sedimented language use presents the possibility that each use, each reiteration, is also something new. In Malawi, as Perullo and Fenn (2003) observed, English is 'the favored language, particularly in young people's mimetic enactment of American hip hop and their appropriation of American hip hop terminology in descriptions of themselves' (p. 47). As they argue, however, the English used is 'radically recontextualised' as terms borrowed from African American English 'take on new sets of meanings' based on Malawian interpretations of American inner city gang life and 'contemporary social experiences of Malawian youth' (p. 41). When we take into account the 'style with which English is used' rather than dwelling only on whether English is used or not (p. 44), English starts to take on a different life. Once the mimetic use of language is seen as *enactment* rather than *copying*, the meanings of language use and choice lie 'not in the semantic realm but in a participation-through-doing that is socially meaningful' (p. 45). Issues of language choice and style 'constitute aspects of discursive and musical practice in Malawian rap culture that are conjoined via language ideologies and are not so easily separable in lived experience' (p. 46). It is this participation through doing, this enactment of language in different contexts, that renders the apparent mimicry of English language hip-hop a site of difference.

This position forces us to reconsider other ways in which we may think about localization. While Too Phat's first verse discussed above links to global hip-hop culture, the second verse discussed in Chapter 1 – 'If I die tonight' – does something a bit different: it excludes the global audience and includes the local with its very specific cultural references to food – Fried Kuey Teow and roti canai. This is, of course, the meat and drink of world Englishes, the localization of English via references to local cultural elements. Later on, however, as the lyrics move to other things to do on the last day, Malique suggests that he would 'line up my shoes one by one/Start with Jordans and end with them Air Force Ones/Put a Post-it on the tongue of each one with the name of each dun/I think I know my homies and who would want which one' (If I die tonight). Here, with the consumerism, the Jordans, post-its and homies, we are surely back in the global world of hip-hop fashion. Or are we? Can we in fact judge so easily what is local and global? While we may be comfortable to say that Fried Kuey Teow is a local reference (though even that, when we take into account other diasporas and travel, may not be so clear), may we assume that other references are not local? Or, put another way, when do Malique's Jordans become local? As in the discussion of hip-hop in Malawi, mimicry and enactment may localize the imitated.

English as a field of change and flow

Clearly we need a more complex theory of localization that can take us beyond a view that local languages, or English that bears particular local features, are the determinants of localization. Looking at rap in Europe, Androutsopoulos and Scholz (2003) use Lull's (1995) framework which posits a three-tiered process for understanding appropriation. The first stage is one of deterritorialization, the removal of a cultural practice from its origins. The middle stage of cultural melding includes transculturation (the production of new cultural forms as different cultural practices move and encounter each other), hybridization (the mixture of cultural forms) and indigenization (imported forms take on local features). Finally, the process moves to one of reterritorialization (the integration of the new practices into local use). Through an analysis of the hybrid 'spaghetti funk' philosophy of Italian rappers Articolo 31, the sampling of traditional Greek *rembetiko* music by the Greek Terror X Crew, lyrics dealing with issues of migration and racism by rappers such as IAM (France) and Advanced Chemistry (Germany), the use of both vernacular/dialect variants of languages and mixtures of English, and the adaptation of rap lyrics to local patterns of rhyme and reference, Androutsopoulos and Scholz reveal what they call the 'double bond of European rap discourse between a global and a local pole. Being a local representative of a global cultural discourse is, we believe, fundamental to European rappers' self-understanding and discursive action' (2003, p. 476).

While the examples of sampling, mixing and localizing discussed here fit closely with the concerns of this chapter, this model of deterritorialization, transculturation and reterritorialization, and the polarity between the local and the global (where one is a 'a local representative of a global cultural discourse'), leave us with a framework that may not adequately capture the dynamics of flow, fixity and fluidity as cultural practices become embedded in different contexts. Such a multi-stage approach to processes of localization, nevertheless, captures some of the dynamics I have been exploring here in terms of the ways hip-hop's *project of realism* is carried out as *a field of change and flow* in relationship to language choice. The widely employed dichotomy which suggests that English serves global purposes while local languages are for local culture is problematic in a number of ways. It is impossible to understand the global spread and use of English without considering the local contexts of its use (Canagarajah, 2005), which include language history and politics, current linguascapes, language ideologies, economy and infrastructure. Thus English (or other so-called metropolitan languages) is already in its use a tropicopolitan language (Aravamudan, 1999) bound up in a diverse set of local relations of language ideology, politics and social life. The local use of English in relation to different cultural formations (such as the messages and ideologies of rap) is always a contextual use influenced by many different community and regional views. There is a constant tension between the global flow of an ideology of authenticity and the local fixity of what authenticity means and how it should be realized. To use English in different contexts is to invoke issues of class, location and identity.

Where English is tied to education and middle-class opportunity, to use English as a person from an impoverished background is potentially also to call on an ambivalent class position. As one young hip-hop fan told me in Brazil, when I asked if 'Rappin Hood', a rap crew from Sao Paolo, used English in their lyrics (apart from the interesting English of their name), to use English would surely not fit with an angry *favela* voice talking of race, poverty, violence and drugs (see Pardue, 2004; and MV Bill, 2002).

In many forms of rap around the world, aside from the indexical use of various forms of hip-hop terminology (DJ, scratch, bomb and so on; and see Preisler, 1999), the use of English may invoke a class position which is incompatible with a voice that wishes to speak from a minoritarian position. In Malaysia, one informant expressed surprise that I was talking to what are disparagingly known as *kutu* – a pejorative Malay term (literally head lice) for the young and unemployed hanging around in malls and shopping centres – on the assumption that local hip-hop artists were members of this population, only to be more surprised to find that various English-language rappers had attended prestigious private schools and studied overseas. To have a command of English sufficient to rap in the language may, in some contexts, imply a very particular class background.

Yet to 'use English' may mean many things. It is widely perceived as the language of modernity, of international communication and of the international music industry. On the one hand, singers may use English extensively in their music – recording tracks or whole CDs in English – as part not only of an appeal to a wider audience, but also to local audiences who may want to hear local bands using English. On the other hand, bands may use various English words and phrases to point indexically to the wider domain of which they and their audience wish to see themselves, and it is not uncommon in many countries, from France to Japan, to employ a speaker of English to add English lyrics to a song. The English used in such contexts may be many things. Cutler (2003) analyses the practice of *chanter en yaourt* (literally, singing in yoghurt) in France, which involves 'the use of an assortment of real and nonsense English words and sounds sung in phonologically and prosodically convincing approximations of English' (p. 329). While such phenomena may appear to be a cheap appeal to English, they also need to be understood as part of an aesthetic appeal to 'meaning that is culturally specific and linked to the unique historical and cultural relationship individuals have to a foreign language and its speakers' (p. 344). Many musicians have to confront the problem that local language and music traditions may be embedded in traditions of style and content (an elevated literary style or a particular romantic tradition, for example) that are anathema to the language, sounds, style and messages they wish to convey. English may at first offer a useful alternative, 'not only as an "international language" but also as the most sonically appropriate linguistic option for underground music' (Wallach, 2003, p. 55). And if a switch to local languages follows, this may then be both in opposition to local musical practices and with an appropriated set of language ideologies that have come through the use of English. On the other hand, as K'Naan (Interview, 25 April 2006) suggests, while English may be a useful medium for getting a political message about Somalia to a wider audience, it may also be a language that is unable to carry the poetic substance of oral traditions in languages such as Somali.

African American English plays a very particular role in global hip-hop, and to use aspects of AAVE – even through a nod in this direction via an indexical 'yo' – is to claim a position of global rap identification. To use English, and particularly AAVE-styled English, may link to a broader circuit of affiliations – both musical and cultural – that imbue the cultural forms (music, graffiti) with aspects of the politics of hip-hop as an angry anti-establishment voice. Yet Rip Slyme's lyrics discussed at the beginning of this chapter – *Yo Bringing That, Yo Bring Your Style* – appear to do little more than invoke a general world of African American-influenced rap lyrics. For others, however, the use of terms such as 'yo' is precisely what needs to be rejected since it stands as an indication of a focus away from the local context. As Australian hip-hop artist Monkimuk says, referring directly to this use of 'yo', 'And me being someone that also raps in indigenous languages, it's really good for the kids in the desert to see that you don't have to be a *yo yo* – an American as I call them – rapping in an American accent. Even if you don't speak English as your first language you can rap in your native tongue' (MM, 4 November 2005).[8]

Rip Slyme's use of English, however, is not limited to such indexical pointing to African American English. The track 'By the Way', which uses the English chorus 'By the Way Five Guy's Name (x3), Five Guy's Name is Rip Slyme 5' ('By the Way', 'Tokyo Classic') throughout, is somewhat different. From the register of the phrase 'by the way'[9] to the pronunciation of 'five guy's name' (with its four or more syllables) and the syntax of the sentence (five guy/possessive particle/name/topic particle/Rip Slyme 5) all suggest Japanese-influenced English. Thus while the lyrics are in English and perform the activity not uncommon to rap of self-reference (announcing the name of the crew), they also locate themselves phonologically and syntactically as Japanese performances in English. This cannot therefore be categorized easily as imitation (which, in any case, is also more complex than often allowed). The problem for frameworks such as world Englishes is that this may be a priori discounted as local English on the basis that no stable variety of English has emerged for internal communication within Japan. English in Japan, from this perspective, is exonormative. While it is certainly true that English is more readily available, for example, to some Malaysians (though this always depends on class, region, ethnicity and education) as a language of local identification, to assume that the use of English in contexts such as Japan is necessarily exonormative or an act of external identification is to overlook the complexities of language use and identity. Such language use confounds these categorizations: it is both local and non-local, both English and Japanese. And as we shall see in Chapter 7, English becomes so embedded in translingual language use that it becomes pointless in many ways to look at languages as separable entities. Thus the issue is not so much one of language choice as of understanding transidiomatic practices, the communicative practices that result from the co-presence of multilingual talk and various media (Jacquemet, 2005; see also Chapter 3).

If we accept the possibility that the mimetic enactment of language may radically recontextualize what superficially may appear to be the same, then the use of English, even the imitation of an African American term, may be full of multiple meanings of identification, localization, imitation and reinterpretation. This takes us back to issues of performativity and the point that language identities are performed in the doing rather than reflecting a prior set of fixed options. Rather than the use of an American accent or American hip-hop idioms being acts of passive imitation per se, we can see that each enactment enfolds the past while enacting the present differently. To use English, therefore, is not to be tied to a past history of English use but is to perform English anew, to be involved in a process of semiotic reconstruction (Kandiah, 1998). While often showing surface-level copying of features, particularly of African American English, the English is always local English, and is used to reflect local themes and taboos. And themes that are taken up and developed may also be those (such as male/female relations) that are already common in the local context. Thus what may look like an imported set of global concerns may in fact be either a local take on more global themes or a local reconstruction of both the global and local. As I shall argue in Chapter 7, such processes of localization destabilize notions of origins, suggesting that hip-hop may be far more local than a notion of de- and reterritorialization may imply. As Gurnah (1997) points out, 'changing patterns in different cultures can *never* reproduce each other, for they are made up of different cultural raw materials forged in variant histories' (p. 126).

Rather than understanding the use of English in rap music merely as an appeal to the international music industry, a reflex of globalization, an indexicalization of an English-speaking world, we also need to consider both the aesthetics of using English and the possibility that in any case English becomes so rapidly part of the local that it is far less clear than it might appear what it means to say something 'in English' (see Pennycook, 2006b). It makes little sense to construct a global (English)/local language dichotomy where one is assumed to be for international intelligibility and the other for local identity. As Pietro Felix explains about Too Phat's lyrics, it may be a very small indication that triggers a sense of what is local: 'There are some words that can be like English and Malay. It is the same pronunciation. It is just that when they pronounce it, the accent they use is in Malay. So all of a sudden, you hear this smooth American flow and then this one word, it is Malaysian. You know? So it is like a little hook somewhere in the song' (PF, 12 December 2003). English becomes local and, as we shall in more detail later in the next chapter, local identities are constantly being refashioned in these contexts. The authenticity that hip-hop insists on is not a question of staying true to a prior set of embedded languages and practices but rather is an issue of performing multiple forms of realism within the fields of change and flow made possible by transmodal and transcultural language use.

7 Language flows,
language mixes

Following the discussion of language use and authenticity in the previous chapter, one might still be tempted to ask whether the direction of influence is nevertheless in one direction: while swarap in Tanzania may have developed its own style that has diverged from North American rap in terms of language, culture, style and ideology, is there any effect in the opposite direction? As Perry (2004) suggests (see Chapter 5), the cultural isolation of the United States may render talk such as Gilroy's (1993) of the 'stereophonic, bilingual, or bifocal cultural forms originated by, but no longer the exclusive property of, blacks dispersed within the structures of feeling, producing, communicating, and remembering that I have heuristically called the black Atlantic world' (p. 3) little more than a romantic fantasy of mutual influence. Pennay (2001, p. 128) comments in his discussion of rap in Germany: 'Regrettably, the flow of new ideas and stylistic innovations in popular music is nearly always from the English-speaking market, and not to it.' Similarly, in her discussion of the Basque rap group Negu Gorriak (featuring the Mugurza brothers), Jacqueline Urla points out that 'unequal relations between the United States record industry and Basque radical music mean that Public Enemy's message reaches the Mugurza brothers in Irun, and not vice versa' (2001, p. 189). Is it then the case that while hip-hop changes and transforms around the world, it is always caught in a one-way flow of spread and diversification?

This chapter explores the question of global flows of hip-hop and language, and opens up a rather different perspective. While it is certainly true that the global rap/hip-hop scene has a limited effect on the dominant US scene, it is also true that there are many other circles of flow. In some ways, US hip-hop simply becomes an irrelevance to the multiple influences on global flows. Or, if not irrelevant, it is only one part of a far more complex picture. And ultimately, rather than the dominance of the US music market being a problem for the rest of the world, it is more the case that this dominance is what leads to the isolation of the US: just as the dominance of English globally has played an important role in the isolation of the US linguistically (Kramsch, 2005; Sonntag, 2003; Venuti, 1997), so the lack of engagement with the global circles of flow limits its linguistic, musical and cultural possibilities. The world of global hip-hop is also one of language mixing, transidiomatic practices and refashioned identities: the flow is always remixed. As hip-hop engages with diverse local practices in different contexts, it draws on multiple local influences, raising questions about its origins. If Italian hip-hop draws on traditions of operatic recitative, if Somali-Canadian hip-hop finds inspiration in the tradition of Somalian oral poetry, if Fijian Australian hip-hop may be seen in terms of island traditions of dance, song, story-telling and carving, if Turkish hip-hop can draw on seventeenth-century minstrels, Malaysian on traditional Malay song and Senegalese on the *griots* of West Africa, it becomes less clear whether this is the localization of hip-hop or the delocalization of local traditions. Or, rather, something else again.

Circles of flow

While it may be true that the effect of global rap on the US is limited, the issue is also not one of unidirectional flow. There are many flows in many directions, and thus we can start to think of alternative frames of analysis by analogy with the black Atlantic, from the hip-hop Pacific to the black Mediterranean or 'Chopstick hip-hop'. As Tony Mitchell (2001a) suggests, if Sydney rappers of Fijian and Tongan background, such as Trey and Posse Koolism, combine with King Kapisi's 'Samoan hip-hop to the world', and if Hawaiian band Sudden Rush's *Ku'e* (Resist) has been influenced by Aotearoa-New Zealand Upper Hutt Posse's *E Tu* (Be Strong), then what we are witnessing is a 'Pacific Island hip-hop diaspora' and a 'pan-Pacific hip-hop network that has bypassed the borders and restrictions of the popular music distribution industry' (p. 31). These circles of hip-hop flow are at times overlapping: Hawaii, for example, links the Pacific to the US, while French-influenced parts of the Pacific, such as French Polynesia (Tahiti) and New Caledonia link the Pacific to the French circuit. As my discussion of *capoeira* at the beginning of Chapter 2 suggested, furthermore, the Pacific has always been a place of multiple criss-crossing movements, and the ways different transcultural forms link across the region produces an intricacy of interactive influences.

In her discussion of *Na Mele Paleoleo* (Hawaiian rap) developed by Sudden Rush, Fay Akindes (2001) argues that by bridging elements of political self-determination with popular culture, this Hawaiian hip-hop has become 'a liberatory discourse for Hawaiians seeking economic self-determination in the form of sovereignty. Sudden Rush ... have borrowed hip hop as a counter-hegemonic transcript that challenges tourism and Western imperialism' (p. 95). Sudden Rush draw on a mixture of indigenous traditions, including *kaona* – a particular Hawaiian style of using metaphor in order to express hidden meanings (a development in part in reaction to Calvinist missionary proscription of sexual reference, and thus seen as an anti-colonial subversion) – as well as direct political messages. As Akindes describes the title track of Ku'e (which means to oppose or resist), 'the main message is a call to reclaim Hawaiian lands and, therefore, economic self-sufficiency and self-determination. The rap is fresh and unfamiliar: it is ne mele paleoleo, Hawaiian hip hop, a cut n' mix of African and Jamaican reggae rhythms, Hawaiian chanting, and subversive rapping in the English and Hawaiian languages' (p. 91).

The use of languages such as Hawaiian – with its links to other Polynesian languages such as Tahitian, Samoan and Maori – is in itself an important political statement. As I suggested in Chapter 6, the politics of rap lyrics need to be understood not only in terms of the interpretable meaning of the lyrics but also in the varieties of language used. Although its use in Hawaii is limited, as Szego (2003) notes in her discussion of Hawaiian schoolchildren learning chanted poetry (*mele*), 'young Native Hawaiians singing and listening to music in their associated language demonstrate how text performed and apprehended outside the domain of language fluency can yield to sonic, semantic, and symbolic interpretation' (p. 320). These students, with a limited capacity in Hawaiian language, 'experienced musically realized text as a gestalt ... when language was fused with musical sound, the interpretive possibilities expanded' (p. 322). This observation brings us back to the discussion of the somatic turn and transmodality: when language is combined with music and bodily movement, it can take on a very different set of meanings beyond those more narrowly understood in discussions of language use in education.

According to Akindes, Sudden Rush 'deliver messages of Hawaiian nationalism in a musical format that speaks to Hawaiian youth' (2001, p. 93) while simultaneously disrupting 'the false and idealistic notion of purity or authenticity in music by contesting the ideas of origins and by exemplifying how music is continually evolving through a constant cut 'n' mixing of melodies, rhythms, styles, and themes' (p. 95). As I suggested above, and as we shall see in greater depth below, this contesting of origins and mixing of styles is a significant way in which identity is refashioned through hip-hop. For Sudden Rush, as for many contemporary musicians, these mixes and reclamations are in no way contradictory: reclaiming a sense of Hawaiian national identity may involve many mixes of language, music and politics. Thus, while it may appear at first sight that Hawaiian rappers are but reflexes of an American music industry, their work is in fact directly in opposition to the American presence in Hawaii, employs a mix of musical, cultural and linguistic influences, and looks outward to the other Pacific Islands rather then over its shoulder towards the colonial power.

'Following the adoption of breakdancing by Maori and Pacific Islander youth', Mitchell (1998a) points out in the context of Aotearoa-New Zealand, 'rap music and hip hop culture became an inevitable medium for musical expressions of Maori militancy' (p. 41). As a result, he suggests (1998b), the already hybrid forms of rap have become further hybridized, producing 'strong musical, political and cultural resonances in Aotearoa'

(p. 168). Maori and other Pacific Islander rappers in Aotearoa-New Zealand 'have substituted Maori and Polynesian cultural expressions for the African-American rhetoric of hip hop'. Upper Hutt Posse in particular combine 'the use of Maori traditional instruments, militant *patere* and *karanga* (raps and calls to ancestors) and invocations of the spirits of the forest (*Tane Mohuta*) and the guardian of the sea (*Tangaroa*), and rhetoric borrowed from the Nation of Islam' (Mitchell, 2003a, p. 13). Auckland has thus become a major centre for Pacific Island music, with many cross-influences from the Samoan, Tongan, Fijian and other islander people there. Samoan King Kapisi urges islanders to engage with their own cultures and histories and to acknowledge the interrelated Pacific: 'I represent for all Pacific peoples from Hawaii 2 Aotearoa' (Fix Amnesia, Savage Thoughts). Kapisi urges the 'Newtown born coconut' (Newtown is a suburb of Auckland with a large Pacific islander population; coconut meaning 'brown on the outside, white on the inside') to forget religion and to 'check your history/Or you might lose yourself and your own identity' (Fix Amnesia).[1] King Kapisi's 'Samoan Hip-hop worldwide' project reconnects the Samoan diaspora, urging them to reconnect with their cultural heritage (Pearson, 2004).

And in the small New Caledonia scene, we see two parts of interlinked flow, the black Pacific and the French Atlantic, Francophone hip-hop and islander identity. Amid the anti-colonial politics of the 1980s in New Caledonia *kaneka* music fused Western music, and particularly reggae, with indigenous musical forms. As Goldsworthy (1998) points out, *kaneka* is a distinctively New Caledonian style of music that results from 'a conscious, deliberate attempt to achieve Kanak cultural identity through a popular music medium' (p. 45). Kanak musicians, he goes on, 'have also strongly identified with this larger picture of black solidarity and anti-hegemonic activity in their pursuit of their own specific goals' (p. 51). Like Sudden Rush in Hawaii, drawing on a mixture of musical styles and articulating an ant-colonial politics, Kaneka music has fused local languages and musical rhythms with Western styles as part of an oppositional politics to French colonial rule. Section Otoktone sing in their CD *On Vient de la Rue* (We're From the Streets) – a name and title that immediately locates these rappers as indigenous (autochtone) and yet part of the hip-hop ideology of the street – of the problems faced by 'la nouvelle génération calédonienne' (the new (New) Caledonian generation), contrasting the colours of New Caledonia seen by the tourists (white sand, blue sea, bronze bodies) with the greys of the buildings and the nickel mines (a constant point of contention in terms of ownership, exploitation and pollution).

The French-language hip-hop scene has been one of the most significant for twenty years, a complex interlocked circle of flow that links the vibrant music scenes in Paris and Marseille in France; Dakar, Abidjan and Libreville in West Africa, and Montreal in Quebec. Hip-hop in France developed in the *banlieues* – the suburban housing projects where many poor, and first and second generation immigrant populations live. Here, in multiethnic mixes of people of Maghreb (Algeria, Tunisia, Morocco), French African (Mali, Senegal, Gabon), French Antilles (La Martinique, Guadeloupe) and other European (Portugal, Romania, Italy) backgrounds, hip-hop emerged as a potent force of new French expression (Cannon, 1997; Faure and Garcia, 2005; Huq, 2001a, b; Prévos, 1998, 2001, 2002). Rap in France 'uses a street-speak version of French that includes African, Arab, gypsy and American roots and is viewed with disapproval by traditionalists for its disregard for traditional rules of grammar and liberal use of neologisms' (Huq, 2001a, p. 74). While Paris became a centre for many movements and crossings of French-language musicians, dancers and artists, the southern port city of Marseille looked more resolutely southwards. Typical of the movement was popular Marseille group IAM, whose members have Madagascaran, Senegalese, Algerian, Spanish, Italian and French backgrounds, and whose album *Ombre est Lumière* Mitchell (2003b) describes as 'one of the all-time masterpieces of world hip-hop' (p. 108). Along with their sharp language use – their album *Métèque et mat* evokes *échec et mat* (checkmate), *Métèque* meaning more or less 'wog' and *mat* from the Arabic 'to die' (see Swedenburg, 2001), while *Ombre est Lumière* (darkness is light) is a play on the French *son et lumière* (sound and light) shows – they developed an ideology which Prévos (2001) calls 'pharaoism'(p. 48) thus both linking to the Arabic background of many French immigrants, and as Swedenburg (2001) argues giving 'Egyptianist Afrocentricity a Mediterranean inflection, asserting a kind of "black Mediterranean" ' (p. 69).

The rap scene in France, as Huq (2001a) describes it, 'stands out as the ideal soundtrack to accompany the post-industrial, post-colonial times ushered in by the new millennium, in which the new tricolore (the French national flag), is black, blanc, beur'[2] (p. 81). While the many flows of immigrant influence into France have thus greatly affected French hip-hop, the 'diasporic flows' (Prévos, 2001, p. 53) of hip-hop back into the wider francophone circle of flow have in turn changed the music and linguascapes of other regions of the world. In Libreville, Gabon, rappers mix English, French and local languages such as Fang and Téké. As Auzanneau (2002, 2003) explains further, English is never used on its own but always in conjunction with French, while vernacular languages may be used on their own, with each other or with French, but never with English. The use of vernacular languages signals a clear identity with the Gabonese community while keeping a distance from France which

> is perceived as economically exploitative, culturally assimilating, and a former colonizer. Within the rap movement, which puts Gabonese culture on a public and perhaps even international stage, vernacular languages are enjoying something of a revalorization. Formerly associated with out-of-date and archaic values (and thus with 'backwardness'), these languages are now becoming languages of 'authenticity' and 'roots' and thus claim for themselves an identiary role both in rap and in the city.
>
> (Auzanneau, 2002, p. 114)

As we shall see later in this chapter, this relationship between hip-hop and 'tradition' is one that takes many interesting forms.

The French that is used in Gabon is subject to both endonormative and exonormative pulls, with the former 'departures from standard French' serving as 'factors of social differentiation and thus identification' (Auzanneau, 2002, p. 108). Libreville's 'relexified French' uses 'borrowings from Gabonese languages, languages of migration, and English (standard and non-standard, but especially slang)' as well as non-standard French lexicon, including various created forms, neologisms and *verlan,* which is not only a form of French slang that reverses standard French (hence the term 'beur' used to refer to people of Arabic descent is derived from 'Arabe' and the term 'verlan' itself derives from the French term 'l'envers' meaning the other way round) but also, as Doran (2004, p. 194) explains,

> a kind of linguistic *bricolage* marked by the multilingualism and multiculturalism present in the communities where it is spoken, which include immigrants from North Africa, West Africa, Asia and the Caribbean. Given the marginal status of these communities vis-à-vis elite Parisian culture, Verlan can be viewed as an alternative code which stands both literally and figuratively outside the hegemonic norms of Parisian culture and language.

When such codes are imported (or to some extent reimported) to the Libreville rap scene, there is a vast array of language and cultural influences at work. The choices they make between languages is crucial: 'the place given to English or to French *verlan* can diminish in favor of terms taken from Libreville French or local languages when the songwriter wishes to negotiate his or her Gabonese identity through the interactions being represented in the song' (Auzanneau, 2002, p. 117). By using relexified French, 'speakers mark their attachment to Gabonese culture at the same time as they make their break with the values of both their own traditional society and the dominant Western society. This variety is the emblem of the rappers' culture and of their *métissée* (mixed) identity as young urbanites' (p. 118).

A similar mixed identity is commonly found in Montreal. Montreal has large immigrant communities, reflecting in part the relationship to the francophone circle of flow. Along with the various Asian, Jewish and well-established communities from Portugal, Italy and Greece, as well as communities from Spanish-speaking countries of South and Central America, there is a strong presence of people of Haitian origin, and North and Sub-Saharan Africa, including Lebanon, Algeria, Morocco, Tunisia, Mali and Senegal. As Impossible from Haitian-origin Muzion puts it,

> Le style montréalais, moi, j'l'aurais défini comme, c'est la seule place où t'as un mélange culturel comme ça, que t'as un mélange des langues

comme ça, que ça soit l'anglais, créole, pis le français, mais un français quand même québécois.

I'd define the Montreal style as, it's the only place where you have a cultural mix like that, where you have a mixture of languages like that, whether it's English, [Haitian] Creole, then French, but all the same a Quebec French.

(cited in Sarkar and Allen, in press)

As Sarkar and Allen note, languages are commonly mixed, partly reflecting the way language is used among urban youth in Montreal – 'en général, on chante, on rap comme on parle' ('in general, we sing, we rap the way we speak') according to J. Kyll of Muzion – but also clearly as a new form of emerging and performative identity. As Sarkar and Allen observe, rappers claim that rather than such language mixes alienating listeners, they enable listeners to relate to diversity in new ways. Thus when French, creole and English is mixed in a line such as 'Tout moune qui talk trash kiss mon black ass du nord' (Sarkar *et al.*, 2005), new possibilities of identification are being opened up. And this language use, they suggest, following J. Kyll, is having an effect on the larger community so that 'Même les Québécois, maintenant, ils commencent à utiliser des slangs créoles' ('Even Québécois now are starting to use [Haitian] Creole slang terms'), adopting terms such as *patnai* (Haitian creole for a good friend). I shall return to the issue of creoles and rap later in this chapter.

Given these mixes, labels such as 'francophone' need to be applied with caution to such circles of flow. While on one level these music scenes are connected by their postcolonial use of French, this French is also widely divergent, and, as with English, cannot be easily assumed to be one entity. As Édouard Glissant (1997) suggests, 'there are several French languages today, and languages allow us to conceive of their unicity [*sic*] according to a new mode, in which French can no longer be monolingual. If language is given in advance, if it claims to have a mission, it misses out on the adventure and does not catch on in the world' (p. 119). The languages and cultures that circulate within these flows are constantly mixed with other languages and cultures, so that new mixtures arrive in new places and remix once again as they become relocalized. As Auzanneau puts it, rappers in Libreville, Gabon, 'are inserted into large networks of communication that confer on them a plurality of identities' using a wide 'diversity of languages with their variants, along with their functioning as markers of identity (of being Gabonese, African, or an urbanite)' (Auzanneau, 2002, p. 120).

There are many such circles of flow, including the Spanish, which connect the hip-hop scenes in Cuba, Spain, Mexico and South America (and which, due to the large Hispanic communities in the US, does have some effect on that market) (Cepeda, 2003; Fernandes, 2003; Pacini Hernandez and Garofalo, 2004), the Lusophone, the Chinese (Ho, 2003) and so on.

These different circles also intersect in many places, above all in Africa. As N'Dongo D from Senegalese group Daara J explains:

> L'Afrique est une plateforme, et le seul lieu d'échange réel entre les peuples, les cultures, les langues .... En Afrique vous trouverez, du portugais, de l'espagnol, du français, de l'anglais tout melangé dans la culture sur le meme continent ... le zone sénégalais c'est un zone francais, l'autre zone c'est un zone anglophone, l'autre zone c'est un zone lusophone, etc etc Donc, malgré ce mélange la, les cultures africaines, les peuples africaines, les ethnies gardent quand meme leurs langues be base, mais pour mieux se comprendre entre eux, on utilise par example le français au Senegal. Donc pour nous, la puissance de la langue ... comme l'a dit Professeur Cheikh Anta Diop ... le développement, c'est l'acceptation d'éléments nouveaux; sans acceptation d'éléments nouveaux, il ny a pas de développement; nous avons accepte d'éléments nouveaux dans les langues, les instruments, etc et nous avons guardé notre base.

> Africa is a platform, and the only real place of exchange between people, cultures and languages. In Africa you will find Portuguese, Spanish, French, English all mixed together in the culture in the same continent.... The Senegalese zone is a French zone, another zone is an English zone, another is Portuguese and so on. So in spite of this mixture, the African cultures, peoples and ethnic groups have still kept their own languages, but to better understand each other, they use French, for example, in Senegal. So for us, the power of language ... as Professor Cheikh Anta Diop[3] said, development is the acceptance of new elements; without accepting new elements, there is no development; we've accepted new elements in languages, instruments and so on, and we've kept our own base.
>
> (Interview, 5 March 2005; my translation)

And just as it is worth being cautious about using these linguistic labels (as we have seen, they are far more mixed and multilingual than these terms allow), so there are other ways in which circles of flow operate. They may, for example, be historical. Daara J's title track 'Boomerang' on the album of the same name is so called (though interestingly using an indigenous Australian weapon) to point to their argument that hip-hop has its origins in Africa and has now returned: 'Born in Africa, brought up in America, hip-hop has come full circle' (Boomerang). According to Faada Freddy, 'this music is ours! It is a part of our culture!' As he explains, the traditional Senegalese form of rhythmic poetry, *tasso*, is the original form of rap:

> You can take somebody away from his home but you cannot rip off his culture. So that's why we arrive at the statement where the American people brought out all that culture that was slumbering at the bottom

of their soul .... And this is ... it was the beginning of rap music. This music went around the world because ... it applied a certain influence over the world and all over. But now just realize that music is coming back home because it is about time that we join the traditional music, we join yesterday to today.

(Interview, 5 March 2005)

This circuit of flow, then, sees hip-hop as an African form that travelled across the Atlantic, was developed in the US and has now returned home. From this perspective, it is worth noting, the global spread of hip-hop is not the proliferation of North American culture but of African culture.

Circuits of flow can operate along lines other than language. Looking at rap by British and French musicians of Islamic background, for example, Swedenburg (2001) argues for 'the importance of paying close attention to popular cultural manifestations of "Islam" in Europe' (p. 76). British band Fun-Da-Mental's engagement with Islam is 'central to its multipronged intervention: Islam instils religioethnic pride among Asian youth, serves as an image of antiracist mobilization, creates links between Asians and Afro-Caribbeans, and shocks and educates white leftists and alternative youth' (Swedenburg, 2001, p. 62). Similarly, Swedenburg argues that French group IAM's Islamic engagement is part of their 'effort to widen the space of tolerance for Arabo-Islamic culture in France, through its lyrical subject matter, its deployment of Arabic words and expressions, and its musical mixes, splattered with Middle Eastern rhythms and samples of Arabic songs' (p. 71). Of course, what is meant by Islam will mean many different things. For some, such as Singaporean Shaheed, 'I am a Muslim, so I don't talk about going to a club and drink and something like that. You know that is against my religion. I might go to a club to enjoy the music but that is about it. I don't tell lies and that way I keep myself real, keep myself true to myself because I have to keep myself protected from all this' (Shaheed, 13 December 2003). Nation of Islam, meanwhile, as K'Naan (K'naan, 25 April 2006) comments, may have more to do with culture and race than with religion, yet their oppositional politics play an important role for both Muslims and non-Muslims, and have thus become influential, for example, in the Maori politics of Upper Hutt Posse (Mitchell, 2003a).

In a rather different context, Malay rappers Too Phat saw both a spiritual and commercial opportunity in developing rap with lyrics from the Koran in Arabic. 'Alhamdulillah' (*360°*), as Pietro Felix explains, was originally conceived as 'an R&B "thankyou, praise Allah" kind of thing', which, they felt, 'sounded very Arabic, it sounded very Malay, more prayer, religious kind of sound', so they got Yasin, an Arabic singer, to do the lyrics. The song is largely a critique of materialist values with thanks to Allah for the gifts they have received – 'I thank Allah for blessing me to be creative/ So here's a diss for me for bein' unappreciative/Wanted a perfect life, yeah smile then die old/Fame, money, women, phat cribos and white gold/' – and a warning for not saying 'alhamdulillah'. As Felix Pietro goes on, 'suddenly we thought "this is great marketing". A lot of Malay kids will love this, plus we can check this out to ... all the way East kind of thing' (PF, 12 December 2003). This plan to gain sales in Middle Eastern countries such as Saudi Arabia, however, was not so successful: 'they didn't want to play it because it seems their censorship board does not allow songs that have anything to do with praise Allah.' Meanwhile, with less strict rules of what can and cannot be done in popular music, as long as, as we saw in the previous chapter, you don't use 'rojak language', the song 'gets great airplay' in Malaysia. 'People were blown away with the song. They never thought a rap song would have Koran lyrics, Arabic lyrics' (PF, 12 December 2003).

While some Islamic states have been less ready to accept such a possibility, other artists are less sure about the overt use of Muslim identity:

> Being a Muslim is something that you do, not talk about .... And I'm a Muslim in that way, in the true way, not in the way that it is holding a banner saying 'I am a Muslim, look at me', instead I am doing what a Muslim is supposed to do. I'm trying to spread some good, trying to be good, trying to not offend people; those are the elements that exist for me. And so it means nothing to say 'I'm a Muslim', it means more to *be* a Muslim.
>
> (K'Naan, Interview, 25 April 2006)

There are, unsurprisingly, therefore a number of different positions on the notion and possibility of Islamic hip-hop. And yet it is clear that from rappers of Turkish background in Germany, such as Islamic Force (see Kaya, 2001, 2002, 2003) to Malaysian Too Phat, from French bands such as IAM to the verbal intifada of Palestinian rappers (Sling Shot Hip Hop, 2006), it is nevertheless possible to talk in terms of what Alim (2005, 2006) has called a *transglobal hiphop ummah*.[4]

The hip-hop culture of collaboration leads to other circuits of flow. Thus Hong Kong DJ Tommy's compilation, 'Respect for Da Chopstick Hip Hop' – the title itself, of course, a play on global (Respect/Da) and local (Chopstick Hip Hop) elements – features MC Yan from Hong Kong, K-One, MC Ill and Jaguar from Japan, and Meta and Joosuc from Korea, with tracks sung in English, Cantonese, Japanese and Korean. Such collaborations are common. Too Phat's *360°*, for example, contains a track '6MC's', featuring Promoe of Loop Troop (Sweden), Vandal of SMC (Canada), Freestyle (Brooklyn, New York) and Weapon X from Melbourne, Australia: 'From sea to sea, country to country/6 MC's bring the delicacies/ It's a meeting of the minds to ease the turmoil/360 degrees around the earth's soil.' Weapon X turns up again on Korean MC Joosuc's track 'Universal Language' (Joosuc also featured on 'Respect for Da Chopstick'), in which Weapon X uses English and Joosuc Korean (with some English). In Joosuc's words:

Lyrics	Transliteration	Translation
Street to street, city to city 흘러가는 정보 check check 필히 또 필히 …	*Street to street, city to city Hul uh ga nun jung bo check check Pil hi tto pil hi …*	Street to street, city to city, information flowing for certain …
시대는 바야흐로 worldwide	*Shi dae nun bah ya hu ro worldwide*	The time is now worldwide
사라져버리는 의미 없는 국경의 체제	*Sa ra juh buh ri nun ui mi um nun gook gyoung ui che je*	The disappearing meaningless boundary systems of countries
그렇다면 사양말고 뻗어나가야지	*Gu ruh tah myun sah yang mahl go bbuh duh nah gah ya ji*	If so, I will also join the flows without any hesitation

As DJ Jun explains, this track 'is about different languages but we are in the same culture which is hip-hop. So language difference doesn't really matter. So hip-hop is one language. That is why it is called universal language' (DJJ, 2 November 2003). From this perspective, then, hip-hop as a culture rises above different languages: the universal language is not English; it is hip-hop.

Mixing and making other Englishes

One thing that also clearly emerges from these accounts of circles of flow is the constant mixing, borrowing, shifting and sampling of music, languages, lyrics and ideas. Let us return to Rip Slyme for a moment. We have already seen in Chapter 6 how this Tokyo band may use snatches of borrowed English – 'Yo Bringing that, Yo Bring Your Style' – as well as more locally produced English – 'Five Guy's Name is Rip Slyme 5' – but in the following example from the track 'Tokyo Classic', we see a more complex mixture.

Lyrics	Transliteration	Translation
錦糸町出 Freaky ダブルの Japanese	*Kinshichoo de freaky daburu no Japanese*	Freaky mixed Japanese from Kinshichoo
'Tokyo Classic'		

By naming Kinshichoo (a suburb of Tokyo) and by doing so in kanji (Japanese characters of Chinese origin), Rip Slyme locate their Japaneseness explicitly, yet at the same time they use the English word for Japanese, seeming in the same instant to refashion their identity from the outside. This Japanese identity is then both 'freaky' and 'double', the latter a recently coined term to describe people of mixed origin. English and Japanese flow across the boundaries of identity, becoming both fixed (Rip Slyme 5, from Kinshichoo) and fluid (Yo, double, Japanese), producing new possibilities of what it means to be Japanese, to use English, to participate globally, to be local.

Other artists present different ways of embedding English in Japanese (or Japanese in English). In the following lyrics, for example, DJ Tonk (Move On) uses the English word 'listen', written in katakana (rissun), followed by 2 (meaning 'to'); and 'our blues moonlight' (in katakana: buruusu muunraito) is juxtaposed with the traditional-sounding Japanese (in kanji) 'under the moonlight' (tsukiakari no shita). Here, then, we have the old and the new, English and Japanese, contrasted, mixed and combined in a way that makes them hard to disentangle.

Lyrics	Transliteration	Translation
リッスン２俺達の ブルース ムーンラ イト 月明かりの下	**rissun** two oretachino **buruusu muunraito** tsukiakari no shita	Listen to our blues moonlight under the moonlight

In the example below from Zeebra's *The Rhyme Animal*, Zeebra plays with the different rhymes in katakana (dynamic, titanic), producing a final mixed rhyme with the Japanese dai (big) and panic (daipanikku – big panic – to rhyme with dainamikku – dynamic). Perhaps what emerges here above all is the sense that English and Japanese become so intertwined, and meaning is so dependent on the mixture of the codes, that the very separability of English and Japanese becomes an impossibility; the very notion of whether English is invading Japanese culture or being used to represent Japanese culture can simply no longer be asked.

Lyrics	Transliteration	Translation
のっけからダイナミック まるでタイタニック 想像を超える大パニック	nokkekara **dainamikku** marude **taitanikku** souzouwo koeru dai **panikku**	From the very beginning, it was dynamic, just like Titanic, and an unimaginable big panic

As with the circles of flow described above, many of these performers are interlinked not only on a personal level (they collaborate, work together, turn up on each other's CDs) but on a more general level of origins, movement and histories. Korean MC JK of popular rap group Drunken Tiger grew up in LA, trying to establish rap in Korean amid the cultural politics of Los Angeles. Likewise, his friend MC Tasha, who, like Ilmari of Rip Slyme, has a mixed cultural and linguistic familial background, describes herself on the track 'Wonder Woman' as 난반먹통 Korean 혈통 (nahn bahn meok tong Korean hyeol tong: half part inkpot and Korean blood, or an ABK – (African) American Born Korean). While her lyrics vary from love songs to a critique of male Korean chauvinism, hypocrisy, domestic violence and relationships between wealthy older men and young girls (Man, Man,

Man), it is the ways in which her lyrics create relations between English and Korean that interest me here. From the opening of 'Memories ... (Smiling Tears)' from *Tasha Hip-Hop Album*, for example, she builds a mixture of English and Korean around the Chinese idiom (commonly used in Korea): 七顚八起 (*chil jeon pahl gi*) meaning: If I'm knocked seven times, I come back on my eighth (or something like 'no pain, no gain').

Lyrics	Transliteration	Translation
Yo if I fall two times I come back on my third 절대로포기않지 and that's my word	*Jeol dae roh poh gi ahnchi*	I never give up
If I fall five times I come harder on my sixth 조금만더가면돼포기않지난아직	*Joh geum mahn deo gah myeon dwae poh gihi ahn chi nahn ah jik*	I'm not far from the goal, I haven't given up yet
If I'm knocked 7 times I come back on my eighth 칠전팔기내인생끝까지가볼래	*Chil jeon pahl gi nae in saeng gyeut ggah gi bohl lae*	Even if I fail seven times, I will try again; I will keep trying until the end of my life
Now knowledge of self thru the pain in this world 난절대로포기않지 and that's my word	*Nahn jeol dae roh poh gi ahn chi*	I never give up

In this example, then, Tasha uses a well-known Korean idiom and embellishes it in the two languages, each phrase working with the other to develop the meaning. Elsewhere, from the track Meditation, Tasha combines English and Korean differently. Unlike the lyrics above, where English and Korean complement each other – the lyrics in English and Korean reinforce the meaning – here she moves from English to Korean across both meaning and sound: 'Rainy day' is echoed immediately in *Naerinae*, also meaning rain, with the same rhyme – day, *Naerinae, igosae, smyeodeunae, goeenae* – repeated through the rest. The common rap feature of repeated rhymes within a sentence is here reproduced across languages.

Lyrics	Transliteration	Translation
Rainy day 내리네 이곳에스며드네 내작은방바닥에고이네	*Naerinae igosae smyeodeunae nae jahggeun bahng bah dahg aeh goeenae*	Rainy day, raining, soaking and gathering on the floor of my small room

This use of rhymes across both languages is a feature of a number of tracks. In 'The Concrete Jungle', she rhymes 돌려 (*dohllyeo* – turning) and 돌려 (*dohllyeo* – taking breath) with 'mirror'. The mixture of English and Korean, held together through repeated ryhmes, creates a new level of meaning.

Lyrics	Transliteration	Translation
고개를 돌려 now check the back mirror 빨간 불에 멈춘 우린 잠시 숨을 돌려	*Goh gae reul dohllyeo ... bbahl gahn boorae meom choon woorin jahmsi soomeul dohllyeo*	Turning her head and checking the back mirror, stopping by a red light and taking breath for a while

What Tasha achieves here is a mixture of Korean and English that combines the different 'flows', sounds and meanings of English and Korean. There are therefore two senses to the flows I have been discussing here. On the one hand, the interlocking circles of flow that produce a constant movement of linguistic, musical and cultural influences around the world. On the other hand, the flows of rap lyrics, which are a crucial part of the aesthetics of MC-ing (having a good flow is widely recognized as central to the art of rap). As Krims points out, the 'rhythmic styles of MC-ing, or "flows", are among the central aspects of rap production and reception, and any discussion of rap genres that takes musical poetics seriously demands a vocabulary of flow' (Krims, 2000, p. 48). It is one thing, however, to master the flow of one language (and there has been much debate over whether some languages are better oriented towards rap flows than others), but it is quite another skill to 'flow-switch' as Tasha does. The skill here is not just to move between languages, creating a set of new meanings by doing so, but also to move in and out of different flows. By artfully integrating the flows of English and Korean rap styles in a bilingual performance, she presents English and Korean in new relationships.

Part of another complex circuit are GHOST 13 ('Guys Have Own Style to Talk' – one group, three rappers): 'Now lisnen up por pabor makinig 2004 rap sa Pinas yumayanig lalong lumalakas never madadaig', rap GHOST 13 from the Philippines in English (Now lisnen up/never), Chavacano (por pabor, please) and Tagalog (rap sa Pinas yumayanig lalong lumalakas [never] madadaig: Listen to 2004 Philippines rap getting stronger and never beaten). GHOST 13 – Blanktape (a name derived originally from his hometown Baliwasan Tabuk), Diorap (from his last name Diola and rap) and L-Sabor (Spanish/Chavacano for flavour or taste) – are from Zamboanga in western Mindanao, known as the City of Flowers:[5] 'Chavacano de Zamboanga siento porsiento ... kami magdidilig sa city of flower' (In Chavacano, Tagalog and English: one hundred per cent Chavacano from Zamboanga ... we water the city of flowers). GHOST 13 use what they call 'halo-halong lenguaje' (mixed language), comprising Tagalog, Visaya, Chavacano and Tausug as well as English in their lyrics.[6] Some tracks, such as Tinambak (Basura), based on the tune of Eminem's 'Without Me', deal with issues such as waste disposal (Capuz, 2005), while others, such as El Templa, Ese Amor Se (El Deverasan) and the track GHOST 13, address their Chavacano and Zamboanga identity: 'Listen everyone we are the only one rap group in the land who represent zamboanga man!/Guyz have own style, style to talk a

while di kami mga wanna [we are not imitators] because we have own identity' (GHOST 13).

Here, then, we have part of the 'Pinoy Rap' circle, linking the vibrant
hip-hop scene in the Philippines (with its debates over the preference for
English over Tagalog for many bands) through the *balikbayan* circuit (those
living outside the Philippines) to American Filipino bands such as Kontrast,
or Apl.de.ap of Black Eyed Peas. In Mindanao we also see the intersec-
tion of Christian and Muslim circuits (while L-Sabor thanks Almighty God,
for Blanktape, 'First and foremost gusto kong magoasalamat kay Allah for
giving me this talent' (CD cover), or as they say in their lyrics, 'Relihiyon
muslim o kristyano masquin' [Muslim or Christian, whatever]). Like many
creole languages, Chavacano is often derided (with terms such as 'Filo-
Spanish'), the term itself being derived from the Spanish *chabacano* (vulgar).
Chavacano is the general term for several Spanish-based creole languages in
the Philippines. Zamboangueño, the most widely spoken and the language
used by GHOST 13, has predominantly Spanish vocabulary and Cebuano
as the substrate language. It remains an important place of identity for these
rappers. Like other creoles, it does not exist in isolation but rather is always
in relation with and accompanied by other languages. To announce this
identity, to place it centrally in the music, is to open an important space for
this language. And GHOST 13, representin' in classic hip-hop style, are very
clearly putting Chavacano on stage here.

The use of creoles in rap can be a sign of street credibility, of local
authenticity. Since creole languages are often viewed as non-standard, local
languages, their very use also provides an avenue for an oppositional stance
in terms of language use rather than lyrical intent. Many creole languages
are tied to slavery, colonialism, migration and the African disapora. From
Jamaican *patwa* in the UK, Haitian creole in Montreal or to Cabo Verde
(Cape Verde) rappers such as The Real Vibe and Black Side in Holland, and,
arguably, from African American English to aboriginal Australian English
(see Chapter 8), to use creole is to invoke a certain cultural politics, to take
up a space within this historical and contemporary circle of flow. As with the
hip-hop crews in Libreville, whose mixing and use of languages was clearly
overt, so the use of creole and other languages by groups such as GHOST
13 is part of an explicit challenge to forms of identity. It is a reclamation of
a space of language mixing that is the historical and geographical norm, but
one that has often been hidden beneath the patina of nationalist language
policy. Such a view ties in with the views on *créolité* of Édouard Glissant
(1997), Patrick Chamoiseau and other French Caribbean writers. In a similar vein to Gilroy's notion of the black Atlantic, we see here a view that
makes creole languages central to the modern world since they take métis-
sage, postcolonial realities and multiple origins as the norm: 'La créolité
est une annihilation de la fausse universalité, du monolinguisme et de la
pureté' (Bernabé *et al.*, 1993, p. 28): créolité is an annihilation of false universality, monolingualism and purity. Multiple identities were invented by

creolization, suggests Raphäel Confiant. As he goes on, 'la mondialisation créole valorise la "diversalité" c'est-à-dire le mélange, le partage des ancêtres et des identités, le non-cloisonnement des imaginaires' (2006, n.p.). Creole globalization – and here Confiant is placing their concept of *créolité* at the centre of a new way of thinking about the world, in a way reminiscent of the the the notion of worldliness discussed in Chapter 2 – valorizes *diversalité* (a term coined by this group of thinkers to refer to a stronger sense of diversity (*diversité*) with its static versions of difference – see p. 20), that is to say mixing, the sharing of ancestors and identities, the non-partitioning of the imaginary.

For these theorists of creolization, then, creole languages, cultures and ways of being should be the model for a new era of globalization/ worldliness. And hip-hop, I am suggesting, is a driving force not only for the use of creoles but for their creation. As Kaya's (2001) study of Turkish hip-hop culture in Berlin suggests, 'Turkish youths have a peculiar language of their own. They speak a creole language. It is a mix of Turkish, German and American-English. This new form of city speech in the migrants' suburbs is a verbal celebration of ghetto multiculturalism, twisting German, Turkish and American slang in resistance to the official language' (p. 147). Creole linguists may object here and point out that this is not a 'true creole', defined usually as a language that has developed from an earlier pidgin when used by children, that now has first-language speakers, with vocabulary often from European languages and grammars derived either from putative universal grammatical forms or from other languages: 'creoles are pidgins which have become native languages for their speakers' (Sebba, 1997, p. 16).[7] Yet while the linguistic emphasis on defining creoles according to strict criteria has done much to avoid the derogatory view of creoles as degenerate languages, this also has its pitfalls. As with much of linguistics the emphasis on disinterested description as a tool to counter discrimination comes at a cost of disengagement with a broader cultural politics (Makoni and Pennycook, 2005, 2006; Pennycook, 2001).

As Degraff (2005) warns us, one of the most dangerous myths of linguistics is 'creole exceptionalism', 'a set of beliefs, widespread among both linguists and nonlinguists, that Creole languages form an exceptional class on phylogenetic and/or typological grounds' (p. 533). These beliefs, Degraff argues, are part of a long discursive chain 'connecting "the problem of slavery" in the New World to European scientific racism. In turn, the discourse of Creole Exceptionalism can be textually linked to certain tropes within a (pseudo-) scientific hegemonic narrative that runs throughout the history of the (post-) colonial Caribbean from the earliest descriptions of its Creole languages' (Degraff, 2005, p. 535). As Sinfree Makoni and I have argued (Makoni and Pennycook, 2006), while Degraff's critique of linguistic studies of creoles and his proposition for a postcolonial creole linguistics opens up an important space for thinking of creoles outside the exceptionalism and exoticization that is so common, the argument might still be made more effective by suggesting not merely that creoles are unexceptional (i.e. we assume creoles to be no more exceptional than other languages) but rather that other languages are exceptional (we take creole languages as the norm, and question the genesis and status of other languages). This is closer to the position of Bernabé *et al.* (1993) discussed above.

There is no space here to do more than touch on this area of debate, so let me return to the question of whether we should only accept Chavacano as a creole (because it is accepted by linguists) and reject Kaya's claim that the language of Turkish hip-hoppers in Berlin is a creole (since it has not developed from a prior pidgin, does not have first language speakers as defined by linguistics, and does not share the features of other creoles). Following in part Mufwene's (2001) argument that, like Degraff's position, creoles 'are not outcomes of abnormal, unusual, or unnatural developments in language evolution' (p. 192), and following his lead in taking a more relaxed definition of creoles – 'in its sociohistorical sense to identify primarily those varieties that have been identified as "creole" or "patois" by nonlinguists' (p. 10) – I think we should take seriously the notion that the transgressive language use of rap, mixing and borrowing, using language from wherever, deliberately changing the possibilities of language use and language combinations, should be seen as a creolizing force. While Chavacano in the Philippines or the creoles of the Caribbean may be older and different in a number of ways, to reject the Turkish-German-English creole of Berlin hip-hop would be to overlook the ways in which languages are created. If, as many people rightly are, we are concerned about the decline of languages in the world (Skutnabb-Kangas, 2000), we might then see hip-hop not, as conservative critics would suggest, as an engine of linguistic degeneration, but rather as a potential driver towards diversity both in terms of what Halliday (2002; and see Pennycook, 2004c) has termed *semiodiversity* – the diversity of meaning within languages – and in terms of *glossodiversity* – the diversity of languages themselves. And if, as Mufwene (2001) argues (see Chapter 2), there is no reason to discount creoles from the purview of world Englishes, then a Turkish-based creole, with German and English relexification, might just have to be considered as one of those other Englishes, as one of the many global Englishes.

New traditions, new places

A key theme in the discussion of the localization of hip-hop has been the question of place. Authenticity, as Connell and Gibson (2003, p. 44) note, has constantly been sought through attempts at 'embedding music in place' but popular music in particular has always escaped such attempts, having 'reflected the fluxes and fluidity of contemporary life, unsettling binary oppositions established in earlier phases of modernity (tradition/ contemporary; authentic/inauthentic; local/global) by refusing to be pinned down'. This unsettling of relations between the contemporary and the traditional is constantly at play in hip-hop. As Auzanneau (2002) points out, while rappers in Libreville use language that marks a very specific attachment to Gabonese culture, they are also at the same time opposing both the values of dominant Western society as well as those of traditional Gabonese society. Local authenticity can neither merely imitate dominant imported practices nor draw unquestioningly on local tradition. Instead, we find new, refashioned languages, cultures, identities and traditions. The ways in which local traditions are taken up, however, have serious implications for how we understand issues of origins and identities.

Let us return for a moment to the third set of Too Phat's lyrics discussed in Chapter 1. Here Too Phat switch to Malay with lyrics that are more localized and speak more to a local community (though since these lyrics are also largely comprehensible to Indonesians, their audience is still potentially large). Although there are a few elements of English, and particularly the English of rap, mixed in (*spit it menarik* – spit it out cool), and while the self-referentiality of the lyrics ('This is the first time, just brilliant, I am rapping in Malay') may still be seen as part of global hip-hop culture, the local references open a new and different issue: when they rap '*Tukang karut moden bercerita pasti girang*' (The modern Master, when he tells stories, is bound to create happiness), they are connecting their rapping to traditional forms of Malay song. Tukang Karut is the lead singer in the Dikir Barat, a chanting/singing form of entertainment popular in Kelantan (in North East Malaysia, seen as the home of many traditional Malay forms of culture); the dikir barat bands can perform all night long, with the Tukang karut ('master of nonsense') singing the main verse and the choir following with a chant taking off from these lyrics. By referring to themselves as the modern Tukang Karut, Too Phat relocate their art in Malay traditional culture. Unlike Daara J's argument that hip-hop has its origins in African culture and has returned home, Too Phat here are pointing to a broader possibility that the localization of hip-hop is not just about local references, local languages, local themes, but may involve the invocation of traditional cultural forms.

Lipperini (1992, cited in Mitchell, 1996) suggests that rap in Italy could be said to have 'dual origins in the oral traditions of the griots of Africa and in the *recitativo* used in early Italian operas in Florence in the sixteenth century, with their *imitar con canto chi parla* (imitating in song a person speaking)' (Mitchell, 1996, p. 163). The German hip-hop scene has a strong Turkish presence (Elfein, 1998),[8] once again suggesting that hip-hop continues to operate as a vehicle for marginalized youth to find expression. According to Kaya (2001), the 'structural outsiderism' of these working-class Turkish youths leads them to look to 'their homeland, religion and ethnicity' as 'their main cultural sources' (p. 155). Kaya goes on to draw a direct link between the medieval Turkish minstrels (*halk ozani*) who 'enlightened the masses with their lyrics' and who later 'used to write and sing poems against the supremacy of the Ottoman rule over the peasantry' (p. 181) and these Berlin-Turkish rappers.

This is not merely a functional argument that rappers are the modern minstrels of the twenty-first century (an interesting supposition in itself), but rather a case for understanding these connections in musical and cultural terms. Thus 'using the traditional Turkish musical genre as the source of their samples and having been guided by the traditional Turkish minstrels in terms of lyrical structure, these contemporary minstrels, or storytellers, tend to be the spokespersons of the Turkish diaspora' (Kaya, 2001, p. 203). Here, then, contemporary rap invokes cultural traditions not only by sampling and reference to musical styles but also by taking up particular social and political functions as story-tellers and critics of the current regime.

A different slant on this may be found in the British group Asian Dub Foundation (ADF), who cut across British cultural boundaries with their Jamaican-influenced rap about young British Asians: 'Young Asian brothers an sisters/Moving forward, side by side/*Naya Zindagi/Naya Jeevan/* New Way New Life.' *Naya Zindagi/Naya Jeevan,*[9] meaning 'new life, new life' in Hindi and Urdu, is a reference to a 1970s BBC programme in the UK aimed at Indian and Pakistani immigrants. Here these second-generation South Asians recall how this programme 'Kept our parents alive/Gave them the will to survive/Working inna de factories/Sometimes sweeping de floor'. But now a new generation has arrived: 'And we're supposed to be cool/Inna de dance our riddims rule/But we knew it all along/Cos our parents made us strong/Never abandoned our culture/Just been moving it along' ('New Way New Life', 2000). Here ADF claim to be both drawing on their parents' South Asian cultural heritage and 'moving it along'. While the 'new life' of the TV series was targeted at helping immigrants to Britain to adapt to their new way of life while also keeping linguistic and cultural connections, the new way/new life of this next generation is shifting this cultural inheritance into quite a different space, an African Caribbean-influenced rap celebration of the new life of second-generation South Asian youths in London, as well as a critique – as in much of their lyrics – of the racism in modern Britain, a space that their factory-working parents who watched *Naya Zindagi/Naya Jeevan* on TV in the 1970s might find it hard to accept as an extension of the cultures they have maintained.

This kind of relationship is widespread in global hip-hop. As we saw earlier, King Kapisi urges Samoans living outside Samoa to re-engage with their cultural heritage. Somali-Canadian MC K'Naan, meanwhile, draws direct links to the oral poetry traditions of Somalia. His track 'Until the Lion Learns to Speak' (*The Dusty Foot Philosopher*, 2005) is a homage to Somali poet Arays Isse Karshe, the particular rhythms that he alone used, and an acknowledgement that 'everything that he talked about was concerning the struggle of the country and its power struggle with independence and colonialism'. In Somalia, K'Naan argues, one's ability to use language is seen as crucial: 'that's really the nature of language in our country. It is so highly regarded. It's your livelihood.' Looking more broadly at Africa, he then suggests that these oral traditions all tie to modern hip-hop. While West

Africa has its *griots,* and Somalia has a long tradition of oral language use, 'any country, any given country in Africa, you will find an ancient form of hip-hop. It's just natural for someone from Africa to recite something over a drum and to recite it in a talking blues fashion, and then it becomes this thing called hip-hop' (K'Naan, interview, 25 April 2006).

MC Trey (*Island Rappers,* 1999), a Fijian Australian rapper, makes similar connections, explaining that she's into hip-hop because, as a transmodal practice, it recalls the transmodality of Fijian performances: 'It has all those elements that you can express yourself ... like in Fiji, they have ... their art and their dancing, and their music ... and I feel that hip-hop has that. It's one of the only modern art forms where you've got ... your breaking, your DJ-ing, graffiti, your MC-ing ... your story-telling.' She goes on: 'I feel that MC-ing is definitely an extension of oral tradition, like just in the islands they used to sit around the Kava Bowl, and their story-telling, you know, a lot of it was passed down through word of mouth, they didn't have much documentation.' Here we have another claim that hip-hop can be a tool in cultural maintenance or revival. This is a form of hip-hop that reflects the oral traditions of Fiji, the art and carving (via graffiti), the dancing and the music. For Trey, these connections are crucial. As she explains on the cover of her CD *Tapastry Tunes,* her label *Tapastry* refers to *tapa,* 'a traditional Fijian cloth made from the inner bark of mulberry trees, decorated with stencilled motifs and repetitive patterns which tell stories of ancient Fijian lifestyles – tapa is of high significance in Fijian culture and always included in traditional, ritualistic and spiritual ceremonies throughout the islands.' As with the Asian Dub Foundation, this pride in a cultural heritage is one that may be hard for a previous generation to identify with: South Asian cultures being moved along through Jamaican rap; Fijian cultures being extended through hip-hop.

This raises some important considerations for how we think about language and culture within global contexts, problematizing arguments over origins. If Trey is linking back to Fijian cultural practices, if Too Phat are the modern descendants of traditional Tukang Karut singers, if ADF are moving their parents' culture along, if K'Naan is continuing in the tradition of Somali oral poetry, and if Islamic Force in Berlin are heirs to the traditions of *halk ozani* minstrels in seventeenth-century Turkey, the idea that hip-hop simply spread from its supposed centre in the US becomes hard to maintain. The new cultural forms produced in the dynamics of localization have multiple lineages. All cultures have produced forms of dance, art and story-telling; and hip-hop cultures – however we understand their origins in New York, influences from the Caribbean, participation in the Black or French Atlantic, or their African roots – can make it possible to reconnect modern urban life with older ways of interlinking stories, music, dance and community life. At the same time, however, such links are by no means simply 'maintaining' traditional culture. The very notion that a modern, urban, commodified, global cultural form such as hip-hop could be involved in cultural maintenance is, on the face of it, rather absurd. And yet, the connections that hip-hop makes possible render other forms of cultural practice possible, and thus cultural and linguistic forms are simultaneously engaged in and changed. Extending Daara J's observation (p. 123, citing Cheikh Anta Diop) that development can only come with change, we might suggest that cultural and linguistic maintenance can only come about through change.

Such an observation may appear paradoxical, but it opens up insights for both language and culture. We can make some similar observations about English and its origins that take us beyond arguments about linguistic spread versus localization. As I have argued elsewhere (Pennycook, 2002a), following Nandy's (1988) observation that 'cricket is an Indian game accidentally discovered by the English' (p. 1) that 'can be given the credit for having introduced into Indian society a new and unique means of cultural self-expression' (p. 2), so we might say English is an Indian language accidentally discovered by the English that can be given the credit for having introduced into Indian society a new and unique means of cultural self-expression. Such an observation takes us beyond the image of a global spread followed by localization, since it suggests that many languages and cultures that are assumed to be imported are always/already local. The language in which these connections are made may be English or other languages: Too Phat make the link to tradition in Bahasa Malaysia; for K'Naan, it is English that helps spread the word but which lacks the poetry of Somali: 'when I compare it to Somali, English is very dry, and also very young sounding' (Interview, 25 April 2006); for King Kapisi and Trey it is predominantly English; for ADF it is a Jamaican style of English; for Turkish hip-hoppers it may be Turkish, German, or, as we saw earlier, perhaps a creolized mix with English. In the end, the question of which language is being used may be virtually irrelevant or unanswerable. These global Englishes become so interlinked with other languages and traditions that the will to name them as a separate code seems at times perverse. Or, to put it another way, English may already have been globally local before it started to spread.

The unifying gregarity of rap as xenoglossic becoming

The above discussion pushes us to think beyond notions of 'language choice' as if the issue were always one of deciding between discrete languages. As Sinfree Makoni and I have argued (Makoni and Pennycook, 2005), many such notions are based on the metadiscursive regimes that divided languages into separate and enumerable objects, overlooking the complex ways in which languages are interwoven and used. Looking at the division between Gaelic and English popular music in Ireland, McCann and Ó Laoire (2003) argue that the issue is not so much 'language choice' as the discursive construction of this 'choice of languages'. As they point out, the construction of a choice between two languages posits 'two radically distinct and symbolically disparate linguistic traditions': on the one hand, an ancient personal, lyrical and more authentic Gaelic tradition; on the other, a more recent, practical, literal, plain and less authentic English tradition (p. 234). As they go on to argue, the 'simplistic nature of the binary opposition' between the two constructs both a 'reified view of "tradition", thereby concealing important questions of social context and personal meaning' and 'an either/or language choice between distinct alternative entities' (p. 234). As many of the above examples show, the notion of language choice between discrete codes makes little sense in contexts where artists take both a far more complex view of tradition, and a very different view of language choice.

The mixed codes of the street, and the hypermixes of hip-hop, pose a threat to the linguistic, cultural and political stability urged by national language policies and wished into place by frameworks of linguistic analysis that posit separate and enumerable languages (Makoni and Pennycook, 1995, 2006). As Jacquemet (2005) puts it, we need not only to understand contact linguistics but to 'examine communicative practices based on disorderly recombinations and language mixings occurring simultaneously in local and distant environments. In other words, it is time to conceptualize a linguistics of xenoglossic becoming, transidiomatic mixing, and communicative recombinations' (p. 274). Hip-hop language use can therefore be read as resistant or oppositional not merely in terms of the lyrics but also in terms of the language choice. Keeping it linguistically real is often a threat to those who would prefer to keep it linguistically pure. For many communities, using a variety of languages, mixing languages together, is the norm. As Sinfree Makoni and I have argued, the notion that people use separate and discrete languages is a very strange language ideology that has arisen at a particular cultural and historical moment. Furthermore, to the extent that many hip-hoppers come from marginalized communities where the strait-jackets of linguistic normativity have had less effect, their mixed-code language will likely reflect local language use. It would be strange for someone from Zamboanga not to use at least Chavacano, Tagalog, Cebuano, Tausug and English in different daily interactions. This is not only a question, however, of reflecting local language use.

Choices in language use are deeply embedded in local conditions, from the economy and the local music industry infrastructure (limited recording facilities militate against local practices and languages) to the historical background to language policies, language ideologies, aesthetics, and other local and regional social and cultural concerns. As Berger (2003) points out, 'while language choice in music may reflect prevailing language ideologies, that influence is often a two-way street; that is, rather than merely reproducing existing ideologies, singers, culture workers, and listeners may use music to actively think about, debate, or resist the ideologies at play in the social world around them' (pp. xiv–xv). According to Gurnah (1997), 'an appropriation of own or other cultures is an active and intellectually intensive and demanding exercise which mobilizes rational and sensual faculties, always' (p. 126). Auzanneau (2002) argues that the language choices which the rappers in Libreville made were clearly intentional. Although at one level these language choices may therefore be viewed as reflecting local diversity, at another level they are also intentionally producing local diversity. As with Baumann's arguments about performance (see Chapter 4), where language is publicly put on display, made available for scrutiny, hip-hop is itself precisely part of the process of change, making new language, new language mixes available to others.

Rather than merely reproducing local language practices, language use in hip-hop may consequently have as much to do with change, resistance and opposition as do lyrics that overtly challenge the status quo. This is particularly true of musicians such as rap artists, whose focus on verbal skills performed in the public domain renders their language use a site of constant potential challenge. The importance of this observation in terms of understanding transcultural flows and global Englishes is that it gives us an insight into the ways in which Englishes are used in relation to other languages to perform, invent and (re)fashion identities across borders. Thus in performing their acts of semiotic reconstruction, it is no longer useful to ask if Rip Slyme are using Japanese English to express Japanese culture and identity as if these neatly pre-existed the performance, or whether Too Phat are native speakers of a nativized variety of English, as if such nationally constructed codes predefine their use, or whether Tasha's bilinguality is unrepresentative of language use in Korea, as if national language policy precludes alternative possibilities, or whether GHOST 13's lyrics reflect local language mixing in Zamboanga, as if language use was so easily captured and represented. When we talk of global English use, we are talking of the performance of new identities.

As the discussion of language ideologies in Chapter 2 suggested, once we understand languages from a local perspective, once we see language ideologies as contextual sets of belief about languages, as cultural and political systems of ideas about social and linguistic relationships (Gal and Irvine, 1995; Irvine, 1989), then the ways in which languages are used and thought about are never just about language but also about community and society, what it means to be a person in a particular context (Woolard, 2004). The performative nature of hip-hop lyrics, therefore, may not only reflect local language conditions but may also actively resist current ways of thinking, and produce new ways of thinking about languages and their meaning. Rap, Auzanneau (2002) suggests, 'is a space for the expression of cultures and identities under construction'. Indeed, 'it is itself a space creating these identities and cultures, as well as codes and linguistic units that will ultimately be put into circulation beyond the songs. Rap thus reveals and participates in the unifying gregarity of the city's activities, and works with the city on the form, functions, and values of its languages' (p. 120). Mixing and sampling is a significant element of hip-hop culture, extending not only to the use of sound samples, different backing tracks and different instruments, but also to the mixing and sampling of languages. Just as lyrics may oppose social orthodoxies, the use of multiple languages may be purposive acts in opposition to ortholinguistic practices, performatively enacting new possibilities for language use and identity.

8   Hip-hop pedagogies and local knowledge

Midnight, the Manning Bar, Sydney University, 4 November 2005. The stage is dark; a figure sits cross-legged on the floor, rubbing a stick between his hands. The audience waits, watching the steady, rhythmic movement. A trail of smoke, a red glow; he blows on a piece of bark and then leaps up waving the smouldering material in his hands. The glow turns to a flame. At some point in the evening I had been musing on the connections between this place, the Manning Bar, and the great Australian historian Manning Clark, who magisterially pronounced at the beginning of his *A History of Australia* that 'Civilisation did not begin in Australia until the last quarter of the eighteenth century' (Clark, 1962, p. 3). Of course, it wasn't named after him – not even a historian of his status could have a bar named after his first name – but the name and the first line of his book resonate. Doubtless, 'civilisation' is meant here in a technical sense – the development of forms of farming and urban settlement with particular social hierarchies and divisions of labour – yet this emphasis on history as the story of civilizations while the rest is lumped into prehistory has always been a very particular vision of people and culture, discounting so many from participation in history. And this fire burning in the darkness on the stage is representing a different history, a history that goes way back further than the arrival of Europeans and their insidious civilization on the shores of Australia, a history of languages, cultures and knowledges that developed over thousands of years on this arid land.

Suddenly the fire is put out. Three MCs – Joel Wenitong (from the Gubbi Gubbi mob[1] from South West Queensland) and brothers Abie and Wok Wright (part of the Wonnurah, Gommeroy, Anawan and Djungutti mobs) of *Local Knowledge* – leap on to the stage, microphones in hand, the last act on the Klub Koori Night, an evening of indigenous Australian hip-hop. Hip-hop, suggests Wire MC, a Gumbayngirri descendant from Bowraville on the mid-north coast of New South Wales, is 'the "new corroboree"[2] for young indigenous Australians, who are looking for a way to express themselves and their culture in a positive way' (Vibe Australia, 2005). This argument immediately recalls the discussion in Chapter 7 about culture and tradition. What relations of culture, change and history are made possible here when hip-hop can be reclaimed as an indigenous cultural practice, or when hip-hop becomes a forum in which indigenous cultural practices can thrive? Lez Beckett's set this evening includes a 'Didge Battle', a battle between a traditionally dressed didgeridoo[3] player, his body painted, seated cross-legged on stage, and the DJ's didgeridoo samples. On the floor in front of the stage there is a break-dancing battle; then we switch back to traditional dance, an emu and a wallaby stalking around the darkened dance floor.

Many of the issues discussed in this book are at play here. If this seems a long way from the Atmosphere nightclub in Kuala Lumpur where I started this book, it is also, at another level, not so far at all. But if, on the other hand, it seems very close – another site of the homogenization of the world through the spread of such cultural practices – it is also a very long way away. Here we have hip-hop that is in complex ways both part of a global hip-hop movement, identifying with the anti-racist struggle of African Americans, using the appeal of a global youth subculture to draw in the young from the streets, yet also deeply local, drawing on oral traditions of aboriginal story-telling, using the transmodal practices of indigenous culture – music, story, dance, painting – to link the body, movement, culture and tradition. Here we see the mobilization of hip-hop as a local form of cultural expression; performance of identities that are refashioned on the stage and on the dance floor. Local Knowledge, the last act, call themselves 'Hip Hop Realists' who are 'telling it like it was, how it is and how it should be. It's rap about real issues and real passion' (Blaktrax, 2005), which takes us back to the discussion in Chapter 6 of authenticity and the global invocation to tell it locally like it is.

English is the dominant language of the evening, but this, as Local Knowledge (Interview, 21 October 2005) insist, is aboriginal English, a language that, as Malcolm (1994) asserts, is 'unique at all levels of linguistic description' (p. 291). Aboriginal English is one of those 'varieties' of English that receives little attention in the world Englishes framework. There are a number of reasons for this, as discussed in Chapter 2, including the orientation towards standardized varieties with a literary heritage (rendering Australian English as the named variety with aboriginal English as a non-standard subcategory, thereby overlooking colonial and postcolonial history, as well as the role of oral cultures); the focus centrally on new Englishes as manifestations of new nations (India, Malaysia, Nigeria, Singapore and so on) and thus the tendency to overlook the tensions surrounding ethnically and racially marked differences within different contexts, such as the difference between black and white South African English (Bruthiaux, 2003); and the inability to deal with creole languages and their speakers (Mufwene, 2001). A good case can be made to view aboriginal English not so much as a variety of Australian English but as an indigenous language that in some forms is mutually comprehensible with English (Eades, 1988, 2004, 2006; Harkins, 1994; Malcolm, 2000). To view aboriginal English as a creole, which, like

African American English, is comprehensible with standardized varieties of English at one level of the continuum, is to acknowledge this history of indigenous Australians' struggle for language and voice within a colonial context. This also ties this use of 'English' not to English-driven globalization but rather to the localized performance of identity through creoles (see Chapter 7). Aboriginal English here becomes part of the worldliness of English, part of the *créolité* defined by Confiant *et al.* Just as Glissant (1997) argues that while he may be separated from 'English-speaking' Caribbean writers such as Derek Walcott by his *langue* (French) but joined by their shared *langage* (what they speak about, their ways of speaking), so aboriginal English may in some ways have more to do with the Chavacano of Zamboanga hip-hop, the Haitian creole of Montreal hip-hop, the Cape Verde creole of Rotterdam hip-hop than the English of Australia.

Local Knowledge, winners of the 2005 Deadly Award[4] for Band of the Year, are carefully named. As Joel explains, they were trying to define what they were all about: 'teaching all the cultural knowledge in a way that's appealing to our young fellas, try to teach about traditional ways, and that life isn't about what a lot of young fellas think life is. And being local mob, being Indigenous mob here from Australia' (Interview, 20 October 2005).[5] The notion of *local knowledge* is a significant one within current postcolonial thinking. Canagarajah (2005) outlines various meanings of the term: from the beliefs and orientations of a community, to knowledge that is seen as unofficial, outside institutionally sanctioned knowledge (including knowledge that doesn't fit academic disciplines); and local or professional knowledge about ways of doing things. Across all these domains, he suggests, local knowledge is 'context-bound, community-specific, and non-systematic because it is generated ground-up through social practice in everyday life' (p. 4). One aspect of the transgressive theory discussed in Chapter 3 is to ask why one version of local knowledge (occidentalist) became non-local, and what kinds of local knowledge could usefully be brought back into play. As Canagarajah argues, this is a complex and difficult question, one that needs to avoid a search for pure traditional local knowledge but instead to work from the *locus of enunciation* (see Mignolo, 2000), to understand that the context from which we speak shapes the knowledge we produce. And this is what hip-hop can be so good at getting at.

The engagement with reality that Local Knowledge insist on is with cultural politics, with local knowledge in communities rather than imported knowledge. It is also about telling it like it should be, about the future. And when Joel explains that they are teaching about being local, it is clear that Local Knowledge are also educators, running 'heaps of workshops all over the country' (Interview, 20 October 2005). As Joel explains, one of the appeals of hip-hop is its orality and transmodality:

> in our communities it's the only form of communication; storytelling, music, dance, creative arts. All that sort of thing is the way we've

communicated and passed our knowledge, and that's one of the big reasons why hip-hop is huge in aboriginal communities. There isn't one aboriginal kid who doesn't like hip-hop because it's that oral communication that we're so used to over the thousands and thousands of years.

It is this theme of hip-hop and education that I shall address in this chapter, not only in terms of the move to bring musical lyrics into the classroom, but also in terms of this much wider use of hip-hop as a means to address young people, as a medium through which people can express themselves, and as a broad cultural movement that has major implications for issues of language, authorship and literacy.

From hip-hop voice to hiphopography

For the purposes of the discussion here I shall draw distinctions among a number of different ways in which popular culture has been taken up in education, from inclusion in the curriculum in order to increase motivation to broader incorporations of hip-hop culture, from informal learning outside educational institutions to hip-hop as a lived curriculum. For some, the inclusion of popular culture in the classroom may be a pragmatic choice aimed not so much at popular culture itself as at its motivational advantages (Beady, 2001) (music or film are often far more likely to attract the attention of students than more standard curricular fodder). These may be standard educational goals (literacy, interpretation, cultural criticism) with popular culture as the 'hook'. Many educational projects have further successfully brought hip-hop culture into the classroom not merely as a means to motivate students but also as a means to connect their outside worlds with what they are doing inside. Rahn's (2002) account of using graffiti in art classes with Cree students in North Quebec suggests that this brought not only motivation but also new forms of community in and outside the school, and connections between 'traditional skills, mentors, and codes' as well as the possibilities for transformation (p. 191). Baker (1991, 1993) meanwhile recounts how he was able to show a class of British high school students, who were struggling to find relevance in Shakespeare's *Henry V*, 'how Henry V was a rapper – a cold dissing, def con man, tougher than leather and smoother than ice, an artisan of words' (1991, p. 227). These and many other projects link the curriculum as normatively conceived to the wider world with which students are engaged.

Indigenous Australian hip-hopper MunkiMuk gives an example of how he uses rap to help students develop their literacy skills:

I was showing them things like rhyming, having a board there and saying what word rhymes with this word. I give them a word, like 'today I woke up and went to school' and ask what rhymes with school and they'll come back with all the 'ool' words, all of them having a go, spitting back all these words at ya. And then I say 'all right, now you've got all the words, let's put them into a sentence. What are we going to say about it?' and they might say 'cool' or something, and I go 'alright, we've got the word cool, it rhymes with school, but what are we going to do with cool?' And they'll come up and start giving you idea of sentences, and I'm trying to involve everyone.

(Interview, 4 November 2005)

Summarizing work on popular culture and education, Norton and Vanderheyden (2004) argue that 'if educators do not take seriously the social and cultural texts that are authorized by youth – which may simultaneously empower them – they run the risk of negating and silencing their students' (pp. 204–205). This critical pedagogical approach to popular culture 'seeks to validate the knowledge that students bring with them to the classroom, knowledge that is constructed within the practices of students' everyday lives outside the classroom' (p. 205). While the use of popular culture as a motivational tool or a means to teach other aspects of the curriculum may not focus on the culture of the popular itself, a critical pedagogical engagement with popular culture, by contrast, has argued that to exclude the popular from educational contexts is to reject student culture and difference. As Giroux and Simon (1989) put it, 'teachers need to find ways of creating a space for mutual engagement of lived difference that does not require the silencing of a multiplicity of voices by a single dominant discourse' (p. 24). In contrast to what Luke (1996) calls the 'logocentric' approaches to critical education that seek to impart what is assumed to be powerful knowledge to their recipients, this 'phonocentric' tradition is concerned primarily with fostering diversity, with allowing the non-powerful knowledges, cultures and voices of the disadvantaged to be heard. As Willis (2003) remarks, 'Educators and researchers should utilize the cultural experiences and embedded bodily knowledge of their students as starting points, not for bemoaning the failures and inadequacies of their charges, but to render more conscious for them what is unconsciously rendered in their cultural practices' (p. 413).

Norton and Vanderheyden go on to suggest that in the Canadian context of their study, lack of knowledge of popular culture may also be part of the marginalization of students from non-mainstream language and cultural backgrounds. Duff (2004) makes a similar point in her study of the infusion of popular cultural references in classroom discourse and the implications particularly for students from non-English-speaking backgrounds: 'Pop culture is a potentially rich, powerful and engaging classroom resource but one that is perhaps less globally accessible than is often assumed .... Even when accessible, the cultural references and English names may be unfamiliar to students' (p. 261). Since such students often lack the means and social networks to engage in forms of locally valued popular culture, they are left out of both formal (classroom references to cultural knowledge) and informal (youth culture) social, linguistic and cultural networks. From this point of view, therefore, the introduction of popular culture such as hip-hop into schools is a question of an inclusionary approach to education in which the languages and cultures of students are seen to be an essential part of any curriculum. As Norton and Vanderheyden (2004) and Duff (2004) suggest, however, students from non-mainstream backgrounds may not have easy access to the cultural resources of other students. It may be important, therefore, both to assist those students with gaining such access and to be cautious about assuming shared popular cultural references across a diverse student body.

The inclusion of popular culture in educational settings is not only a question of bringing cultural forms and practices into classrooms but also of a wider engagement with literacy and educational practices in the broader community. As Hull and Schultz (2001, p. 604) suggest in the context of literacy:

> Given the vast gulfs that separate and continue to widen between children and youth who flourish in school and those who do not, between the privileged and the disenfranchised, there is no better time for literacy theorists and researchers, long practiced in detailing the successful literate practices that occur outside school, to direct their energies toward investigating potential relationships, collaborations, and helpful divisions of labor between schools and formal classrooms and the informal learning that flourishes in a range of out-of-school settings.

Rather than taking the school–popular culture link therefore to be only one of using popular culture in the classroom, the argument here is that by learning from the multiple forms of education outside formal settings that use and work though the cultures of hip-hop, education may be greatly enriched.

If we take Preisler's (1999; and see Chapter 1) Danish break-dancers Out of Control with their English vocabulary of hip-hop terminology from windmills, back spins, turtles and back spreads to tags, bombs, jams, ciphers, burn-offs, cut-backs, cross-faders, hang-outs and low-lifes, we have a number of options. As Preisler (1999) points out in the Danish context, and as Ibrahim's (1999) example of African youths in Canada suggests, English may be learned as much through informal domains of popular culture as through formal classroom domains. Thus 'informal use of English – especially in the form of code-switching – has become an inherent, indeed a defining, aspect of the many Anglo-American-oriented youth subcultures which directly or indirectly influence the language and other behavioural patterns of young people generally' (p. 244). Our response to this may be to include this in the curriculum, or even, as Preisler paradoxically ends up arguing, to emphasize standard international English instead. More useful, however, is to try to understand how and why these young people have engaged with and learned from this cultural domain and what implications this may have for education more generally. We need other ways of thinking about popular cultural forms such as hip-hop beyond inclusion and validation in the curriculum.

Alim (2004) has developed what he calls 'hiphopography' in order to take advantage of the ways students engage with forms of language and culture outside school. Seeing how his students were attentive to language, style, sociolinguistic features and the role of hip-hop culture in their lives, he trained the ninth and eleventh grade students in 'ethnographic field methods (such as participant observation and interviewing) with the aim of helping them to document their own language and culture' (p. 9). These young 'hiphopographers' then documented the linguistic practices of the expressive hip-hop culture of their local community, including local terminology in the community such as 'Rogue', which is apparently limited to the local context around the high school (p. 240). These hiphopographies allowed these students to become far more aware of local language use, which was often gravely misunderstood by the local teachers. As a project in critical language awareness, or what Alim (in press b) has called Critical Hip Hop Language Pedagogies (CHHLP), this work helps students to discover how language is used in local contexts, how hip-hop language plays a particular role in creative expression, and what the implications are for the different forms of language used in different contexts (inside and outside school) and different communities.

The language of hip-hop is significant here for several reasons. As Alim (in press a) argues, and as I suggested in Chapter 7, it is often overtly used as an oppositional challenge to mainstream language ideologies. As Bauman and Briggs (1996; and see Chapter 4) argue, furthermore, performance invites critical reflection on communicative processes, drawing attention to speech as social action. In this view, then, verbal performances put language on display, making language available to scrutiny. The flows and mixes of Tasha, Rip Slyme, Zeebra or GHOST 13 discussed in Chapter 7, for example, make visible the possibility of a relationship between English and other languages that undermines the monolingual fallacies that underlie many assumptions about language pedagogy and identity. The changed spellings, the word plays, the rhymes bring language to the fore. From the titles of groups – Teh Tarik Crew, juxtaposing a Malay tea style with a hip-hop crew, Rip Slyme with their Japanese reversal of 'Lips Rhyme' (the title of their first hit), New Caledonian Section Otoktone with their reference to indigeneity, or Local Knowledge, bringing together both ethnography and indigenous politics – to the lyrics of tracks that bring issues of language culture and identity to the fore – from Daara J's 'Born in Africa, growing up in America, rap has just gone around to come back' (Boomerang) to Chinese American Jin's track 'Learn Chinese', where he declares 'Y'all gonna learn Chinese' and 'Every time they harass me, I wanna explode/We should ride the train for free/We built the railroads' (Jin, 2004) or ADF's 'Dis is England's new voice/Censorship for years/But now dem have no choice/Running thru de playground/We could never have known/Dat in de future/Our role models would be home grown' (New Way/New Life), or many, many other examples – the hip-hop world puts language on display.

According to Rose (1994), rap should be seen not as having some primordial oral origins as if it simply emerged from African American oral practices or links back in an unbroken line of orality to African cultures. Drawing on Walter Ong's notion of 'postliterate orality' to describe 'orally influenced traditions that are created and embedded in a postliterate, technologically sophisticated context' (Rose, 1994, p. 86), Rose draws attention to the ways in which rap music 'blurs the distinction between literate and oral modes of communication' (p. 85). Rather, she suggests, the lyrical skills of MC-ing suggest a more complex form of *postliterate orality* produced amid complex literacy skills and in a culture of sampling and borrowing. Rap lyrics put language on display, make features of rhyme, rhythm, dialect and difference salient in ways that other textual formations may not. Rap therefore presents a significant tool for language awareness. As I suggested in Chapter 7, the language shifts and mixes used by various performers are by no means unintentional or mere reflections of local traditions. As Auzanneau (2002) points out, the rappers in Libreville were very aware of what they were doing. Thus the verbal performance of rap is in itself an explicit engagement with language, form and style that can be a significant tool for developing language awareness. An interesting example of this is the track 'Bakardi Slang' on Kardinal Offishall's *Quest for Fire*, which plays on the differences between African American and Caribbean language styles of Toronto (T Dot) rappers:

> We don't say, 'You know what I'm sayin''
> T dot say's 'Ya dun know'
> We don't say, 'hey that's the breaks'
> We say 'Yo, a so it go'

The whole track is constructed around this comparison of linguistic styles. Whether used formally as a pedagogical tool or in its more general use as a tool of linguistic awareness, such highlighting of linguistic difference is of particular use for a meta-understanding of language. As Bronwen Low (2001) argues, also drawing on Kardinal Offishall's lyrics, rap of this sort is important not only as a tool for engaging student interests but also 'as a site of knowledge about contemporary currents in poetry' (p. 15). The spoken poetry of rap, it seems, may be affecting current language use, having played an important role in the re-emergence of poetry as performance (culminating, for example, in the development of *Def Poetry Jam*[6]), which has in turn spawned the development of *poetry slams*. As Sydney poet Jess Stalenberg says, 'If you listen to a lot of new poets, a lot of them have a very strong rhyme .... It's the funky new thing to have a rhyme, a rhythm, a bit of free-style freedom in what you're saying, and that all comes from hip-hop' (cited in Lobley, 2004, p. 5).

Low (2001) goes on to suggest that if 'education can consider rappers not only as poets but as theorists and agents of linguistic and communicative change' (p. 28), the language of rap may be used to explore a range of questions to do with standard languages, stigmatized varieties, orality, literacy and so on. For MunkiMuk, this is also part of a broader agenda to do with language choice:

> Because American culture and influence is a big thing, and because hip-hop is an American thing – just to show them you can do it with an Australian accent, or, if you actually speak in native tongue then you can rap in your native language. Once they see me do it, they start getting into it and rapping in their own tongue. For some of these people, English is like their fifth language, so I try to get them to do it in lingo. And there's a whole bunch of kids out there who are rapping in lingo these days, which you've got to love.
>
> (Interview, 4 November 2005)

These projects in language awareness, hiphopography, rapping in lingo, do several things. Rather than viewing hip-hop as a hook to motivate students or as a cultural archive to be included in the curriculum, they look outward into the larger world of which classrooms are a part. As they do so, they shift a sense of what school knowledge is and of how it relates to the larger context. As Rupa Huq (2001a) notes in the context of using French rap in French classes, the messages, languages and ethnicities of French rap are 'redefining what it is to be French' (p. 75). Ibrahim's (2001) 'pedagogy of the imaginary', drawing on bell hooks's (1994) transgressive pedagogy discussed in Chapter 3, points to the 'horizon of possibilities of using Black cultural productions, particularly musical, literary, and cinematic represen-tations, as moments of rupture to what hooks calls "colonial imperialist paradigms" where Black identities are represented "one-dimensionally"' (p. 98). Here, hip-hop pedagogies are being used to transgress, rupture and change how identities are defined through language. The transgressive arts of hip-hop present rich possibilities for such transformative pedagogies.

Hip-hop culture, broadly understood, provides a very particular cultural and ideological background as transgressive art, as a challenge to norms of language, identity and ownership. Aspects of this broad cultural formation include 'an enthusiastic embracing of new technology and mass culture, a challenging of modernist notions of aesthetic autonomy and artistic purity, and an emphasis on the localised and temporal rather than the putatively universal and eternal' (Shusterman, 2000, p. 61). Of particular interest, however, is the 'recycling appropriation rather than unique originative creation, an eclectic mixing of styles' (ibid.), or what Potter calls 'the relentless sampling of sonic and verbal archives' (1995, p. 53). DJ Spooky (aka That Subliminal Kid) (Miller, 2004) describes sampling as 'a new way of doing something that's been with us for a long time: creating with found objects. The rotation gets thick. The constraints get thin. The mix breaks free of the old associations' (p. 25). As he goes on to argue, 'creativity rests in how you recontextualize the previous expression of others, a place where there is no such thing as an "immaculate perception"' (p. 33). Echoing the ideas of Bakhtin (1981, 1986) and Barthes (1977), this argument challenges notions of authorship, originality and creativity.

Rahn (2002) similarly observes that 'biting' – the graffiti writers' term for copying other people's work – is 'completely accepted as a way to transfer knowledge and is considered a form of flattery to copy one's mentor' (p. 206). While this is not always the case – 'biting' often carries negative connotations of inappropriate borrowing – the sampling culture of hip-hop does suggest different ways of understanding ownership and creativity. DJ Spooky's notion of recontextualizing the previous expression of others and Rahn's contention that copying a mentor is a sign of flattery may even for some bring echoes of what has often been described (sometimes derided) as 'Confucian' ways of learning and respecting authority (for a critique of these discourses, see Kubota, 1999, 2004). Aside from the irony that hip-hop culture may be mobilizing supposedly Confucian-style forms of imitation and respect, it is worth observing that hip-hop pedagogy may be reinvesting in traditional forms of learning and imitation. As Christen (2003) shows, organized graffiti crews 'resemble medieval guilds or trade unions, with apprentices assisting on works designed by masters, often painting backgrounds and filling in outlines in preparation for the finer detailed work' (p. 63). While graffiti may for some appear too transgressive an activity to engage with educationally, it nevertheless may embody what may also be seen as traditional pedagogical forms. On the other hand, if we note the discussion in Chapter 6 about imitation as a form of re-enactment, a recontextualization that produces something new, it could also be argued that the emphasis on imitation is equally an engagement with the contemporary, post-authorial era (see Pennycook, 1996).

Rice's (2003) 'hip-hop pedagogy' of writing based around a 'whatever pedagogy' of hip-hop takes up issues of digital borrowing by developing 'a writing practice that models itself after digital sampling's rhetorical strategy of juxtaposition' (p. 453). Starting with the premise that 'teaching research-based argumentation and critique in composition studies is like learning how to perform hip-hop music' (p. 453), Rice's choice of hip-hop 'as a model for the composition essay' is an 'attempt to draw upon a dominant form of contemporary culture familiar to the majority of students I encounter in my classrooms' (p. 453). Thus this is not an attempt to validate knowledge embedded in hip-hop culture but rather to engage with a set of styles, beliefs and practices that are part of hip-hop. Rice focuses on 'the way hip-hop constructs discourse, the way it produces rhetorical meaning through its complex method of digital sampling, and how such a rhetoric functions within he scope of argumentation' (p. 454). Rice relates Barthes's understanding of how texts draw together words from the tissues of culture around them to hip-hop's sampling of 'whatever': 'The coincidental overlap of Barthes's and hip-hop's usage of the whatever leads me to look to both for instructions on how to create this unnamed way of writing' (p. 458). He concludes that the alternative practices in hip-hop pedagogy are a place to begin questioning 'our ability to resist dominant modes of thinking, to engage with consumerism while working against it, to spark the resistance, whatever' (p. 469).

More broadly, the point here is that hip-hop is part of a cultural movement that challenges notions of origins, ownership and authorship. As has been argued in the context of plagiarism (Chandrasoma *et al.*, 2004; Pennycook, 1996) there is good cause to rethink the ways in which we consider textual ownership in the current era, acknowledging that all texts are constituted through intertextual relationships. More broadly still, the argument here is that hip-hop both produces and is produced by a cultural context that often thinks differently about questions of language, writing, identity and ownership from the mainstream discourses of the academy. As we saw in the previous chapters, hip-hoppers may have very different ideas about what it means for something to be real, how they relate to communities, how language operates. To the extent that this broad cultural movement influences youth in different ways across the world – always appropriated, always locally inflected – it is important that educators take this into account. Inclusion in the curriculum from this point of view, therefore, is not so much a question of using lyrics or discussing issues in popular culture as it is about engaging much more broadly with a cultural movement that has many different inflections across the globe.

'Down with' Dewey and the lived curriculum

While an important first step in dealing with popular culture is to get beyond the dismissive hierarchies of high and low culture, or the tendencies to view popular culture as only commercial, as 'mere entertainment', it is equally important to understand it as much more than a motivational tool or a bank of knowledge to be validated and incorporated into a school curriculum. McCarthy *et al.* (1999) note, 'Contemporary curriculum and educational researchers writing on the topic of schooling have tended to ignore the critical role played by popular culture in the production of the differential social identities of school youth' (p. 1). While conservative discourses have eschewed any engagement with popular culture, decrying it as corruptive of young minds and attempting to ban it from any educational context, more inclusive educationalists have overlooked ways in which popular music is 'at the epicenter of practices of discursive identity formation for the young'

(p. 2). Popular culture has to do with desire, mobility and multiple identifications: the ways in which people relate to style (clothing, music, looking cool), to community (friends, enemies, in-groups, out-groups), to pleasure (listening, watching, feeling, being liked), to images of how to be in the world (sexy, sporty, smart). It has to do with complex ways in which we construct our identities both on a level of choice to associate with certain people, sounds, images and lifestyles, and with more basic preferences and desires.

As discussed in Chapter 5, the 'fifth element' in hip-hop is sometimes described as knowledge. As Afrika Bambaataa puts it, 'there is only one school and that's the learning, evolving, going through the different phases or cycles school of hip-hop. That is the real hip-hop school' (Bambaataa, 2005). Thus it might be argued that the fifth element of hip-hop is best conceived of not as knowledge but as the process by which knowledge is acquired, namely education.[7] It is no coincidence that Daara J chose for themselves a name that can be translated as 'school of life'. As discussed in the previous chapters, there are very real reasons why we should take hip-hop seriously as a cultural, political, philosophical and educational movement. Shusterman (2000) argues that 'rap philosophers are really "down with" Dewey, not merely in metaphysics but in a noncompartmentalized aesthetics which highlights social function, process, and embodied experience' (p. 73). Shusterman's principal interest here is the relation between rap and Dewey's pragmatist philosophy of aesthetics. For Dewey (1959 [1934]), aesthetics needed to be more broadly understood, taken away from the limited domain of high art, and brought instead into the realm of the everyday. Aesthetics is about *experiencing* beauty and pleasure. Similarly, Dewey's (1966 [1916]) educational philosophy was centred around a view that we learn by doing, that education should not be abstracted from daily life, that learning was a social activity, and that education should be about the education of the whole person as learner, person and citizen. From this point of view, then, we can start to see hip-hop not as a means to do pedagogy but as pedagogy itself.

Popular culture may be understood as part of a way of life, a bodily orientation, a habitus, rather than curricular knowledge. To think of hip-hop in pedagogical terms, therefore, requires an understanding of popular culture as a site of pedagogy. As Dimitriadis points out, 'contemporary youth are increasingly fashioning notions of self and community outside of school in ways that educators have largely ignored' (2001, p. xi). Ibrahim's (1999) research on the ways in which African students studying in a Franco-Ontarian school in Canada identify with forms of hip-hop shows that it is their identification outside the classroom with forms of African American culture that drive their identifications through English. As these students enter the racialized world of North America, they 'become Black', starting to redefine their identities in terms of the available social and cultural categories on the new continent. In doing so, they increasingly start to identify with forms of black culture and black language, particularly hip-hop and black English. Rap and hip-hop, he shows, are 'influential sites in African students' processes of becoming Black, which in turn affected what and how the students learned' (p. 364). The choice of these cultural forms and the position on the margins associated with being Black was 'simultaneously an act of investment, an expression of desire, and a deliberate counterhegemonic undertaking' (p. 365). In this sense, as Dimitriadis (2001) argues, hip-hop is 'a lived curriculum, one which has suffused young people's lives in ways that belie the kinds of formal and distant identifications we might expect from more traditional educational practices' (p. 124).

Hip-hop has therefore become a vehicle for a wide range of educational projects. As Pardue comments in the Brazilian context, 'Hip-hoppers have become increasingly persuasive that their work is educational because they reach large populations of urban youth that previously were isolated from public education' (Pardue, 2004, p. 412). This occurs in a number of ways: hip-hop workshops typically run for youths in local community contexts may focus on aspects of the music industry, developing skills in literacy, break-dancing, music or graffiti, or on hip-hop as a means of local expression. As Phreaze (Jay), the facilitator of a hip-hop workshop in Sydney explains, 'the main thing is just to get them to use their vocab. Because that's the main thing when it comes to lyricism, like, especially now when people are rapping about crap [laughs], you know ... about chains and money and you know, like just rubbish and one syllable words throughout their entire song' (Interview, 14 September 2005). Thus the focus for the disadvantaged youths attending this workshop (many of aboriginal and Islander origin, some already with a history of drug use and detention), is on both localizing the focus away from the culture of bling, and developing the means to articulate local experiences in more complex ways.

A number of hip-hop groups have become involved in local educational initiatives, where their popularity and relation to local understanding can be effective in addressing issues from drug abuse to violence. Much of Local Knowledge's educational work is via workshops aimed to address specific concerns in local communities. Joel describes one workshop they did as part of a programme to address issues of domestic violence:

> heaps of the kids who were in Juve [Juvenile detention] were into hip-hop so they wanted to use that to teach these kids – not just offenders, and they were all mainstream, not just indigenous kids – what is sexual assault, that it's not just rape, but it's also things like saying stuff about females that are inappropriate. So I came in and got them all to put it into songs and it was really successful because then the songs got put on radio. So the kids themselves became the ambassadors for this kind of issue, and it was good, especially when a lot of them were themselves offenders.

Detention centres (prison, juvenile detention) are a significant site for hip-hop work. As Joel notes, many young people in detention are into hip-hop and this gives them an important means of learning and expression. As one indigenous participant in the Back 2 da Lab 2 workshop[8] put it, he has 'thought of heaps of songs, but haven't wrote them down yet. Yeh, still got them in me head. So, like, haven't wrote them down, cause I'm still working on my beat, yeh.' Many of the songs were formed in 'juve': 'When you're locked up and shit, y'know. You 're kicking back in your room, y'know. Can't think about your family and shit. So all you can do is talk about it. Yeh, I just put it in my rap rhymes. It's the way I put it anyway' (Interview, 15 September 2005).[9]

Pardue's (2004) study of hip-hop 'as an alternative system of education' in Brazil also focuses on juvenile detention workshops, where 'hip-hoppers and psychologists alike argued that hip-hop is *um meio* (a vehicle) through which education can be effective' (p. 417) . These workshops, run by posse Hausa, focused on issues such as sexually transmitted diseases and HIV/AIDS. Hip-hop instructors in the youth prison (FEBEM) Pardue studied

> did not necessarily intend or believe that students would become rappers, DJs, graffiti artists, or B-boys. Rather, the hip-hop elements were viewed as vehicles to open up FEBEM youth to other ways of interacting with the world. Through activities involving composition, language, sound, images, and body movement, hip-hop instructors urged the FEBEM youth to reconsider their places and roles in life.
>
> (Pardue, 2004, p. 424)

From this perspective, then, hip-hop pedagogy is a vehicle to reach young people not only to educate on specific topics (domestic violence, drug use, sexually transmitted diseases) or to develop intellectual and somatic skills (music, literacy, dance), but also as a means to broaden an understanding of one's position in life. 'Brazilian hip-hoppers implicitly employ a Freirean approach to education as they insist that the experience of misery, racism, poverty, and violence is a legitimate departure for learning' (Pardue, 2004, p. 429). Hip-hop pedagogy thus becomes a means for an engagement with far more than music, writing and dancing: it is about reconsidering one's place in life.

While these workshops use hip-hop to engage young people through informal pedagogical interactions, we can also view hip-hop activities themselves as educational. 'Although seldom recognized as such', Christen (2003) notes, 'graffiti crews are also educational organizations that promote valuable learning among their members' (p. 58). Invoking John Dewey's (1966) description of peer learning groups as aiming to influence the mental and moral disposition of their members, Christen observes that while graffiti crews were originally designed to support the painting of 'pieces' (graffiti terminology for art works, from masterpieces), they become organizations where more experienced members pass on their skills and knowledge to their eager disciples. Indeed, as noted above, these crews operate in some ways like medieval guilds. Graffiti, he argues, 'provides poor and disadvantaged adolescents with knowledge, skills, and values important for success in the mainstream. At the same time, it bonds young people to their urban neighborhoods, empowering them to challenge the dominant society and to transform rather than escape their communities' (p. 58). The education in such crews is therefore both conservative and transgressive, teaching skills that may be used in other contexts as well as a critical understanding of social power and the possibility for alternatives.

Söderman and Folkestad (2004), in their study of informal learning by Swedish MCs, conclude that 'the changeable element of hip-hop fits well with the educational discourse of *life-long learning*' (p. 325). They also point out that the re-emergence of the Greek notion of *mousiké* in Scandinavian educational discourse, referring to the integration of dance, visual arts, music and literature, links in interesting ways with the elements of hip-hop culture. Just as hip-hop gives us a more integrated and transmodal mode of engagement, and, as we saw in the previous chapter in the discussion of how such transmodal integration may link back to traditional cultural ways of doing things (as Trey argued in the case of Fiji, for example; see Chapter 7), so we might suggest here that hip-hop pedagogies link not only to Deweyan notions of pragmatic philosophy, aesthetics and education, and to Freirean-based transformative pedagogies, but also to Greek concepts of integrated action (which, of course, as Daara J, drawing on Senegalese thinker Cheikh Anta Diop's arguments, pointed out in Chapter 7, takes us ultimately back to Egypt and to Africa), and to local pedagogies everywhere, from Fiji to aboriginal Australia, from Cree students in North Quebec (see Rahn, 2002) to students in detention centres in Brazil. And as it links, it also transforms, changing the nature of those cultural forms it appropriates.

Hip-hop pedagogies, therefore, are not just about using popular culture as a motivational factor in the curriculum; nor are they to do only with the inclusion of student culture in the curriculum and the development of voice; they do not stop either at issues of awareness raising, of helping students to understand the connections between the languages of the street and the codes of education. The transcultural contexts, transmodal practices and transtextual understandings of language made possible by the transgressive art of hip-hop open up new ways of thinking about education that are not merely to do with experiential or lifelong learning, about informal education in the streets, but rather offer a new and transgressive set of opportunities for connecting education, the streets, disadvantage, language and culture. Hip-hop rethreads the lines of tradition, making it possible simultaneously to engage in these global cultural practices and to reinvent connections to local practices. By putting language on display, by mixing languages in new and inventive combinations, by drawing connections across time and space, hip-hop enables the refashioning of social futures.

Transgressive hip-hop pedagogies, therefore, redraw the lines of language, learning and engagement.

Teaching with the flow

According to McCarthy *et al.* (2003, p. 462),

> the great task confronting educators as we move into the 21st century is to address the radical reconfiguration and cultural rearticulation now taking place in educational and social life. These developments are foregrounded and driven by the logics of globalization, the intensification of migration, the heightened effects of electronic media, the proliferation of images, and the everyday work of the imagination. All these developments have shifted the commonly taken-for-granted stabilities of social constructs such as 'culture,' 'identity,' 'nation,' 'state,' and so forth.

This book has been trying to open up these questions through an exploration of the global spread of hip-hop and the global spread of English. Both, I have been arguing, have major implications for education: English presents us not only with basic pedagogical questions of form and access – what should be taught to whom – but also with questions of how cultural forms are interrelated with language use, and how the appropriation of language and culture presents different possibilities for imagined identities, imagined traditions and imagined languages.

As Willis (2003) suggests, working-class youth in the UK 'find more passion and acceptable self-identity through music on MTV, wearing baseball caps and designer shoes, and socializing in fast-food joints than they do through traditional class-based forms' (p. 402). As we have seen at numerous points in this book, this is equally true of different youth around the world (with obvious caveats concerning class and culture): Too Phat were guests at a South East Asia MTV show, wore their baseball caps at the right angle, had a good collection of footwear (from Jordans to Air Force Ones) and were happy to hang out in fast-food joints. This is the new global world of refashioned youth identifications. At the same time, of course, Too Phat's fast-food joints included Chinese and Indian food stalls, plates of fried kuey tow and roti canai, and, as I suggested in Chapter 6, their shoes were fast becoming local. My argument here is that as educators we need to grasp the different digital worlds of identification that our students inhabit as well as this interplay between the flow, fixity and fluidity of culture, language and identity.

Popular culture not only raises the question of the permeability of classroom walls (Pennycook, 2000b) (discourses and identities are constructed across the educational boundaries of walls, desks, tests and texts) but also links students across time and space. As Connell and Gibson (2003, p. 271) suggest, music forms 'transnational networks of affiliation, and of material and symbolic interdependence .... Music nourishes imagined communities, traces links to distant and past places.' The fluidity and (downloadable) availability of music, its link to place and imagined community, and the possibilities it presents for diverse identifications, render popular culture a more dynamic space than one of knowledge validation, curricular inclusion or community engagement. A brief analogy may be useful here. In his discussion of anthropological frames for looking at culture, Clifford (1997) compares the colonial tradition of 'living among fellow whites, calling up "informants" to talk culture in an encampment or on a veranda, sallying forth to "do the village"' (p. 20) with the subsequent move from the balcony to the ethnographer's tent, with anthropologists required 'to live full time in the village, learn the language, and be a seriously involved participant observer' (p. 20). And yet, as Clifford notes, this era of anthropology 'represented a powerful localizing strategy: centering "the culture" around a particular locus, "the village," and a certain spatial practice of dwelling/ research which itself ... depended on a complementary localization – that of "the field"' (p. 20). The research location – typically a village – became a bounded site, the place in which culture existed. What is missing here, suggests Clifford, is 'the wider global world of intercultural import–export in which the ethnographic encounter is always already enmeshed' (p. 23). Rather than the localizing strategy of the field, Clifford argues for the image of 'travel', with its emphasis on movement, encounter and change, for 'once the representational challenge is seen to be the portrayal and understanding of local/global historical encounters, co-productions, dominations, and resistances, then one needs to focus on hybrid, cosmopolitan experiences as much as on rooted, native ones' (p. 24).

We could conduct a similar mapping of understandings of education. While educational research has commendably moved from 'black box' views of classrooms as sites of measurable input and output to understandings of education as a complex site of cultural encounter, the next step – to move beyond the localizing strategy of the field – is still under way. For Clifford, the image of cultural encounter is not so much the tent in the village but rather 'a hotel lobby, urban café, ship, or bus' (p. 25). Centrally, then, the focus is on culture as travel rather than place, on movement, change and mixing, on encounters between people on different trajectories. There is no longer a space here to assume that while the anthropologist may have travelled to 'get there', the people he or she encounters have always 'been there'. For education, then, the representational challenge is the portrayal and understanding of local/global historical encounters, co-productions, dominations and resistances; the focus is not so much on the bounded culture of educational institutions as on hybrid, cosmopolitan (or tropicopolitan) experiences. From this point of view, the locus of educational encounter is not the village culture of the classroom observed from the ethnographer's seat in the corner, but rather the educational equivalent of the hotel lobby, ship or bus: the shopping mall, skateboarding scene or fast-food hangout. The point, however, is not just to relocate our pedagogical gaze to the street, but to understand the fluidity, fixity and flow of cultural movement. The examples at the end of Chapter 7 – where Trey reconnects to Fijian cultural practices, Too Phat are the modern descendants of traditional Tukang Karut singers, K'Naan draws inspiration from Somali oral poetry, ADF are moving their parents' culture along, and Islamic Force are heirs to the traditions of *halk ozani* minstrels in seventeenth-century Turkey – in conjunction with the circuits of flow that enable hip-hoppers to see themselves as part of a multidimensional world, enable a very different image of cultural engagement.

This is also why the issues of performance and performativity discussed in Chapter 4 are so important here. On the one hand, we can start to see how the embodied engagement with language performances creates a far deeper set of affective and emotional affiliations than the rationalist projects of standard language curricula. On the other hand, a performative understanding of language suggests that identities are formed in the linguistic performance rather than pregiven, and that language use is an act of identity which calls that language into being. The notion of performativity, then, can take us beyond views of language and identity that tie them to location and origins, and instead opens up possibilities for seeing how languages, identities and futures are constantly being refashioned. In both the claims that hip-hop is a language itself, a language that transcends assumed divisions between languages, and the mixing of English with other languages, we can see the performative possibilities of a constantly shifting range of identifications. Engagement with hip-hop, Ibrahim (2001) suggests, is about being 'able to "see" multiple ways of speaking, being, and learning' (p. 99). To teach with the flow, then, suggests not so much an incorporation of hip-hop texts into the curriculum as an opening up of possible languages and identities, an engagement with multiple ways of speaking, being and learning.

As Willis says with respect to popular culture more broadly, and as I would argue with respect to hip-hop, its educational acceptance 'does not mean a lazy throwing open of the school doors to the latest fad, but rather committing to a principled understanding of the complexity of contemporary cultural experience' (Willis, 2003, p. 411). The location of classrooms within global transcultural flows implies that they can no longer be considered as bounded sites, with students entering from fixed locations, with identities drawing on local traditions, with curricula as static bodies of knowledge. Popular music, as Connell and Gibson (2003) argue, unsettles common distinctions between the local and global, the traditional and contemporary, and reflects the flows, fluxes and fluidity of life in an era of globalization. Students refuse attempts to be pinned down, despite the array of educational technologies (tests, uniforms, architecture, psychological theories of identity) designed to do so. Popular music 'remains an important cultural sphere in which identities are affirmed, challenged, taken apart and reconstructed' (Connell and Gibson, 2003, p. 117). If we believe that education needs to proceed by taking student knowledge, identity and desire into account, we need to engage with multiple ways of speaking, being and learning, with multilayered modes of identity at global, regional, national and local levels.

Unless we get in touch with this as educators, the flow will pass us by. We will end up like a bookstore at an international airport, selling whatever goods passing travellers feel may fill their empty travel time. Languages will flow and change around us, new combinations of languages and cultures will be put together, texts will be sampled and mixed in ever new juxtapositions. Students are in the flow; pedagogy needs to go with the flow.

Notes

1 Hip hop be connectin'

1 Too Phat are Malique Ibrahim (Mista Malique) and Johan Ishak (Joe Flizzow).
2 Lyrics from 'Just a lil' bit' featuring Warren G, from *360°*. Positive Tone (2002).
3 I have chosen to write the term 'hip-hop' in this form throughout the book except where used differently (without the hyphen as 'hip hop', for example) in quotations. The term *hip-hop* is generally used to refer to the broad cultural formation of rap, break-dancing, graffiti and DJ-ing, though it also sometimes refers more restrictedly to rap. In this book I try to use the term always to refer to the broader culture, though the focus on rap music at times restricts this usage.
4 'If I die tonight' feautring Liyana, *360°*. Positive Tone (2002). The track is a reference to, and includes a sample from, 2Pac's 'If I die 2Nite'.
5 Interestingly, this Malaysian dance form has its origins in Portuguese folk dance, dating from the Portuguese occupation of Malacca.
6 I coined this term in Pennycook (2003a) to refer to the combination of rap and English, but like the other terms discussed here (e.g. Blinglish), I feel it does not adequately capture the complexity of the issues at stake.
7 Ala Canggung (do you wanna have a party?) featuring Lil' Marissa, from *360°*. I am indebted to Lee Su Kim for linguistic and cultural assistance with these and other Malaysian lyrics.

Translation
You are attracted to the lyrics, they make you feel good
Mr Malique, Joe Flizzow and T-Bone spit it out cool
Our hit is really great, can make people move
The modern Master, when he tells stories, is bound to create happiness
This is the band that will get rid of all feelings of sadness
First time, just brilliant, I am rapping in Malay

2 Other Englishes

1 I have categorized these different approaches to the global spread of English in various ways, including not only the homogeny versus heterogeny positions but also in terms of liberal pluralism, linguistic imperialism, language rights and so forth (see Pennycook, 1999, 2000a).
2 These issues are partly addressed in their later book, *Multitude* (Hardt and Negri, 2004).
3 Mignolo uses the French, Spanish and Portuguese terms. In common use the two terms are more or less synonymous. I have translated *mondialization* here as *worldliness,* a term I used in earlier attempts (e.g. 1994) to deal with these issues

to cover both globalization and worldliness. It may be a more effective term in the more limited sense I am trying to give it here.

4 Mignolo also uses the term in the sense that Occidentalism pre-dated orientalism, that the *Indias Occidentales* became part of the European imaginary before its engagement with the East. Given the European history of Crusades, trade and exploration in 'the East' prior to this era of colonialism, however, this argument may need modification. A different sense of Occidentalism is given by Chen (1995) for whom Occidentalism is a Chinese, or other Asian, construction of its Western other: 'As a result of constantly revising and manipulating imperialistically imposed Western theories and practices, the Chinese Orient has produced a new discourse marked by a particular combination of the Western construction of China with the Chinese construction of the West, with both of these components interacting and interpenetrating each other'(pp. 4–5).

3 Transgressive theories

1 The *ruud bwai* 'is a figure – young, urban, black and angry – that has come to haunt the middle-class imaginary of post-independence Jamaica, a figure signifying not merely a lack of the esteemed rationality and preferred values of respectable society but a positive contempt for, and refusal of, them' (Scott, 1999, p. 210).

2 *Jouissance* is usually left untranslated into English, sitting as it does somewhere between and beyond pleasure and desire. It has been widely used by many French scholars from Lacan, Derrida and Barthes to Kristeva, Irigaray and Cixous.

4 Performance and performativity

1 My translations from the French. Italics are in the original.

5 Taking the vernacular voices of the popular seriously

1 For example, Adams and Winter (1997), Alim (2002, 2003, 2004, 2006) Auzanneau (2002, 2003), Cutler (1999), Hill (1995, 1998, 1999), Newman (2001, 2005), Rampton (1995, 1999).

2 The level of debate around such concerns in applied linguistics (e.g. in Seidlhofer, 2003) lacks the sophistication of understanding to be found in cultural studies.

3 Cited in Scott, 1999 (pp. 215–216). I am tempted to leave this 'untranslated' in the context of the discussion in Chapter 2 of other Englishes. Does it disqualify this as English if it has to be translated? Nevertheless, for the record: We refuse to be what you wanted us to be/We are what we are/that's the way it's going to be/(if you don't know)/You can't educate us for no equal opportunity/Talking 'bout my freedom/People/freedom and liberty.

4 See Chapter 3. The *ruud bwai* is the black urban and angry youth of post-independence Jamaica, expressing contempt for the middle-class tropes of rationality and respectable society (Scott, 1999, p. 210).

5 Teh Tarik, literally 'pulled tea', is a popular drink in Malaysia, usually bought at outdoor stalls. It is made from tea and condensed milk and gets its name from the manner of pouring the tea from a height, creating a froth. This and other quotes from artists in the following chapters is drawn from the ARC-funded Research Project, Postoccidental Englishes and Rap.

6 The other two are a collapsing of the distinction between 'consumption' and 'production', with 'profound implications for questions of audience and authenticity'; and a 'situatedness within a long and complex musical continuum' (Potter, 1995, p. 53).

7 All translations from the German are my own for articles in Androutsopoulos (2003).

6 English and the global spread of authenticity

1 Senegalese singer Youssou N'Dour's CD *Coono du Réér* (*Nothing's in Vain*) has songs in Wolof (Sagal Ko – Honour Her), French (C'est l'amour – It's Love) and English (So Many Men). Angélique Kidjo (2001), from Benin, described as 'a bonafide global phenonenon' whose musical style encompasses 'afro-funk, reggae, samba, salsa, gospel, jazz, zairean rumba, souk and makossa' (CD cover), includes tracks in Fon, Yoruba, French and English.
2 The feeling of existence or being. The term is from Jean-Jacques Rousseau, and connects also to Heidigger's *Sein* and *Dasein*, and Sartre's *l'etre*.
3 This is similar in some ways to Foucault's (1970) project, which also sought, as Dreyfus and Rabinow (1982) explained it, to get beyond the structuralist assumption of overarching order and the hermeneutic position that gives absolute priority to the observing subject. It is intriguing, therefore, given Fairclough's (2003) position on critical realism, that it was in many ways this relation between structuralism and hermeneutics that has been played out repeatedly in the debates between Fairclough and Widdowson over critical discourse analysis (see Seidlhofer, 2003).
4 As Bhaskar goes on to explain, his position 'entails acceptance of (i) the principle of *epistemic relativity*, which states that all beliefs are socially produced, so that all knowledge is transient, and neither truth-values nor criteria of rationality exist outside historical time. But it entails the rejection of (ii) the doctrine of *judgemental relativism,* which maintains that all beliefs are equally valid, in the sense that there can be no rational grounds for preferring one to another. It thus stands opposed to epistemic absolutism and epistemic irrationalism alike. Relativists have wrongly inferred (ii) from (i), while anti-relativists have wrongly taken the unacceptability of (ii) as a *reductio* of (i)' (1989, pp. 23–24).
5 The Malay term *rojak*, meaning mixture or salad – typically a mix of pineapple, cucumber, tofu and *jicama* in a *belacan* sauce – is used commonly to refer to the multicultural and multilingual mixture of Malaysian society.
6 Underground Indonesian rap artists Balcony and Homicide (2003) use both Indonesian and English in their lyrics.
7 There is a nice irony here, however, given that the group with the Malay music have called themselves Too Phat, while the group rejecting such forms of localization have nevertheless embedded themselves locally with the name Teh Tarik Crew.
8 This and other data from Australian contexts is drawn from a second Australian Research Council (ARC)-funded project, *Local Noise: Indigenising Hip Hop in Australasia* (DP055937) with Tony Mitchell.
9 This feels like a translation of the Japanese *tokorode*, a phrase whose register differs somewhat from the English 'by the way'.

7 Language flows, language mixes

1 The cover of King Kapisi's 'Samoan hip-hop worldwide' album *Savage Thoughts* depicts Kapisi walking on water, an image that recalls the well-known chapel window in St Faith's church in Rotorua (NZ). The figure of Jesus wearing a traditional Maori Korowai cloak is sandblasted on a plate glass window in the church so that he appears to be walking on the water of Lake Rotorua. King Kapisi, also in traditional dress, seems to echo this image. Thus while the first image is a Maori Christian appropriation of Jesus, the second is a Samoan reappropriation.

2 The phrase 'Black, Blanc, Beur' – Black, White, Arab – emerged in relation to the French World Cup-winning team and in reaction to the Bleu, Blanc, Rouge (the blue white and red of the national flag) nationalism of le Pen's racist and anti-immigrant *Front National.*

3 Cheikh Anta Diop (1923–1986) was a famous Senegalese historian and one of the strongest advocates of an Afrocentric world view. His argument that the African background of the Egyptian pharaos had been overlooked by European anthropologists and historians makes an important link here with the pharaoism of IAM.

4 Ummah (or umma) is an Arabic word meaning community or nation. In the Islamic context it is used to mean the community of believers or the Muslim world (*ummat al-mu'minin*).

5 Also known, from different viewpoints, as the front line against Muslim insurgency in Mindanao or independence from the Philippines.

6 GHOST 13 claim to use Tagalog, Visaya, Chavacano and Tausug. My informants, however, have also suggested some lyrics are in Cebuano, Kapampangan (Pampangueno) and other languages. What is perhaps of most interest here is that opinions differ about which languages are being used, and speakers of different Philippine languages claim to understand and name some sections but not others. This speaks to the whole larger problem of the naming and circumscribing of languages (see Makoni and Pennycook, 2005).

7 Sebba does go on to complexify this initial definition somewhat, though it would seem that this stands as a fairly common general definition in linguistics.

8 For issues in Turkey itself, see Solomon (2005).

9 Bhaskaran Nayar has informed me that it should be ' "Nay*i* Zindagi, Naya Jeevan" (since Zindagi is feminine, it has to take the feminine form of the adjective)'. I am also indebted to Bhaskaran for explaining some of the multiple layers of meaning in this phrase.

8 Hip-hop pedagogies and local knowledge

1 'Mob' is the common aboriginal English term for a 'tribe', 'clan' or 'group'.

2 Corroboree is a traditional ceremonial meeting of aboriginal Australians.

3 The didgeridoo is possibly the world's oldest wind instrument.

4 The Deadly Awards recognize excellence in aboriginal and Torres Strait Islander music, sport, entertainment, the arts and community achievement.

5 This interview was done by co-researchers Tony Mitchell and Nick Keys as part of the Local Noise project. See also Mitchell (2006).

6 *Def Poetry Jam* is the Broadway stage adaptation of the television show created by Russell Simmons, co-founder of the hip-hop label Def Jam.

7 This issue was raised by Tony Mitchell in an interview with Australian MC Maya Jupiter when he asked: 'It seems to me that teaching is becoming one of the five elements of hip hop' (Mitchell, 2004, p. 38), to which she replied: 'Definitely. Ask Morganics [another Australian hip-hop artist]. It is just passing on what you know and what is wrong with that?' I am here trying to develop this insight to make broader connections between hip-hop and education.

8 This workshop was observed as part of the Local Noise research project, with Celina McEwen as principal researcher. This workshop, run by Phreaze, was the second of the Back 2 Da Lab workshops.

9 This interview was part of a video project by Reem Algharabali and Linda Gustavsson, made during the Back 2 Da Lab 2 ethnographic study.

Bibliography

Discography

Angélique Kidjo (2001) *Keep on Moving: The Best of Angélique Kidjo*. Wrasse Records.

Asian Dub Foundation (ADF) (2000) *Community Music*. London Records 90.

Balcony and Homicide (2003) *Hymne penghitam langit dan prosa tanpa tuhan*. Harder Records, Bandung, Indonesia.

Bob Marley and the Wailers (1979) *Survival*. Tuff Gong.

Daara J (2004) *Boomerang*. Wrasse Records.

DJ Tommy (2001) *Respect for da chopstick hip hop*. Warner Music Hong Kong.

DJ Tonk (2004) *Move On*. Featuring Mili, K-On. Funai Entertainment, Japan.

GHOST 13 (2004) *GHOST 13*. GMA Records, Philippines.

Jin (2004) *The Rest is History*. Virgin Records.

Kardinall Offishall (2001) *Quest for Fire*. MCA Records.

JOOSUC (2002) *Welcome to the Infected Area*. Universal/MP, Korea.

King Kapisi (2001) *Savage Thoughts*. Festival Records (NZ).

K'Naan (2005) *The Dusty Foot Philosopher*. Salt X Records.

Kru (1999) *Formula Luarbiasa*. EMI (Malaysia).

MV Bill (2002) *Declaração de Guerra*. Natasha Records, Rio de Janeiro.

Poetic Ammo (1998) *It's a Nice Day to be Alive*. Postive Tone, Kuala Lumpur.

Rip Slyme (2002) *Tokyo Classic*. Warner Music Japan.

Section Otoktone (2003) *On vient de la rue* ... New Caledonia, Nouméa.

Sudden Rush (1997) *Ku'e*. Way Out West Production.

Tasha (n.d.) *Hiphop Album*. Gemini Bobos Entertainment, Korea.

The Real Vibe (1999) *Unidade*. Mesapro, Schiedam (Holland).

Too Phat (2000) *Plan B*. Positive Tone.

Too Phat (2002) *360°*. EMI (Malaysia).

Two Up (2002) *Tastes Like Chicken*. Village Idiot Records.

Youssou N'Dour (2002) *Nothing's in Vain (Coono du Réér)*. Nonesuch Records.

Zeebra (1998) *The Rhyme Animal*. Polystar, Japan.

Filmography

Island Style, dir. Carla Drago, SBS TV, 1999.

Publications

Adams, K. and Winter, A. (1997) Gang graffiti as a discourse genre. *Journal of Sociolinguistics*, 1(3), 337–360.

Adorno, T. (1975) Culture industry reconsidered. *New German Critique*, 6 (Autumn), 12–19.

Africultures (2004) http://www.africultures.com/index.asp?menu=revue_affice_artic le&no=3312&section=cahier. Last accessed 28 April 2006.

Akindes, F.Y. (2001) Sudden rush: *Na Mele Paleoleo* (Hawaiian Rap) as liberatory discourse. *Discourse*, 23(1), 82–98.

Alim, H.S. (2002) Street-conscious copula variation in the hip hop nation. *American Speech*, 77(3), 288–304.

Alim, H.S. (2003) 'We are the streets': African American language and the strategic construction of a street-conscious identity. In S. Makoni, G. Smitherman, A. Ball and A. Spears (eds) *Black Linguistics: Language, Society and Politics in Africa and the Americas*. New York: Routledge, pp. 40–59.

Alim, H.S. (2004) *You Know My Steez: An Ethnographic and Sociolinguistic Study of Styleshifting in a Black American Speech Community*. Durham, NC: American Dialect Society and Duke University Press.

Alim, H.S. (2005) Exploring the transglobal hip hop ummah. In M. Cooke and B. Lawrence (eds) *Muslim Networks from Hajj to Hip Hop*. Chapel Hill and London: The University of North Carolina Press, pp. 264–274.

Alim, H.S. (2006) *Roc the Mic Right: The Language of Hip Hop Culture*. London and New York: Routledge.

Alim, H.S. (in press a) Hip hop nation language. In E. Finegan and J. Rickford (eds) *Language in the USA*. New York: Cambridge University Press.

Alim, H.S. (in press b) Critical hip hop language pedagogies: combat, consciousness, and the cultural politics of communication. *Journal of Language, Identity and Education*, 6(2).

Anderson, B. (1983) *Imagined Communities: Reflections on the Origin and Spread of Nationalism*. London: Verso.

Androutsopoulos, J. (2003) Einleitung. In J. Androutsopoulos (ed.) *HipHop: Globale Kultur – Lokale Praktiken*. Bielefeld: Transcript Verlag, pp. 9–23.

Androutsopoulos, J. and Scholz, A. (2003) Spaghetti funk: appropriations of hip-hop culture and rap music in Europe. *Popular Music and Society*, 26(4), 463–479.

Appadurai, A. (1996) *Modernity at Large: Cultural Dimensions of Globalization*. Minneapolis: University of Minnesota Press.

Appadurai, A. (2001) Grassroots globalization and the research imagination. In A. Appadurai (ed.) *Globalization*. Durham, NC: Duke University Press, pp. 1–21.

Aravamudan, S. (1999) *Tropicopolitans: Colonialism and Agency, 1688–1804*. Durham, NC: Duke University Press.

Austin, J.L. (1962) *How To Do Things with Words: The William James Lectures Delivered at Harvard University in 1955*. Oxford: Clarendon Press.

Austin, J.L. (1971) Performative-constative. In J. Searle (ed.) *The Philosophy of Language*. Oxford: Oxford University Press [Austin's paper originally given in 1958].

Auzanneau, M. (2002) Rap in Libreville, Gabon: an urban sociolinguistic space. In A-P. Durand (ed.) *Black, Blanc, Beur: Rap Music and Hip-hop Culture in the Francophone World*. Lanham, MD: The Scarecrow Press, pp. 106–123.

Auzanneau, M. (2003) Rap als Ausdrucksform afrikanischer Identitäten. In J. Androutsopoulos (ed.) *HipHop: Globale Kultur – Lokale Praktiken*. Bielefeld: Transcript Verlag, pp. 190–215.

Bachman, L. (1990). *Fundamental Considerations in Language Testing*. Oxford: Oxford University Press.

Bailey, R. (1991) *Images of English: A Cultural History of the Language*. Ann Arbor: University of Michigan Press.

Baker, H. (1991) Hybridity, the rap race, and pedagogy for the 1990s. *Black Music Research*, 11(2), 217–228.

Baker, H. (1993) *Black Studies, Rap and the Academy*. Chicago, IL: University of Chicago Press.

Bakhtin, M. (1981) *The Dialogic Imagination: Four Essays*, trans. C. Emerson and M. Holquist. Austin: University of Texas Press.

Bakhtin, M. (1986) *Speech Genres and Other Late Essays*. Austin: University of Texas Press.

Bambaataa 2005 http://www.globaldarkness.com/articles/true_meaning_of_hip_hop_bambaata.htm.

Barthes, R. (1977) *Image, Music and Text*. London: Fontana Press.

Bauman, R. (1992) Performance. In R. Bauman (ed.) *Folklore, Cultural Performances, and Popular Entertainments*. New York: Oxford University Press, pp. 41–49.

Bauman, R. (2004) *A World of Others' Words: Cross-cultural Perspectives on Intertextuality*. Oxford: Blackwell.

Bauman, R. and Briggs, C. (1996) Poetics and performance as critical perspectives on language and social life. *Annual Review of Anthropology*, 19, 59–88.

Bauman, R. and Briggs, C. (2003) *Voices of Modernity: Language Ideologies and the Politics of Inequality*. Cambridge: Cambridge University Press.

Beady, C. (2001) Whatever it takes 2 motivate 2-daze youth. *Education Week*, 20(30), 39–40.

Benjamin, W. (1969) *Illuminations: Essays and Reflections*. New York: Schocken Books.

Bennett, A. (2000) *Popular Music and Youth Culture: Music, Identity and Place*. Basingstoke: Palgrave.

Bennett, A. (2003) HipHop am Main: Die Lokalisierung von Rap-Musik und HipHop Kultur. In J. Androutsopoulos (ed.) *HipHop: Globale Kultur – Lokale Praktiken*. Bielefeld: Transcript Verlag, pp. 26–42.

Bennett, A. (2004) Hip-hop am main, rappin' on the tyne: hip-hop culture as a local construct in two European cities. In M. Forman and M.A. Neal (eds) *That's the Joint! The Hip-hop Studies Reader*. New York: Routledge, pp. 177–200.

Berger, H. (2003) Introduction: The politics and aesthetics of language choice and dialect in popular music. In H. Berger and M. Carroll (eds) *Global Pop, Local Language*. Jackson: University Press of Mississippi, pp. ix–xxvi.

Bernabé, J., Chamoiseau, P. and Confiant, R. (1993) *Éloge de la créolité*. Paris: Gallimard.

Bhabha, H. (1994) *The Location of Culture*. London: Routledge.

Bhaskar, R. (1989) *Reclaiming Reality: A Critical Introduction to Contemporary Philosophy*. London: Verso.

Bhatt, R. (2005) Expert discourses, local practices, and hybridity: the case of Indian Englishes. In S. Canagarajah (ed.) *Reclaimimg the Local in Language Policy and Practice*. Mahwah, NJ: Lawrence Erlbaum, pp. 25–54.

Blaktrax (2005) http://www.sbs.com.au/blaktrax/index.html?id=849. Last accessed 1 May 2006.

Bloom, A. (1987) *The Closing of the American Mind*. New York: Simon & Schuster.

Bourdieu, P. (1982) *Ce que parler veut dire: L'économie des échanges linguistiques*. Paris: Fayard.

Bourdieu, P. (1984) *Distinction: A Social Critique of the Judgement of Taste*. Cambridge, MA: Harvard University Press.

Bourdieu, P. (1991) *Language and Symbolic Power*. Oxford: Polity Press.

Bozza, A. (2003) *Whatever You Say I Am: The Life and Times of Eminem*. London: Bantam.

Branson, J. and Miller, D. (2000) Maintaining, developing and sharing the knowledge and potential embedded in all our languages and cultures: on linguists as agents of epistemic violence. In R. Phillipson (ed.) *Rights to Language: Equity, Power and Education*. Mahwah, NJ: Lawrence Erlbaum, pp. 28–32.

Brantlinger, P. (1983) *Bread and Circuses: Theories of Mass Culture as Decay*. Ithaca, NY: Cornell University Press.

Bruthiaux, P. (2003) Squaring the circles: issues in modeling English worldwide. *International Journal of Applied Linguistics*, 13 (2), 159–177.

Brutt-Griffler, J. (2002) *World English: A Study of its Development*. Clevedon, Multilingual Matters.

Butler, J. (1990a) *Gender Trouble: Feminism and the Subversion of Identity*. London: Routledge.

Butler, J. (1990b) Performative acts and gender constitution. In S.E. Case (ed.) *Performing Feminisms: Feminist Critical Theory and Theatre*. Baltimore, MD: Johns Hopkins University Press, pp. 270–282.

Butler, J. (1993) *Bodies that Matter: On the Discursive Limits of 'Sex'*. London: Routledge.

Butler, J. (1997) *Excitable Speech: A Politics of the Performative*. London: Routledge.

Butler, J. (1999) Performativity's social magic. In R. Shusterman (ed.) *Bourdieu: A Critical Reader*. Oxford: Blackwell, pp. 113–128.

Butler, J. (2004) *Undoing Gender*. New York: Routledge.

Caillois, R. (1988) *L'Homme et le sacré*. Paris: Gallimard.

Cameron, D. (1990) Demythologizing sociolinguistics: why language does not reflect society. In J. Joseph and T. Taylor (eds) *Ideologies of Language*. London: Routledge, pp. 79–96.

Cameron, D. (1995) *Verbal Hygiene*. London: Routledge.

Cameron, D. (1997) Performing gender identity: young men's talk and the construction of heterosexual masculinity. In S. Johnson and U.H. Meinhof (eds) *Language and Masculinity*. Oxford: Blackwell, pp. 47–64.

Cameron, D. and Kulick, D. (2003) *Language and Sexuality*. Cambridge: Cambridge University Press.

Canagarajah, S. (1999a) *Resisting Linguistic Imperialism in English Teaching*. Oxford: Oxford University Press.

Canagarajah, S. (1999b) On EFL teachers, awareness and agency. *ELT Journal*, 53(3), 207–214.

Canagarajah, S. (2000) Negotiating ideologies through English: strategies from the periphery. In T. Ricento (ed.) *Ideology, Politics, and Language Policies: Focus on English*. Amsterdam: John Benjamins.

Canagarajah, S. (2004) Subversive identities, pedagogical safe houses, and critical learning. In B. Norton and K. Toohey (eds) *Critical Pedagogies and Language Learning*. Cambridge: Cambridge University Press, pp. 116–137.

Canagarajah, S. (2005) Reconstructing local knowledge, reconfiguring language studies. In S. Canagarajah (ed.) *Reclaimimg the Local in Language Policy and Practice*. Mahwah, NJ: Lawrence Erlbaum, pp. 3–24.

Canale, M. (1983). From communicative competence to communicative language pedagogy. In J.C. Richards and R.W. Schmidt (eds) *Language and Communication*. London: Longman pp. 2–25.

Canale, M. and Swain, M. (1980) Theoretical bases of communicative approaches to second language teaching and testing. *Applied Linguistics*, 1, 1–47.

Cannon, S. (1997) Paname city rapping: B-boys in the *Banlieues* and beyond. In A. Hargreaves and M. McKinney (eds) (1997) *Post-colonial Cultures in France*. London: Routledge, pp. 150–166.

Capuz, R. (2005) When hip-hop is novelty. *Manila Standard Today*, 25 October.

Case, S.-E. (ed.) (1990) *Performing Feminisms: Feminist Critical Theory and Theatre*. Baltimore, MD: Johns Hopkins University Press.

Castells, M. (2000) *The Rise of the Network Society. The Information Age. Economy, Society and Culture. Volume 1* (2nd edn). Oxford: Blackwell.

Cepeda, M.E. (2003) *Mucho Loco* for Ricky Martin: or the politics chronology, crossover, and language within the Latin(o) music 'boom'. In H. Berger and M. Carroll (eds) *Global Pop, Local Language*. Jackson: University Press of Mississippi Press, pp. 113–129.

Chakrabarty, D. (2000) *Provincializing Europe: Postcolonial Thought and Historical Difference*. Princeton, NJ: Princeton University Press.

Chalfant, H. and Prigoff, J. (1987) *Spraycan Art*. London: Thames & Hudson.

Chandrasoma, R., Thompson, C. and Pennycook, A. (2004) Beyond plagiarism – transgressive and non-transgressive intertextuality. *Journal of Language, Identity and Education*, 3 (3), 171–193.

Chang, J. (2005) *Can't Stop Won't Stop: A History of the Hip-hop Generation*. New York: St Martin's Press.

Chen, X.-M. (1995) *Occidentalism: A Theory of Counter-discourse in Post-Mao China*. New York: Oxford University Press.

Chomsky, N. (1965) *Aspects of the Theory of Syntax*. Cambridge, MA: MIT Press.

Christen, R.S. (2003) Hip hop learning: graffiti as an educator of urban teenagers. *Educational Foundations*, 17(4), 57–82.

Clark, M. (1962) *A History of Australia*. Carlton, Vic.: University of Melbourne Press.

Clifford, J. (1988) *The Predicament of Culture: Twentieth Century Ethnography Literature and Art*. Cambridge, MA: Harvard University Press.

Clifford, J. (1997) *Routes: Travel and Translation in the Late Twentieth Century*. Cambridge, MA: Harvard University Press.

Cohn, B. (1996) *Colonialism and its Forms of Knowledge*. Princeton, NJ: Princeton University Press.

Condry, I. (2001) A history of Japanese hip-hop: street dance, club scene, pop market. In T. Mitchell (ed.) *Global Noise: Rap and Hip-hop Outside the USA*. Middletown, CT: Wesleyan University Press, pp. 222–247.

Confiant, R. (2006) Créolité et francophonie: un éloge de la diversalité. http://www.palli.ch/~kapeskreyol/articles/diversalite.htm. Last accessed 12 April 2006.

Connell, J. and Gibson, C. (2003) *Sound Tracks: Popular Music, Identity and Place.* London: Routledge.

Corson, D. (1997) Critical realism: an emancipatory philosophy for applied linguistics? *Applied Linguistics*, 18(2), 166–188.

Cronin, M. (2003) *Translation and Globalization.* London: Routledge.

Crystal, D. (1997) *English as a Global Language.* Cambridge: Cambridge University Press.

Culler, J. (2000) Philosophy and literature: the fortunes of the performative. *Poetics Today*, 21(3), 503-519.

Cutler, C.A. (1999) Yorkville crossing: white teens, hip hop, and African American English. *Journal of Sociolinguistics*, 3(4), 428–442.

Cutler, C.A. (2003) '*Chanter en yaourt*' pop music and language choice in France. In H. Berger and M. Carroll (eds) *Global Pop, Local Language.* Jackson: University Press of Mississippi, pp. 329–348.

Darby, D. and Shelby, T. (2005) From rhyme to reason: this shit ain't easy. In D. Darby and T. Shelby (eds) *Hip Hop and Philosophy: Rhyme 2 Reason.* Chicago, IL: Open Court, pp. xv–xvii.

Dasgupta, P. (1993) *The Otherness of English: India's Auntie Tongue Syndrome.* New Delhi: Sage.

Davies, A. (1999) *An Introduction to Applied Linguistics: From Theory to Practice.* Edinburgh: Edinburgh University Press.

Degraff, M. (2005) Linguists' most dangerous myth: the fallacy of Creole exceptionalism. *Language in Society*, 34, 533–591.

Deleuze, G. and Guattari, F. (1987) *A Thousand Plateaus: Capitalism and Schizophrenia*, trans. B. Massumi; original 1980. London: Continuum.

Derrida, J. (1982) *Margins of Philosophy.* Chicago, IL: University of Chicago Press.

Dewey, J. (1959/1934) *Art as Experience.* New York: Capricorn Books.

Dewey, J. (1966/1916) *Democracy and Education.* New York: The Free Press.

Dimitriadis, G. (2001) *Performing Identity/Performing Culture: Hip Hop as Text, Pedagogy, and Lived Practice.* New York: Peter Lang.

Doran, M. (2004) Negotiating between *Bourge* and *Racaille*: Verlan as youth identity practice in suburban Paris. In A. Pavlenko and A. Blackledge (eds) *Negotiation of Identities in Multilingual Contexts.* Clevedon, OH: Multilingual Matters, pp. 93–124.

Dreyfus, H. and Rabinow, P. (1982) *Michel Foucault: Beyond Structuralism and Hermeneutics.* Chicago, IL: University of Chicago Press.

Duff, P. (2004) Intertextuality and hybrid discourses: the infusion of pop culture in educational discourse. *Linguistics and Education*, 14, 231–276.

Durand, A.P. (ed.) (2002) *Black, Blanc, Beur: Rap Music and Hip-hop Culture in the Francophone World.* Lanham, MD: The Scarecrow Press.

Durkheim, E. (1961) *The Elementary Forms of the Religious Life.* New York: Collier.

Eades, D. (1988) 'They don't speak an Aboriginal language, or do they?' In I. Keen (ed.) *Being Black: Aboriginal Cultures in Settled Australia.* Canberra: Aboriginal Studies Press, pp. 97–115.

Eades, D. (2004) Understanding Aboriginal English in the legal system: a critical sociolinguistics approach. *Applied Linguistics*, 25(4), 491–512.

Eades, D. (2006) Lexical struggle in court: Aboriginal Australians versus the state. *Journal of Sociolinguistics*, 10(2), 153–181.

Elder, C. (2004) Introduction to Part II: Applied Linguistics (A-L). In A. Davies and C. Elder (eds) *Handbook of Applied Linguistics*. Oxford: Blackwell, pp. 423–430.

Elflein, D. (1998) From Krauts with attitudes to Turks with attitudes: some aspects of hip hop history in Germany. *Popular Music*, 17(3), 255–265.

Errington, J. (2001) Colonial linguistics. *Annual Review of Anthropology*, 30, 19–39.

Fairclough, N. (1992) *Discourse and Social Change*. Oxford: Polity Press.

Fairclough, N. (2000) Multiliteracies and language: orders of discourse and intertextuality. In B. Cope and M. Kalantzis (eds) *Multiliteracies: Literacy Learning and the Design of Social Futures*. London: Routledge, pp. 162–181.

Fairclough, N. (1995) *Critical Discourse Analysis*. London: Longman.

Fairclough, N. (2003) *Analysing Discourse: Textual Analysis for Social Research*. London: Routledge.

Fanon, F. (1967) *The Wretched of the Earth*. Harmondsworth: Penguin.

Faure, S. and Garcia, M.C. (2005) *Culture hip-hop: Jeunes des cités et politiques publiques*. Paris: La Dispute/SNEDIT.

Fenn, J. and Perullo, A. (2000) Language choice and hip hop in Tanzania and Malawi. *Popular Music and Society*, 24(3), 77–98.

Fernandes, S. (2003) Fear of a black nation: local rappers, transnational crossings, and state power in contemporary Cuba. *Anthropological Quarterly*, 76(4), 575–608.

Florence, N. (1998) *bell hooks' Engaged Pedagogy: A Transgressive Education for Critical Consciousness*. Westport, CT: Bergin & Garvey.

Forman, M. (2002a) 'Keeping it real?': African youth identities and hip hop. In R. Young (ed.) *Music, Popular Cultures, Identities*. Amsterdam: Rodopi, pp. 101–132.

Forman, M. (2002b) *The 'Hood Comes First: Race, Space and Place in Rap and Hip Hop*. Middletown, CT: Wesleyan University Press.

Foucault, M. (1970) *The Order of Things: An Archaeology of the Human Sciences*. New York: Vintage Press.

Foucault, M. (1977) A preface to transgression. In D.F. Bouchard (ed.) *Language, Counter-memory, Practice*. Ithaca, NY: Cornell University Press, pp. 15–52.

Foucault, M. (1980) *Power/Knowledge: Selected Interviews and Other Writings, 1972–1977*, ed. C. Gordon. New York: Pantheon Books.

Foucault, M. (1984) What is Enlightenment? In P. Rabinow (ed.) *The Foucault Reader*. New York: Pantheon, pp. 32–50.

Foucault, M. (1986) *Care of the Self: Volume 3 of The History of Sexuality*, trans. R. Hurley. New York: Random House.

Frith, S. (1996) Music and identity. In S. Hall, and P. Du Gay (eds) *Questions of Cultural Identity*. London: Sage.

Gal, S. and Irvine, J. (1995) The boundaries of languages and disciplines: how ideologies construct difference. *Social Research*, 62 (4), 967–1001.

Giddens, A. (1999) *Runaway World: How Globalisation is Reshaping our Lives*. London: Profile Books.

Gilroy, P. (1993) *The Black Atlantic: Modernity and Double Consciousness*. London: Verso.

Giroux, H. and Simon, R. (1989) Popular culture as pedagogy of pleasure and meaning. In H. Giroux and R. Simon (eds) *Popular Culture, Schooling and Everday Life*. Toronto: OISE Press, pp. 1–30.

Glissant, E. (1997) *Poetics of Relation*, trans. B. Wing. Ann Arbor: University of Michigan Press.

Goldsworthy, D. (1998) Indigenization and socio-political identity in the *kaneka* music of New Caledonia. In P. Hayward (ed.) *Sound Alliances: Indigenous Peoples, Cultural Politics and Popular Music in the Pacific*. London: Cassell, pp. 45–61.

Grossberg, L. (1989) Pedagogy in the present: politics, postmodernity, and the popular. In H. Giroux and R. Simon (eds) *Popular Culture, Schooling and Everday Life*. Toronto: OISE Press, pp. 91–115.

Grossberg, L. (1992) *We Gotta Get Out of this Place: Popular Conservativism and Postmodern Culture*. New York: Routledge.

Gurnah, A. (1997) Elvis in Zanzibar. In A. Scott (ed.) *The Limits of Globalization*. London: Routledge, pp. 116–142.

Habermas, J. (1984) *The Theory of Communicative Action*, trans. T. McCarthy. Boston, MA: Beacon Press.

Hagège, C. (2006) *Combat pour le Français: Au nom de la diversité des langues et des cultures*. Paris: Odile Jacob.

Halliday, M.A.K. (1978) *Language as Social Semiotic: The Social Interpretation of Language and Meaning*. London: Edward Arnold.

Halliday, M.A.K. (2002) *Applied Linguistics as an Evolving Theme*. Plenary address to the Association Internationale de Linguistique Appliqué (AILA), Singapore, December.

Hamilton, A. (2003) Rip-off rap case ends in dreadlock. *The Weekend Australian*, June, 7–8.

Hanson, J. (1997) The mother of all tongues. Review of D. Crystal, *English as a Global Language*. Cambridge: Cambridge University Press. *Times Higher Education Supplement*, 1288, 11 July, p. 22.

Hardt, M. and Negri, A. (2000) *Empire*. Cambridge, MA: Harvard University Press.

Hardt, M. and Negri, A. (2004) *Multitude: War and Democracy in the Age of Empire*. New York: Penguin.

Harkins, J. (1994) *Bridging Two Worlds: Aboriginal English and Crosscultural Understanding*. St Lucia: University of Queensland Press.

Harland, R. (1987) *Superstructuralism: The Philosophy of Structuralism and Post-structuralism*. London: New York.

Harris, R. (1980) *The Language-makers*. Ithaca, NY: Cornell University Press.

Harris, R. (1981) *The Language Myth*. London: Duckworth.

Harris, R. (1988) Murray, Moore and the myth. In R. Harris (ed.) *Linguistic Thought in England, 1914–1945*. London: Duckworth, pp. 1–26.

Harris, R. (1990) On redefining linguistics. In H. Davis and T. Taylor (eds) *Redefining Linguistics*. London: Routledge, pp. 18–52.

Harris, R. (1998) *Introduction to Integrational Linguistics*. London: Pergamon Press.

Hebdige, D. (1979) *Subculture: The Meaning of Style*. London: Routledge.

Hesmondhalgh, D. and Melville, C. (2001) Repercussions of hip-hop in the UK. In T. Mitchell (ed.) *Global Noise: Rap and Hip-hop Outside the USA*. Middletown, CT: Wesleyan University Press, pp. 86–110.

Higgins, M. and Coen, T. (2000) *Streets, Bedrooms and Patios: The Ordinariness of Diversity in Urban Oaxaca*. Austin: University of Texas Press.

Hill, J. (1995) Junk Spanish, covert racism, and the (leaky) boundary between public and private spheres. *Pragmatics*, 5, 197–212.

Hill, J. (1998) Language, race, and white public space. *American Anthropologist*, 100, 680–689.

Hill, J. (1999) Styling locally, styling globally: what does it mean? *Journal of Sociolinguistics*, 3(4), 542–556.

Ho, W.C. (2003) Between globalisation and localisation: a study of Hong Kong popular music. *Popular Music*, 22(2), 143–157.

Hogben, L. (1963) *Essential World English*. London: Michael Joseph.

Holborow, M. (1999) *The Politics of English: A Marxist View of Language*. London: Sage.

hooks, bell (1994) *Teaching to Transgress: Education as the Practice of Freedom*. New York: Routledge.

Hopper, P. (1998) Emergent grammar. In M. Tomasello (ed.) *The New Psychology of Language*. Mahwah, NJ: Lawrence Erlbaum, pp. 155–175.

Horkheimer, M. and Adorno, T. (1944/1986) *Dialectic of Enlightenment*. New York: Continuum.

Hull, G. and Schultz, K. (2001) Literacy and learning out of school: a review of theory and research. *Review of Educational Research*, 71(4), 575–611.

Huq, R. (2001a) The French connection: Francophone hip hop as an institution in contemporary postcolonial France. *Taboo: Journal of Education and Culture, 5* (2 – Special themed issue), 69–84.

Huq, R. (2001b) Rap à la française: Hip hop as youth culture in contemporary postcolonial France. In A. Furlong and I. Guidikova (eds) *Transitions of Youth Citizenship in Europe: Culture, Subculture and Identity*. London: Council of Europe Publishing, pp. 41–60.

Hutnyk, J. (2000) *Critique of Exotica: Music, Politics and the Culture Industry*. London: Pluto Press.

Hymes, D. (1972) On communicative competence. In J.B. Pride and J. Holmes (eds) *Sociolinguistics*. Harmondsworth: Penguin, pp. 269–293.

Ibrahim, A. (1999) Becoming black: rap and hip-hop, race, gender, identity and the politics of ESL learning. *TESOL Quarterly*, 33(3), 349–370.

Ibrahim, A. (2001) 'Hey, whadap homeboy?' Identification, desire and consumption – hip hop, performativity, and the politics of becoming black. *Taboo: Journal of Education and Culture, 5* (2 – Special themed issue), 85–102.

Irvine, J. (1989) When talk isn't cheap: language and political economy. *American Ethnologist*, 16, 248–267.

Jacquemet, M. (2005) Transidiomatic practices, language and power in the age of globalization. *Language and Communication*, 25, 257–277.

Jagose, A. (1996) *Queer Theory*. Melbourne: Melbourne University Press.

Jameson, F. (1998) Notes on globalization as a philosophical issue. In F. Jameson and M. Miyoshi (eds) *The Cultures of Globalization*. Durham, NC: Duke University Press.

Janks, H. (2000) Domination, access, diversity and design: a synthesis for critical literacy education. *Educational Review*, 52(2), 175–186.

Jenkins, R. (1983) *Lads, Citizens and Ordinary Kids: Working Class Youth Lifestyles in Belfast*. London: Routledge & Kegan Paul.

Jenks, C. (2003) *Transgression*. London: Routledge.

Jervis, J. (1999) *Transgressing the Modern: Explorations in the Western Experience of Otherness*. Oxford: Blackwell.

Jinman, R. (2004) A hip-hop odyssey. *Sydney Morning Herald, 48 Hours*, p. 1.

Jones, K.M. (1994) *Say it Loud: The Story of Rap Music*. Brookfield, CO: The Millbrook Press.

Joseph, J. (2004) *Language and Identity, National, Ethnic, Religious*. Basingstoke: Palgrave Macmillan.

Journal of Hip Hop (2005) 1(1). Hip Hop Matters.

Judge fails to unravel rap lyrics Guardian Unlimited (2003) http://www.guardian. co.uk/uk_news/story/0,3604,971776,00.html. Accessed 9 June 2003.

Kachru, B. (1985) Standards, codification, and sociolinguistic realism: the English language in the Outer Circle. In R. Quirk and H.G. Widdowson (eds) *English in the World: Teaching and Learning the Language and Literatures*. Cambridge: Cambridge University Press, pp. 11–30.

Kachru, B. (1986) *The Alchemy of English: The Spread, Functions and Models of Non-native Englishes*. Oxford: Pergamon Press.

Kachru, B. (1992) *The Other Tongue: English Across Cultures*. Urbana: University of Illinois Press (2nd edn).

Kachru, B. (1997) World Englishes and English-using communities. *Annual Review of Applied Linguistics*, 17, 66–87.

Kachru, B. and Nelson, C. (1996) World Englishes. In S. McKay and N. Hornberger (eds) *Sociolinguistics in Language Teaching*. Cambridge: Cambridge University Press, pp. 71–102.

Kandiah, T. (1998) Epiphanies of the deathless native users' manifold avatars: a post-colonial perspective on the native-speaker. In R. Singh (ed.) *The Native Speaker: Multilingual Perspectives*. New Delhi: Sage, pp. 79–110.

Kaya, A. (2001) *'Sicher in Kreuzberg' Constructing Diasporas: Turkish Hip-hop Youth in Berlin*. Bielefeld: Transcript Verlag.

Kaya, A. (2002) Aesthetics of diaspora: contemporary minstrels in Turkish Berlin. *Journal of Ethnic and Migration Studies*, 28 (1), 43–62.

Kaya, A. (2003) 'Scribo ergo sum': Islamic force und Berlin-Türken. In J. Androutsopoulos (ed.) *HipHop: Globale Kultur – Lokale Praktiken*. Bielefeld: Transcript Verlag, pp. 246–272.

Kearney, R. (1988) *The Wake of Imagination*. Minneapolis: University of Minnesota Press.

Kitwana, B. (2002) *The Hip Hop Generation: Young Blacks and the Crisis in African-American Culture*. New York: BasicCivitas Books.

Kramsch, C. (1993) *Context and Culture in Language Teaching*. Oxford: Oxford University Press.

Kramsch, C. (1999) Global and local identities in the contact zone. In C. Gnutzmann (ed.) *Teaching and Learning English as a Global Language: Native and Non-native Perspectives*. Tübingen: Stauffenburg Verlag, pp. 131–143.

Kramsch, C. (2000) Social discursive constructions of self in L2 learning. In J. Lantolf (ed.) *Sociocultural Theory and Second Language Learning*. Oxford: Oxford University Press, pp. 133–154.

Kramsch, C. (2005) Post 9/11: foreign languages between knowledge and power. *Applied Linguistics*, 26, 545–567.

Kress, G. (2003) *Literacy in the New Media*. London: Routledge.

Kress, G. and van Leeuwen, T. (1996) *Reading Images: The Grammar of Visual Design*. London: Routledge.

Kress, G. and van Leeuwen, T. (2001) *Multimodal Discourse: The Modes and Media of Contemporary Communication*. London: Arnold.

Krims, A. (2000) *Rap Music and the Poetics of Identity.* Cambridge: Cambridge University Press.

Krishnaswamy, N. and Burde, A. (1998) *The Politics of Indians' English: Linguistic Colonialism and the Expanding English Empire.* Delhi: Oxford University Press.

Kroskrity, P.V. (2000) Regimenting languages: language ideological perspectives. In P.V. Kroskrity (ed.) *Regimes of Language: Ideologies, Politics and Identities.* Santa Fe, NM: School of American Research Press, pp. 1–34.

Kubota, R. (1999) Japanese culture constructed by discourses: implications for applied linguistics research and ELT. *TESOL Quarterly,* 33 (1), 9–35.

Kubota, R. (2002) The impact of globalization on language teaching in Japan. In D. Block and D. Cameron (eds) *Globalization and Language Teaching.* London: Routledge, pp. 13–28.

Kubota, R. (2004). Critical multiculturalism and second language education. In B. Norton and K. Toohey (eds) *Critical Pedagogies and Language Learning.* Cambridge: Cambridge University Press, pp. 30–52.

Lacan, J. (1992) *The Ethics of Psychoanalysis 1959–1960,* trans. D. Porter, ed. J.A. Miller. London: Routledge.

Laclau, E. (1989) Preface. In S. Žižek *The Sublime Object of Ideology.* London: Verso, pp. ix–xv.

Larkey, E. (2003) Just for fun? Language choice in German popular music. In H. Berger and M. Carroll (eds) *Global Pop, Local Language.* Jackson: University Press of Mississippi, pp. 131–151.

Latour, B. (1993) *We Have Never Been Modern,* trans. C. Porter. Cambridge, MA: Harvard University Press.

Latour, B. (1999) *Pandora's Hope: Essays on the Reality of Science Studies.* Cambridge, MA: Harvard University Press.

Lawe Davies, C. (1993) Aboriginal rock music: space and place. In T. Bennett, S. Frith, L. Grossberg, J. Shepherd and G. Turner (eds) *Rock and Popular Music: Politics, Policies, Institutions.* London: Routledge, pp. 249–265.

Lawson, B. (2005) Microphone commandos: Rap music and political philosophy. In D. Darby and T. Shelby (eds) *Hip Hop and Philosophy: Rhyme 2 Reason.* Chicago, IL: Open Court, pp. 161–172.

Leech, G. (1974) *Semantics.* Harmondsworth: Penguin.

Lensmire, T.J. and Beals, D.E. (1994) Appropriating others' words: traces of literature and peer culture in a third-grader's writing. *Language in Society,* 23 (3), 411–426.

Le Page, R. and Tabouret-Keller, A. (1985) *Acts of Identity: Creole-based Approaches to Language and Ethnicity.* Cambridge: Cambridge University Press.

Levy, C. (2001) Rap in Bulgaria: between fashion and reality. In T. Mitchell (ed.) *Global Noise: Rap and Hip-hop Outside the USA.* Middletown, CT: Wesleyan University Press, pp. 134–148.

Lipperini, L. (1992) Se sei un ladro dillo col rap. *La Republica,* 22 August, p. 25.

Lipsitz, G. (1994) *Dangerous Crossroads: Popular Music, Postmodernism and the Politics of Place.* London: Verso.

Lobley, K. (2004) Poetry in motion. *The Sydney Morning Herald Metro Magazine,* 26 November to 2 December, p. 5.

Lockard, C. (1998) *Dance of Life: Popular Music and Politics in Southeast Asia.* Honolulu: University of Hawaii Press.

Low, B. (2001) 'Bakardi slang' and the language and poetics of t dot hip hop. *Taboo: Journal of Education and Culture*, 5 (2 – Special themed issue), 15–31.

Luke, A. (1996) Genres of power? Literacy education and the production of capital. In R. Hassan and G. Williams (eds) *Literacy in Society*. London: Longman, pp. 308–338.

Lull, J. (1995) *Media, Communication, Culture. A Global Approach*. Cambridge: Polity Press.

Lynskey, D. (2004) Straight outta Africa. *Guardian Weekly*, 24 December to 6 January, p. 27.

Lyotard, J-F. (1984) *The Postmodern Condition: A Report on Knowledge*. Minneapolis: University of Minnesota Press.

McCann, A. and Ó Laoire, L. (2003) 'Raising one higher than the other': the hierarchy of tradition in representations of Gaelic- and English-language song in Ireland. In H. Berger and M. Carroll (eds) *Global Pop, Local Language*. Jackson: University Press of Mississippi, pp. 233–265.

McCarthy, C., Giardina, M., Harewood, S. and Park J.K. (2003) Contesting culture: identity and curriculum dilemmas in the age of globalization, postcolonialism, and multiplicity. *Harvard Educational Review*, 73(3), 449–465.

McCarthy, C., Hudak, G., Allegretto, S., Miklaucic, S. and Saukko, P. (1999) Introduction: Anxiety and celebration: popular music and youth identities at the end of the century. In C. McCarthy, G. Hudak, S. Miklaucic and P. Saukko (eds) *Sound Identities: Popular Music and the Cultural Politics of Education*. New York: Peter Lang, pp. 1–16.

McConaghy, C. (2000) *Rethinking Indigenous Education: Culturalism, Colonialism and the Politics of Knowing*. Flaxton: Post Pressed.

Macdonald, N. (2001) *The Graffiti Subculture: Youth, Masculinity and Identity in London and New York*. London: Palgrave.

McNamara, T. (1995) Modelling performance: opening Pandora's box. *Applied Linguistics*, 16(2), 159–179.

McPherson, L. (2005) Halfway revolution: from the Gangsta Hobbes to radical liberals. In D. Darby and T. Shelby (eds) *Hip Hop and Philosophy: Rhyme 2 Reason*. Chicago, IL: Open Court, pp. 173–182.

Makoni, S. (1998a) African languages as European scripts: the shaping of communal memory. In S. Nuttall and C. Coetzee (eds) *Negotiating the Past: The Making of Memory in South Africa*. Oxford: Oxford University Press, pp. 242–248.

Makoni, S. (1998b) In the beginning was the missionaries' word: the European invention of an African language: the case of Shona in Zimbabwe. In K.K. Prah (ed.) *Between Distinction and Extinction: The Harmonisation and Standardisation of African Languages*. Johannesburg: University of Witwatersrand Press, pp. 157–164.

Makoni, S. and Pennycook, A. (2005) Disinventing and (re)constituting languages. *Critical Inquiry in Language Studies: An International Journal*, 2(3), 137–156.

Makoni, S. and Pennycook, A. (2006) Disinventing and reconstituting languages. In S. Makoni and A. Pennycook (eds) *Disinventing and Reconstituting Languages*. Clevedon, Multilingual Matters, pp. 1–41.

Malcolm, I.G. (1994) Discourse and discourse strategies in Australian aboriginal English. *World Englishes*, 13(3), 289–306.

Malcolm, I.G. (2000) Aboriginal English: from contact variety to social dialect. In J. Siegel (ed.) *Processes of Language Contact: Studies from Australia and the South Pacific*. Montreal: Fides, pp. 123–144.

Massumi, B. (2002) *Parables for the Virtual: Movement, Affect, Sensation.* Durham, NC: Duke University Press.

Maxwell, I. (2003) *Phat Beats, Dope Rhymes: Hip Hop Down Under Comin' Upper.* Middletown, CT: Wesleyan University Press.

Metcalf, T. (1995). *Ideologies of the Raj.* Cambridge: Cambridge University Press.

Mignolo, W. (2000) *Local Histories/Global Designs: Coloniality, Subaltern Knowledges, and Border Thinking.* Princeton, NJ: Princeton University Press.

Miller, P. (DJ Spooky (aka That Subliminal Kid)) (2004) *Rhythm Science.* Cambridge, MA: MIT Press.

Mitchell, T. (1996) *Popular Music and Local Identity: Rock, Pop and Rap in Europe and Oceania.* London: Leicester University Press.

Mitchell, T. (1998a) *He waiata na Aotearoa:* Maori and Pacific Islander music in Aotearoa/ New Zealand. In P. Hayward (ed.) *Sound Alliances: Indigenous Peoples, Cultural Politics and Popular Music in the Pacific.* London: Cassell, pp. 26–44.

Mitchell, T. (1998b) The *Proud* Project and the 'Otara Sound': Maori and Polynesian pop in the mid-1990s. In P. Hayward (ed.) *Sound Alliances: Indigenous Peoples, Cultural Politics and Popular Music in the Pacific.* London: Cassell, pp. 158–172.

Mitchell, T. (1999) Another root: Australian hip hop as a 'glocal' subculture. *UTS Review,* 5(1), 126–141.

Mitchell, T. (2001a) Introduction: Another root – Hip-Hop outside the USA. In T. Mitchell (ed.) *Global Noise: Rap and Hip-hop Outside the USA.* Middletown, CT: Wesleyan University Press, pp. 1–38.

Mitchell, T. (2001b) Kia kaha! (be strong!): Maori and Pacific Islander hip-hop in Aotearoa – New Zealand. In T. Mitchell (ed.) *Global Noise: Rap and Hip-hop Outside the USA.* Middletown, CT: Wesleyan University Press, pp. 280–305.

Mitchell, T. (2003a) Doin' damage in my native language: the use of 'resistance vernaculars' in hip hop in France, Italy, and Aotearoa/New Zealand. In H. Berger and M. Carroll (eds) *Global Pop, Local Language.* Jackson: University Press of Mississippi, pp. 3–17.

Mitchell, T. (2003b) Review of *Black Blanc Beur. European Journal of Communication,* 19(1), 106–110.

Mitchell, T. (2003c) Australian hip hop as a subculture. *Youth Studies Australia,* 22(2), 40–47.

Mitchell, T. (2003d) Indigenising hip hop: an Australian migrant youth subculture. In M. Butcher and M. Thomas (eds) *Ingenious: Emerging Youth Cultures in Urban Australia.* Sydney: Pluto Press, pp. 198–213.

Mitchell, T. (2004) Australian hip hop: coming out from under. *Music Forum,* 10(4), 30–34.

Mitchell, T. (2006) Keeping Koori culture alive: an interview with Local Knowledge. *Music Forum,* 12(2), 32–34.

Moffatt, L. and Norton, B. (2005) Popular culture and the reading teacher: a case for feminist pedagogy. *Critical Inquiry in Language Studies: An International Journal,* 2(1), 1–12.

Mohanty, S. (1997) *Literary Theory and the Claims of History: Postmodernism, Objectivity, Multicultural Politics.* Ithaca, NY: Cornell University Press.

Morgan, M. (2001) 'Nuthin' but a G thang': grammar and ideology in hip hop identity. In S. Lanehart (ed.) *Sociocultural and Historical Contexts of African American English.* Philadelphia, PA: John Benjamins, pp. 187–209.

Morgan, M. (2005) After ... word! The philosophy of the hip-hop battle. In D. Darby and T. Shelby (eds) *Hip Hop and Philosophy: Rhyme 2 Reason.* Chicago, IL: Open Court, pp. 205–211.

Mufwene, S. (1994) New Englishes and criteria for naming them. *World Englishes,* 13(1), 21–31.

Mufwene, S. (1998) Native speaker, proficient speaker and norms. In R. Singh (ed.) *The Native Speaker: Multilingual Perspectives.* New Delhi: Sage, pp. 111–123.

Mufwene, S. (2001) *The Ecology of Language Evolution.* Cambridge: Cambridge University Press.

Muggleton, D. (2000) *Inside Subculture: The Postmodern Meaning of Style (Dress, Body, Culture).* Oxford: Berg Publishers.

Mühlhäusler, P. (1992) What is the use of studying pidgin and creole languages? *Language Sciences,* 14(3), 309–316.

Mühlhäusler, P. (2000) Language planning and language ecology. *Current Issues in Language Planning,* 1 (3), 306–367.

Nandy, A. (1988) *The Tao of Cricket: On Games of Destiny and the Destiny of Games.* New Delhi: Penguin.

Nelson, C. (1999) Sexual identities in ESL: queer theory and classroom inquiry. *TESOL Quarterly,* 33 (3), 371–391.

Newman, M. (2001) 'Not dogmatically; it's about me': ideological conflict in a high school rap crew. *Taboo: A Journal of Culture and Education,* 5 (2), 51–68.

Newman, M. (2005) Rap as literacy: a genre analysis of hip-hop ciphers. *Text,* 25(3), 399–436.

Nip Hop (2004) http://www.gijigaijin.dreamstation.com/Introduction.html. Last accessed 12 June 2004.

Norris, S. (2004) *Analyzing Multimodal Interaction: A Methodological Framework.* London: Routledge.

Norton, B. (2000) *Identity and Language Learning: Gender, Ethnicity and Educational Change.* Harlow: Longman/Pearson.

Norton, B. and Vanderheyden, K. (2004) Comic book culture and second language learners. In B. Norton and K. Toohey (eds) *Critical Pedagogies and Language Learning.* Cambridge: Cambridge University Press, pp. 201–221.

Ortiz, R. ([1940]1995) *Cuban Counterpoint: Tobacco and Sugar.* Durham, NC: Duke University Press.

Osumare, H. (2001) Beat streets in the global hood: connective marginalities of the hip hop globe. *Journal of American and Comparative Cultures,* 24(1/2), 171–181.

Pacini Hernandez, D. and Garofalo, R. (2004) The emergence of 'rap Cubano': an historical perspective. In S. Whiteley, A. Bennett and S. Hawkins (eds) *Music, Space and Place: Popular Music and Cultural Identity.* Aldershot: Ashgate Publishing, pp. 89–107.

Parakrama, A. (1995) *De-hegemonizing Language Standards: Learning from (Post)colonial Englishes About 'English'.* Basingstoke: Macmillan.

Pardue, D. (2004) 'Writing in the margins': Brazilian hip-hop as an educational project. *Anthropology and Education,* 35(4), 411–432.

Pearson, S. (2004) Pasifik/NZ frontiers – New Zealand-Samoan hip hop, music video and diasporic space. *Perfect Beat,* 6 (4), 55–66.

Peirce (Norton-Peirce), B. (1995) Social identity, investment, and language learning. *TESOL Quarterly* 29, 9–31.

Peirce, C.S. (1992) *Selected Philosophical Writings,* Vol. 1. Bloomington: Indiana University Press.

Peirce, C.S. (1998) *Selected Philosophical Writings,* Vol. 2. Bloomington: Indiana University Press.

Pennay, M. (2001) Rap in Germany: the birth of a genre. In T. Mitchell (ed.) *Global Noise: Rap and Hip-hop Outside the USA.* Middletown, CT: Wesleyan University Press, pp. 111–133.

Pennycook, A. (1985) Actions speak louder than words: paralanguage, communication and education. *TESOL Quarterly,* 19 (2), 259–282.

Pennycook, A. (1994) *The Cultural Politics of English as an International Language.* London: Longman.

Pennycook, A. (1996) Borrowing others' words: text, ownership, memory and plagiarism. *TESOL Quarterly,* 30 (2), 201–230.

Pennycook, A. (1998) *English and the Discourses of Colonialism.* London: Routledge.

Pennycook, A. (1999) Pedagogical implications of different frameworks for understanding the global spread of English. In C. Gnutzmann (ed.) *Teaching and Learning English as a Global Language. Native and Non-native Perspectives.* Tübingen: Stauffenberg.

Pennycook, A. (2000a) English, politics, ideology: from colonial celebration to postcolonial performativity. In T. Ricento (ed.) *Ideology, Politics, and Language Policies: Focus on English.* Amsterdam: John Benjamins, pp. 107–120.

Pennycook, A. (2000b) The social politics and the cultural politics of language classrooms. In J.K. Hall and W. Eggington (eds) *The Sociopolitics of English Language Teaching.* Clevedon, Multilingual Matters, pp. 89–103.

Pennycook, A. (2001) *Critical Applied Linguistics: A Critical Introduction.* Mahwah, NJ: Lawrence Erlbaum.

Pennycook, A. (2002a) Turning English inside out. *Indian Journal of Applied Linguistics,* 28(2), 25–43.

Pennycook, A. (2002b) Language and linguistics/discourse and disciplinarity. In C. Barron, N. Bruce and D. Nunan (eds) *Knowledge and Discourse: Towards an Ecology of Language.* London: Longman/Pearson, pp. 13–27.

Pennycook, A. (2003a) Global Englishes, Rip Slyme and performativity. *Journal of Sociolinguistics,* 7(4), 513–533.

Pennycook, A. (2003b) Beyond homogeny and heterogeny: English as a global and worldly language. In C. Mair (ed.) *The Cultural Politics of English.* Amsterdam: Rodopi, pp. 3–17.

Pennycook, A. (2003c) Lingüística aplicada pós-ocidental. In M.J. Coracini and E.S. Bertoldo (eds) *O Desejo da Teoria e A Contingência da Prática: Discursos sobre e na Sala de Aula.* Campinas: Mercado de Letras, pp. 21–60.

Pennycook, A. (2004a) Critical applied linguistics. In A. Davies and C. Elder (eds) *Handbook of Applied Linguistics.* Oxford: Blackwell, pp. 784–807.

Pennycook, A. (2004b) Performativity and language studies. *Critical Inquiry in Language Studies: An International Journal,* 1(1), 1–19.

Pennycook, A. (2004c) Language policy and the ecological turn. *Language Policy,* 3, 213–239.

Pennycook, A. (2005) Teaching with the flow: fixity and fluidity in education. *Asia Pacific Journal of Education,* 25(1), 29–43.

Pennycook, A. (2006a) Language policy and postmodernism. In T. Ricento (ed.) *An Introduction to Language Policy: Theory and Method.* London: Blackwell, pp. 60–76.

Pennycook, A. (2006b) The myth of English as an international language. In S. Makoni and A. Pennycook (eds) *Disinventing and Reconstructing Languages*. Clevedon, Multilingual Matters, pp. 90–115.

Pennycook, A. (2006c) Uma linguística aplicada transgressiva. In LP Moita Lopes (ed.) *Por uma linguística aplicada indisciplinar*. São Paulo: Parábola, pp. 67–84.

Pennycook, A. and Coutand-Marin, S. (2003) Teaching English as a missionary language. *Discourse: Studies in the Cultural Politics of Education*, 17(3), 337–353.

Pennycook, A. and Makoni, S. (2005) The modern mission: the language effects of Christianity. *Journal of Language, Identity and Education*, 4(2), 137–156.

Perry, I. (2004) *Prophets of the Hood: Politics and Poetics in Hip Hop*. Durham, NC: Duke University Press.

Perullo, A. and Fenn, J. (2003) Language ideologies, choices, and practices in East African hip hop. In H. Berger and M. Carroll (eds) *Global Pop, Local Language*. Jackson: University Press of Mississippi, pp. 19–51.

Phillipson, R. (1992) *Linguistic Imperialism*. Oxford: Oxford University Press.

Phillipson, R. (1994) English language spread policy. *International Journal of the Sociology of Language*, 107, 7–24.

Phillipson, R. (1999) Voice in global English: unheard chords in Crystal loud and clear. Review of D. Crystal, *English as a Global Language*. Cambridge: Cambridge University Press. *Applied Linguistics*, 20(2), 265–276.

Phillipson, R. (2003) *English Only Europe? Challenging Language Policy*. London: Routledge.

Phillipson, R. (2005) L'anglais, un impérialisme linguistique qui ne date pas d'aujourd'hui. In L.-J. Calvet and P. Griolet (eds) *Impérialismes linguistiques hier et aujourd'hui*. Aix-en-Provence: Inalco-Édisud, pp. 159–171.

Phillipson, R. and Skutnabb-Kangas, T. (1996) English only worldwide or language ecology? *TESOL Quarterly*, 30 (3), 429–452.

Potter, R. (1995) *Spectacular Vernaculars: Hip-hop and the Politics of Postmodernism*. Albany, NY: State University of New York Press.

Poynton, C. (1993) Grammar, language and the social: poststructuralism and systemic-functional linguistics. *Social Semiotics*, 3(1), 1–21.

Pratt, M.L. (1987) Linguistic utopias. In N. Fabb *et al.* (eds) *The Linguistics of Writing*. Manchester: Manchester University Press, pp. 48–66.

Pratt, M.L. (1992) *Imperial Eyes: Travel Writing and Transculturation*. London: Routledge.

Preisler, B. (1999) Functions and forms of English in a European EFL country. In T. Bex and R. Watts (eds) *Standard English: The Widening Debate*. London: Routledge, pp. 239–267.

Prévos, A.J.M. (1998) Hip hop, rap, and repression in France and the United States. *Popular Music and Society*, 22(2), 67–84.

Prévos, A.J.M. (2001) Postcolonial popular music in France: rap music and hip-hop culture in the 1980s and 1990s. In T. Mitchell (ed.) *Global Noise: Rap and Hip-hop Outside the USA*. Middletown, CT: Wesleyan University Press, pp. 39–56.

Prévos, A.J.M. (2002) Two decades of rap in France: emergence, developments, prospects. In A-P. Durand (ed.) *Black, Blanc, Beur: Rap Music and Hip-hop Culture in the Francophone World*. Lanham, MD: The Scarecrow Press, pp. 1–21.

Price, S. (1996) Comments on Bonny Norton Peirce's 'Social identity, investment, and language learning': a reader reacts .... *TESOL Quarterly*, 30(2), 331–337.

Price, S. (1999) Critical discourse analysis: discourse acquisition and discourse practices. *TESOL Quarterly,* 33(3), 581–595.

Rahn, J. (2002) *Painting Without Permission: Hip-hop Graffiti Subculture.* Westport, CO: Bergin & Garvey.

Rajagopalan, K. (1999) Of EFL teachers, conscience and cowardice. *ELT Journal,* 53(3), 200–206.

Rajagopalan, K. (2000) On Searle [on Austin] on language. *Language and Communication,* 20(4), 347–391.

Rajagopalan, K. (2004) The philosophy of applied linguistics. In A. Davies and C. Elder (eds) *A Handbook of Applied Linguistics.* Oxford: Blackwell, pp. 397–420.

Rampton, B. (1995) *Crossing: Language and Ethnicity Among Adolescents.* London: Longman.

Rampton, B. (1999) Styling the Other: Introduction. *Journal of Sociolinguistics,* 3(4), 421–427.

Rasmussen, D. (1990) *Reading Habermas.* Oxford: Blackwell.

Rasolofondraosolo, Z. and Meinhof, U. (2003) Popular Malagasy music and the construction of cultural identities. *AILA Review,* 16, 127–148.

Rice, J. (2003) The 1963 hip-hop machine: hip-hop pedagogy as composition. *CCC,* 54(3), 453–471.

Richardson, E. and Lewis, S. (2000) 'Flippin' the script'/'Blowin' up the spot': Puttin' hip-hop online in (African) America and South Africa. In G. Hawisher and C. Selfe (eds) *Global Literacies and the World-wide Web.* London: Routledge, pp. 251–276.

Riley, A. (2005) The rebirth of tragedy out of the spirit of hip hop: a cultural sociology of gangsta rap music. *Journal of Youth Studies,* 8 (3), 297–311.

Rivera, R. (2003) *New York Ricans from the Hip Hop Zone.* New York: Palgrave Macmillan.

Rose, T. (1994) *Black Noise, Rap Music and Black Culture in Contemporary America.* Hanover and London: Wesleyan University Press.

Said, E.W. (1978) *Orientalism.* London: Routledge & Kegan Paul.

Said, E.W. (2001) Overlapping territories: the world, the text, and the critic [1986]. In G. Viswanathan (ed.) *Power, Politics and Culture: Interviews with Edward W. Said.* London: Bloomsbury, pp. 53–68.

Sarka, M. and Allen, D. (in press) Hybrid identities in Quebec Hip-Hop: Language, territory, and ethnicity in the mix. *Journal of Language, Identity and Education,* 6(2).

Sarkar, M., Winer, L. and Sarkar, K. (2005) Multilingual code-switching in Montreal hip-hop: mayhem meets method, or, 'Tout moune qui talk trash kiss mon black ass du nord'. In J. Cohen *et al.* (eds) *ISB4: Proceedings of the 4th International Symposium on Bilingualism.* Somerville, MA: Cascadilla Press, pp. 2057–2074.

Sartre, J-P. (2003) *Being and Nothingness: An Essay on Phenomenological Ontology,* trans. H.E. Barnes; introduction by M. Warnock). London: Routledge.

Saussure, F.D. ([1915]1983) *Course in General Linguistics,* trans. R. Harris. La Salle, IL: Open Court.

Scholz, A. (2003) Rap in der Romania. Glocal approach am Beispiel von Musikmarkt, Identität, Sprache. In J. Androutsopoulos (ed.) *HipHop: Globale Kultur–Lokale Praktiken.* Bielefeld: Transcript Verlag, pp. 147–167.

Scollon, R. and Scollon, S.W. (2003) *Discourses in Place: Language in the Material World.* London: Routledge.

Scott, D. (1999) *Refashioning Futures: Criticism After Postcoloniality*. Princeton, NJ: Princeton University Press.

Scott, J. (1985) *Weapons of the Weak: Everyday Forms of Peasant Resistance*. New Haven, CT: Yale University Press.

Scott, J. (1990) *Domination and the Arts of Resistance: Hidden Transcripts*. New Haven, CT: Yale University Press.

Searle, J. (1969) *Speech Acts: An Essay in the Philosophy of Language*. Cambridge: Cambridge University Press.

Sebba, M. (1997) *Contact Languages: Pidgins and Creoles*. Basingstoke: Palgrave.

Seidlhofer, B. (ed.) (2003) *Controversies in Applied Linguistics*. Oxford: Oxford University Press.

Shuker, R. (2001) *Understanding Popular Music* (2nd edn). London: Routledge.

Shuker, R. (2002) *Popular Music: The Key Concepts*. London: Routledge.

Shusterman, R. (2000) *Performing Live: Aesthetic Alternatives for the Ends of Art*. Ithaca, NY: Cornell University Press.

Shusterman, R. (2005) Rap aesthetics: violence and the art of keeping it real. In D. Darby and T. Shelby (eds) *Hip Hop and Philosophy: Rhyme 2 Reason*. Chicago, IL: Open Court, pp. 54–64.

Singh, J. (1996) *Colonial Narratives/Cultural Dialogues: 'Discoveries' of India in the Language of Colonialism*. London: Routledge.

Singh, P. and Doherty, C. (2004) Global cultural flows and pedagogic dilemmas: teaching in the global university contact zone. *TESOL Quarterly*, 38 (1), 9–42.

Skutnabb-Kangas, T. (2000) *Linguistic Genocide in Education – Or Worldwide Diversity and Human Rights?* Mahwah, NJ: Lawrence Erlbaum.

Sling Shot Hip Hop: The Palestinian Lyrical front (2006) http://slingshothiphop.com/. Last accessed 28 April 2006.

Smith, D. (1999) *Writing the Social: Critique, Theory, and Investigations*. Toronto, Ontario, Canada: University of Toronto Press.

Smitherman, G. (1994) *Black Talk: Words and Phrases from the Hood to the Amen Corner*. Boston, MA: Houghton Mifflin.

Smitherman, G. (2000) *Talking the Talk: Language, Culture, and Education in African America*. London: Routledge.

Söderman, J. and Folkestad, G. (2004) How hip-hop musicians learn: strategies in informal creative music making. *Music Education Research*, 6(3), 313–326.

Solomon, T. (2005) 'Living underground is tough': authenticity and locality in the hip-hop community in Istanbul, Turkey. *Popular Music*, 24(1), 1–20.

Sonntag, S. (2003) *The Local Politics of Global English: Case Studies in Linguistic Globalization*. Lanham, MD: Lexington Books.

Spivak, G.C. (1993) *Outside in the Teaching Machine*. New York: Routledge.

Stapleton, K. (1998) From the margins to mainstream: the political power of hip-hop. *Media, Culture and Society*, 20, 219–234.

Star Online, The http://202.186.86.35/news/story.asp?file=/2004/4/25/focus/7818109&newspage, Sunday, 25 April 2004.

Steiner, G. (1975) *After Babel*. Oxford: Oxford University Press.

Stiglitz, J. (2002) *Globalization and its Discontents*. Harmondsworth: Penguin.

Sunderland, J., Rahim, F.A., Cowley, M., Leontzakou, C. and Shattuck, J. (2000) From bias 'in the text' to 'teacher talk around the text': an exploration of teacher discourse and gendered foreign language textbook texts. *Linguistics and Education*, 11(3), 251–286.

Swedenberg, T. (2001) Islamic hip-hop vs Islamophobia. In T. Mitchell (ed.) *Global Noise: Rap and Hip-hop Outside the USA*. Middletown, CT: Wesleyan University Press, pp. 57–85.

Szego, C. (2003) Singing in Hawaiian and the aesthetics of (in)comprehensibility. In H. Berger and M. Carroll (eds) *Global Pop, Local Language*. Jackson: University Press of Mississippi, pp. 291–328.

Talib, I. (2002) *The Language of Postcolonial Literatures: An Introduction*. London: Routledge.

Taylor, C. (1991) *The Ethics of Authenticity*. Cambridge, MA: Harvard University Press.

Taylor, T.D. (1997) *Global Pop: World Music, World Markets*. London: Routledge.

Thomas, N. (1994). *Colonialism's Culture: Anthropology, Travel and Government*. Oxford: Polity Press.

Threadgold, T. (1997) *Feminist Poetics: Poiesis, Performance, Histories*. London: Routledge.

Tollefson, J. (2000) Policy and ideology in the spread of English. In J.K. Hall and W. Eggington (eds) *The Sociopolitics of English Language Teaching*. Clevedon, OH: Multilingual Matters, pp. 7–21.

Too Phat for Germany (2002) http://www.youthquake.nst.com.my. Sunday, 15 December.

Toolan, M. (2003) An integrational linguistic view of coming into language. In J. Leather and J. van Dam (eds) *Ecology of Language Acquisition*. Dordrecht: Kluwer Academic, pp. 123–139.

Toop, D. (1991) *Rap Attack 2: African Rap to Global Hip Hop*. London: Serpent's Tail.

Tsuda, Y. (1994) The diffusion of English: Its impact on culture and communication. *Keio Communication Review*, 16, 49–61.

Tsuda, Y. (1995) *Eigo shihai no koozoo: Nihonjin to ibunka communication* [*The Structure of English Imperialism: Japanese and Foreign Cultural Communication*]. Tokyo: Daisan Shokan.

Urban Dictionary http://www.urbandictionary.com/define.php?term=blinglish. Last accessed 14 March 2006.

Urla, J. (2001) 'We are all Malcolm X!' Negu Gorriak, hip-hop, and the Basque political imaginary. In T. Mitchell (ed.) *Global Noise: Rap and Hip-hop Outside the USA*. Middletown, CT: Wesleyan University Press, pp. 171–193.

van Leeuwen, T. (1999) *Speech, Music, Sound*. London: Macmillan.

van Lier, L. (2004) *The Ecology and Semiotics of Language Learning*. Dordrecht: Kluwer.

Venn, C. (2000) *Occidentalism: Modernity and Subjectivity*. London: Sage.

Venuti, L. (1998) *The Scandals of Translation: Towards an Ethics of Difference*. London: Routledge.

Vibe Australia (2005) http://www.vibe.com.au/vibe/corporate/celebrity_vibe/showceleb.asp?id=450. Last accessed 1 May 2006.

Vygotsky, L.S. (1986) *Thought and Language*. Cambridge, MA: MIT Press.

Walcott, R. (1997) *Black Like Who?* Toronto: Insomniac Press.

Walcott, R. (1999) Performing the (Black) postmodern: rap as incitement for cultural criticism. In C. McCarthy, G. Hudak, S. Miklaucic and P. Saukko (eds) *Sound Identities: Popular Music and the Cultural Politics of Education*. New York: Peter Lang, pp. 97–117.

Wallach, J. (2003) 'Goodbye my blind majesty': music, language, and politics in the Indonesian underground. In H. Berger and M. Carroll (eds) *Global Pop, Local Language*. Jackson: University Press of Mississippi, pp. 53–86.

Weedon, C. (1987) *Feminist Practice and Poststructuralist Theory*. Oxford: Blackwell.

Welsch, W. (1999) Transculturality: the puzzling form of cultures today. In M. Featherstone and S. Lash (eds) *Spaces of Culture: City, Nation World*. London: Sage, pp. 194–213.

Wermuth, M. (2001) Rap in the low countries: global dichotomies on a national scale. In T. Mitchell (ed.) *Global Noise: Rap and Hip-hop Outside the USA*. Middletown, CT: Wesleyan University Press, pp. 149–170.

Westbrook, A. (2002) *Hip Hoptionary: The Dictionary of Hip Hop Terminology*. New York: Broadway Books.

Widdowson, H.G. (2001) Coming to terms with reality: applied linguistics in perspective. In D. Graddol (ed.) *Applied Linguistics for the 21st Century, AILA Review*, 14, 2–17.

Wikipedia: Hip-hop (2005) http://en.wikipedia.org/wiki/Hip_hop. Last accessed 6 May 2006.

Willis, P. (1977) *Learning to Labour: How Working Class Kids get Working Class Jobs*. Farnborough: Saxon House.

Willis, P. (2003) Foot soldiers of modernity: the dialectics of cultural consumption and the 21st-century school. *Harvard Educational Review*, 73(3), 390–415.

Woolard, K. (2004) Is the past a foreign country?: Time, language origins, and the nation in early modern Spain. *Journal of Linguistic Anthropology*, 14(1), 57–80.

Yano, Y. (2001) World Englishes in 2000 and beyond. *World Englishes*, 20(2), 119–131.

Young, R. (1995) *Colonial Desire: Hybridity in Culture, Theory and Race*. London: Routledge.

Young, R. (2001) *Postcolonialism: An Historical Introduction*. Oxford: Blackwell.

Žižek, S. (1989) *The Sublime Object of Ideology*. London: Verso.

Žižek, S. (2004) Knee-deep. Review of *Free World: Why a Crisis of the West Reveals the Opportunity of our Time* by T. Garton Ash. *London Review of Books*, 26 (17), 2 September.

Zuberi, N. (2001) *Sounds English: Transnational Popular Music*. Urbana: University of Illinois Press.

Zulu Nation (2005) http://www.zulunation.com/afrika.htm. Last accessed 5 July 2005.

Index

Related titles from Routledge

Roc the Mic Right: The language of Hip Hop Culture

H. Samy Alim

Complementing a burgeoning area of interest and academic study, *Roc the Mic Right* explores the central role of language within the Hip Hop Nation (HHN). With its status convincingly argued as the best means by which to read Hip Hop culture, H. Samy Alim then focuses on discursive practices, such as narrative sequencing and ciphers, or lyrical circles of rhymers. Often a marginalised phenomenon, the complexity and creativity of Hip Hop lyrical production is emphasised, whilst Alim works towards the creation of a schema by which to understand its aesthetic.

Using his own ethnographic research, Alim shows how Hip Hop language could be used in an educational context and presents a new approach to the study of the language and culture of the Hip Hop Nation: 'Hiphopography'. The final section of the book, which includes real conversational narratives from Hip Hop artists such as The Wu-Tang Clan & Chuck D, focuses on direct engagement with the language.

A highly accessible and lively work on the most studied and read about language variety in the United States, this book will appeal not only to language and linguistics researchers and students, but holds a genuine appeal to anyone interested in Hip Hop or Black African Language.

ISBN10: 0-415-35877-9 (hbk)
ISBN10: 0-415-35878-7 (pbk)

ISBN13: 978-0-415-35877-4 (hbk)
ISBN13: 978-0-415-35878-1 (pbk)

Available at all good bookshops
For ordering and further information please visit:
www.routledge.com

Related titles from Routledge

Hiphop Literacies

Elaine Richardson

Hiphop Literacies is an exploration of the rhetorical, language and literacy practices of African Americans, with a focus on the Hiphop generation. Richardson analyses the lyrics and discourse of Hiphop, explodes myths and stereotypes about Black culture and language and shows how Hiphop language is a global ambassador of the English language and American culture. In locating rap and Hiphop discourse within a trajectory of Black discourses, Richardson examines African American Hiphop in secondary oral contexts such as rap music, song lyrics, electronic and digital media, oral performances and cinema.

Hiphop Literacies brings together issues and concepts that are explored in the disciplines of folklore, ethnomusicology, sociolinguistics, discourse studies and New Literacies Studies.

Elaine Richardson is Associate Professor of English and Applied Linguistics at Pennsylvania State University. She is the author of *African American Literacies* (Routledge, 2003) and co-editor of *Understanding African American Rhetoric: Classical Origins to Contemporary Innovations* (Routledge, 2003).

ISBN13: 978- 0-415-32928-6 (hbk)
ISBN13: 978-0-415-32927-9 (pbk)

Available at all good bookshops
For ordering and further information please visit:
www.routledge.com

Related titles from Routledge

Word from the Mother

Geneva Smitherman

Word from the Mother presents a definitive statement on African American Language (AAL) from the internationally respected linguist, Geneva Smitherman. Her message is clear: all Americans, regardless of cultural background, must appreciate the linguistic conventions and richness of AAL if they are to participate in society as informed citizens.

Illuminated by Geneva Smitherman's evocative and inimitable writing style, the work gives an overview of past debates on the speech of African Americans and provides a vision for the future. The author explores the contributions of AAL to mainstream American English, and includes a list of idioms and expressions as a suggested linguistic core of AAL.

As global manifestations of Black Language increase, Geneva Smitherman argues that, through education, we must broaden our conception of AAL and its speakers, and examine the implications of gender, age and class on AAL. Most of all, we must appreciate the artistic and linguistic genius of AAL, presented in this book through Hip Hop song lyrics and the rhyme and rhetoric of the Black speech community.

Word from the Mother is an essential read for students of African American speech, language and culture and sociolinguistics, as well as the general reader interested in the worldwide "crossover" of Black Popular Culture.

ISBN13: 978- 0-415-35875-0 (hbk)
ISBN13: 978-0-415-35876-7 (pbk)

Available at all good bookshops
For ordering and further information please visit:
www.routledge.com